SEVEN LEADERS

Preachers and Pastors

SEVEN LEADERS

Preachers and Pastors

Iain H. Murray

THE BANNER OF TRUTH TRUST

THE BANNER OF TRUTH TRUST
3 Murrayfield Road, Edinburgh EH12 6EL, UK
P O Box 621, Carlisle, PA 17013, USA

❧

ISBN
Print: 978 1 84871 739 8
EPUB: 978 1 84871 741 1
Kindle: 978 1 84871 742 8

❧

Typeset in 11/14 pt Galliard BT
at the Banner of Truth Trust, Edinburgh, UK

Printed in the USA
by Versa Press, Inc.,
East Peoria, IL

For the Rising Generation
Preparing to Preach the Gospel in Australia
And Their Wives

God of Eternity, Lord of the Ages,
Father and Spirit and Saviour of men!
Thine is the glory of time's numbered pages;
Thine is the power to revive us again.

Ernest N. Merrington
New South Wales and Queensland, 1905–1923
Senior Presbyterian Chaplain
First Australian Expeditionary Force

W. J. Grier
Leicester Ministers' Conference, 1975.

Contents

Contents

Endpapers

  Front: A view over Lake Bala, Wales
      © iStockphoto.com/StevenHogg

  Rear: An aerial photograph of Grace Community
      Church, Roscoe Blvd, Sun Valley, CA

Introduction

THESE pages originated in an invitation to speak on 'Preachers and Pastors' to students for the ministry at the Presbyterian Theological College in Melbourne in March 2014. Chapters 3, 4, 5, and 7 come from addresses given on that occasion. At the request of the students, one of my subjects is a leader who continues in his ministry at the present time. Chapter 2 was originally an address given at the Crieff Fellowship in Scotland in 2009. Chapter 1 on John Elias, I wrote for these pages, regarding him as too important to leave out. Edward Morgan's *Memoir of John Elias* was a biography which meant a great deal to me over sixty years ago. Although Elias died in 1841, his life retains a message immensely relevant to the church today.

By the early part of the last century, the 'pipelines' which carried knowledge of spiritual history were fractured by those who wanted the churches taken in a new direction. Few played an equal part in restoring knowledge of what had been lost than William 'Jim' Grier. Without his guidance many of us would have been the poorer, and thankfulness for what he was enabled to do prompted the chapter under his name.

Of three of the seven men, Archibald Brown, D. M. Lloyd-Jones, and John MacArthur, I have already written biographies. To give some new material and comment on them, and to help bring them closer to the younger generation, they are included here. While Lloyd-Jones and W. J. Grier were the only two among the seven who met one another, I have been repeatedly struck by the spiritual similarities they all shared, despite the differences of time and place. That ought not to be surprising for it is the same head of the church who prepares those whom he sends. Even so, faithful men are not the same in their gifts, opportunities and circumstances. For each Christ has a distinct calling, as he cautioned Simon Peter, 'If I want him to remain till I come, what is that to you? You follow me!' (John 21:22). God does not make replicas. We are to learn from leaders yet be imitators of none.

I am a believer in giving dates. They are important to an understanding of history and their study will often throw light on the providence of God.

While my hope is that this book will assist younger men called to the ministry of the gospel, it is not meant for them alone. All Christians ought to be able to pass on what 'we have heard and known and our fathers have told us' (Psa. 78:3). When history is forgotten, it is later generations who suffer. The past is rich with wisdom which will never be out of date. When the lonely island of St Kilda once appealed for 'a good minister' be sent to them, they were asked, 'What kind of minister would you have to be sent?' The reply was, 'One that will tell us of our danger and preach Christ to us.'

Preachers and pastors do not arise apart from churches, and their usefulness is in large measure related to their people's prayerful understanding and support. No one preaches in a vacuum. The usefulness of a church is bound up with the inter-dependence of pastors and people.

When John Angell James (1785–1859) was near the end of his much-used ministry he expressed thoughts which must resonate with all who approach the conclusion of their service:

> Standing, as I now do, in the prospect of the close of my ministry, of the eternal world, and of my summons to the presence of the great Lord of all, the salvation of souls, as the object of the ministry, appears to me, more than ever before, in all its awful sublimity. Everything else, as compared with this, seems but as the small dust of the balance. To my younger brethren I say, You are engaged in the greatest work in the universe.

Numbers of my generation owe a great debt to the Evangelical Library in London, an institution which has inspired many by calling attention to the riches of the past. At the annual meeting of the library, in November 1961, Dr Lloyd-Jones closed the proceedings with the words:

> O Lord, we thank Thee for the ministry of those long since gone to their reward and who are with thee. We thank Thee that they are still speaking. We pray Thee that Thou wouldst speak to us more and more through them that they may enable us to speak. We thank Thee for all whom Thou hast raised up in past centuries to speak Thy word with holy boldness, without fear or favour. Lord, make us fit to follow in their train. Make us worthy, O God, of the heritage they have sent down to us. Teach us, O Lord, to prize the things that we have, and all that Thou hast made possible to us through them.[1]

I am thankful to Peter Hastie, Principal of the Presbyterian Theological College at Melbourne, for the invitation that prompted this book. Other friends, for whose help I am indebted, include, John Aaron, Ernest Brown, John Grier, and Phil Johnson. As ever, the work of my colleagues in the Banner of Truth Trust has gone into this book at every stage and is much appreciated. None of the seven leaders recorded here would have been what they were without their wives. The presence of the latter is the great unseen story of Christian ministry. A book is needed on the work of a preacher's wife. But it is known to heaven and known to every one of us who has been, and is, so blessed. To God be the praise!

Iain H. Murray
Edinburgh, January 4, 2017

---

[1] There is an important insight into the ministry of Dr Lloyd-Jones which cannot be set down on paper. Fot those who were never present at Westminster Chapel in the time of his ministry, something valuable can now be learned about the congregational worship from the website which has recovered hymn singing from that period. See https://www.youtube.com/playlist?list=PLA75QZVS1VQJdyG7Kua8w-bR9nLyGoe6c

A Time Chart

- John Elias 1774–1841
- Andrew Bonar 1810–1891
- Archie Brown 1844–1922
- Kenneth MacRae 1883–1963
- Martyn Lloyd-Jones 1899–1981
- W. J. Grier 1902–1983
- John MacArthur 1939–

—1750
—1775
—1800
—1825
—1850
—1875
—1900
—1925
—1950
—1975
—2000
—2015

1

John Elias and Revival

'The fall of man and his total depravity; the wretchedness of his condition under the curse and wrath of God; his complete inability to save himself; and free salvation by God's sovereign grace and love; Christ as full Saviour, appropriate to the chief of sinners; inviting the lost to come to him and believe in him; and urging believers to be "careful to maintain good works'. This was the substance of their preaching ... This is the kind of preaching which conquered Wales."'

Goronwy P. Owen,
quoted in R. Tudur Jones,
John Elias, Prince of Preachers, p. 20.

'The thought of sin in the sight of God—how terrible it must be! Never has there been a revival but that some of the people, especially at the beginning, have had such visions of the holiness of God, and the sinfulness of sin, that they have scarcely known what to do with themselves.'

D. Martyn Lloyd-Jones, Revival, p. 157.

'A young preacher who had a high opinion of himself and his learning, once said to an old man who had been one of John Elias's hearers, "If John Elias were alive now, he would not be counted as much of a preacher." The old man became thoroughly agitated: "Oh, indeed! You never heard him, my boy. Nobody who ever heard him would speak like that."'

The Calvinistic Methodist Fathers of Wales, vol. 2, p. 720.

I N the upper story of an old house, close to Baker Street in central London, there existed a room more akin to a barn, stored in every corner with books from across the centuries. This was the Evangelical Library, the brainchild of its founder, Geoffrey Williams, and in the 1950s, when most men of his age had retired, he was daily to be found in the small space reserved as his office in a corner. This was an inner sanctum, not open to the public, but Williams was a tutor as well as a librarian, and some of us were given sight of a glass-fronted cupboard on the wall to the left of the fireplace. This contained yet more books, and it was their subject which made them his special collection. They all dealt with the revivals of the past, and the privileged place he gave to them was indicative of the purpose for which the Evangelical Library existed in his eyes. He was no mere book-lover; he had a higher concern in view. It was from the shelves of that cupboard that I first saw two books, the one a *Memoir of John Elias* (1844) by Edward Morgan, and the other, the *Letters, Essays, and other Papers of John Elias* (1847). Now, more than sixty-years later, I well remember the thrill of being introduced to those books, and I hope this chapter will pass on to others what was given to me.[1]

YOUTH, ANGLESEY, AND MARRIAGE

In Caernarvonshire, four miles from Pwllheli, in north-west Wales, John Jones was a weaver and owner of a small farm. The 1770s were hard times, employment was scarce, and when his son married, John Jones provided the young couple a home on the same farm. This may have been normal enough. It was less normal that when Elias, grandson of John Jones, was born on May 6, 1774, the grandfather came to have the chief influence in shaping the child's future. Unlike Elias's parents, John Jones was a serious Christian and as soon as the boy was old enough to walk he would take him to the parish church of Abererch. The community was all Welsh-speaking and literacy by no means universal, but grandfather Jones set himself to teach Elias to read with the Bible as the text book. By the age of seven the child had read from Genesis to the middle of Jeremiah. At that point the reading stopped when Elias caught smallpox. He was seriously ill, lost his memory, and became blind. When the child opened his eyes again after two weeks, his distressed grandfather was at the bedside and checked his condition with the question, 'My dear boy, do you remember what your lesson is?' 'I answered Yes', Elias later recalled, 'and mentioned some chapter in Jeremiah. The old man rejoiced greatly when he saw that I could remember in spite of my affliction.'

Once able to read, Elias was largely self-educated. He knew no English but had access to a few Puritan books in Welsh, and his love of reading was such that, it is said, he kept the butter from his bread to make 'reed candles' by which he could read when the family had gone to bed.[2]

North Wales was at this date beginning to emerge from profound spiritual darkness. There was little or no light in most of the parish churches, and Nonconformist chapels were few. A great change was coming, not from existing institutions, but from the so-called 'Methodists', evangelicals from within the Church of England who multiplied in spite of the opposition of the denomination of their upbringing. The label, originally given to them as a term of abuse, came to refer to 'all who were evangelical in belief, who sought to live godly lives, and who endeavoured to save the souls of their fellow men'.[3] In Wales the prefix 'Calvinistic' was later added after the Wesleyans became active in the country.

By the time Elias was a teenager he would walk with his grandfather on Sundays to wherever they knew there would be a sermon, and when John Jones became too old to do this, the youngster would go alone. By this means he came into contact with groups of Methodists, many of them young people, who were forming themselves into societies. This followed the pattern already well established in South and Mid-Wales where there was a network of societies, linked by Association meetings held for preaching and wider unity. In 1792, at about the age of eighteen, Elias went to an Association established at Bala among the mountains of North Wales. The site was the result of the settlement in that village of Thomas Charles, a Church of England clergyman whose convictions had debarred him from the pulpits of his own denomination.[4]

The previous autumn a great revival had begun in Bala. In a letter of December 7, 1791, Charles wrote that,

> a general concern about eternal things swallowed up every other concern. And a spirit of conviction spread so rapidly, that there was hardly a young person in the neighbourhood but began to enquire, 'What will become of me?' The work has continued to go on ever since with unabated power and glory. ... I bless God for these days and would not have been without seeing what I now see in the land. No; not for the world.[5]

On May 2, 1792, Charles wrote to a correspondent in Scotland:

> That it is a work of God I am not left to doubt in the least degree: it carries along with it every scriptural satisfactory evidence that we can possibly desire; such as deep conviction of sin, of righteousness and of judgment; great reformation of manners; great love for and delight in the word of God, in prayer, in spiritual conversation, and Divine ordinances. ... I am far from expecting that all who have experienced Divine influences are savingly wrought upon, and soundly converted. If that were the case, all the country would be converted. ... As to the further spread of the work, the prospect, in our country, in general, is very pleasing. In Carnarvonshire and Anglesey

congregations are very numerous and very large. Thousands flock together at the sound of the gospel trumpet, and hear with great earnestness and attention.[6]

This was the situation into which Elias was introduced after he had walked the forty miles across the mountains of Snowdonia to the Bala Association. An incident on the journey was remembered by others walking in the same group:

> At Ffestiniog, on the way to Bala, they held a prayer meeting. A request was made for a copy of the Bible but apparently nobody had one. At length, the quiet serious young man who was a stranger to most of the company said that he had a copy and, when he produced it from his pocket, he was asked to read a chapter. 'He did so', said one old man, 'in such a manner as to make the chapter seem new to us all.'[7]

Unwise attempts were later made to fix the time of Elias's conversion but there is no date when he passed from death to life. All he says himself is that he became a 'professor of religion' in 1792.

From the age of twelve he had been working for his parents as a weaver, and it was this trade which led him to better employment at another farm. What made it better was not the remuneration but the family with whom he now stayed, and where the head of the household was a Methodist leader in a small society at Hendre Howell. Here the youth was among 'godly people, quiet, kind, brotherly, of a tender conscience and brokenness of heart'. Although the societies were not churches, evidence of spiritual life was required for attendance at a society meeting (as distinct from a gathering for preaching). About the end of September 1793 Elias became a member. Encouraged by his witness and prayerfulness, his friends at Hendre Howell recommended him to the monthly meeting which examined men who appeared gifted to preach. The interview with him was on Christmas Day, 1794. Only seven months past his twentieth birthday, 'I saw myself very deficient in my views of the glory of Christ and experience of his love, so as to speak clearly and fervently of him to the people.' He was accepted, although with a condition proposed by one of his examiners, a man with the same names as his grandfather, John Jones. I have to this point referred to Elias by the Christian name of his father, who was Elias Jones. In truth the youth's real Christian name to this point was John, but when he told his questioner that he was 'John Jones', the older man exclaimed, 'Good gracious, call the boy John Elias, or else we shall all be John Joneses before long!'

While no one thought Elias was lacking in fervency, the monthly meeting recognized how further education would aid his usefulness. Thus at the same time as Elias began to preach, he came under the personal care of Evan Richardson, a leading preacher among the Calvinistic Methodists. None of these preachers were salaried at this time, and depended on another occupation—often that of their wives—for their livelihood. In Richardson's case he had a school in Caernarvon, where he taught English, Greek, Latin, French, and Hebrew. He would later say of Elias, 'I never had any one like him, so desirous of learning.' An anecdote suggests that the process was not without difficulties. It is said that as Richardson was one day passing behind the desk at which Elias sat, he glanced to see how his work was progressing. Instead he found the pupil absorbed in making a sermon. 'It is of little use', the teacher is reported to have said, 'preaching is like a fire burning in his bones.'[8]

Elias mastered English at Caernarvon, and perhaps enough of the original languages of Scripture to enable him to use commentaries effectively. Recalling this time in later years, he reflected,

> I was given help to work diligently at night until I acquired in some degree a general knowledge of the things that were most necessary for me. But I am still learning, even in my sixty-seventh year, and see a greater need of knowledge.[9]

Edward Morgan adds, 'He was blessed above all with that knowledge which flesh and blood cannot attain to.'

That Elias's life-work was to be in preaching was now apparent to all. It is said, 'Elias appeared like a comet, in full blaze, at the beginning of his ministry.' It was his freedom in prayer which was especially noted, as at an association at Llanfair Caereinion in April 1796, when there was more comment on 'the wonderful prayer of the boy from Caernarvonshire than anything else in that association'.[10]

It was while Elias was at school with Evan Richardson that an event occurred which introduced the pupil to the place where so much of his life was to be spent. Across the Menai Straits from Caernarvon lies Anglesey, an island twenty-nine miles long by twenty-two broad, and on an occasion when Richardson was unable to fulfil a preaching engagement there, at Bronddu, he sent Elias in his place. The disappointment of the people in seeing a young stranger vanished once the service began and they heard him praying as one that 'had reached the mercy-seat and stood before the divine presence'. The meeting was remembered for years to come, and Elias was at once given invitations to preach in different parts of the island.

Despite its clergy and twenty-seven Church of England parishes, Anglesey had for long been one of the most materialistic and immoral parts of Wales. From that period the island was now gradually emerging, yet much of the old behaviour continued. Sundays were usually spent in all kinds of entertainment. The contents of ships driven ashore from the wild Irish Sea were still plundered, it being the popular belief that local people had the right to what was washed up on their shores. Addiction to alcohol was widespread, and encouraged by many social occasions. Thomas Charles saw the beginnings of change for the better when he visited the island in 1785. A few years later, as already noted, he was amazed at the hunger with which the word of God was being heard in Anglesey.

One convert of these years in Anglesey was the teenage daughter of Richard Broadhead, a well-to-do landowner whose connection was with the privileged few of social standing. Part of Elizabeth Broadhead's education had been in England, and part with a clergyman uncle who served one of the island's parishes. Like most of his fellow clergy, he was opposed to evangelical belief. On one occasion, when he heard that his niece had been in the home of a Methodist, he did not speak to her for three weeks. Another relative of Elizabeth's was an aunt who lived at Bronddu and it was here that, 'quite accidentally', Elizabeth heard a Methodist preacher. There is no record of who she heard, or of how close in time it was to the first visit of Elias to the same place. What she heard filled her mind and brought the beginning of a new life. The change was costly. Her father regarded belonging to the Church of England as part of his nationality, and he virtually disowned his eldest daughter. Shut out of her home, as well as that of her uncle, her only help came from another uncle, on her mother's side, who provided a simple house for her in the village of Llanfechell. Here, determined to support herself, Elizabeth Broadhead opened a shop.

The nearest Methodist meeting place meant a four-mile walk to Llanrhuddlad, and on her first visit there, the gathering was 'amazed on seeing this beautiful young girl, dressed in fineries, coming amongst them'.[11] At what date John Elias met his future wife is not recorded. We only know the outcome: they were married in Anglesey on February 22, 1799. There was no wedding present or assistance of any kind from her father. Antagonism to his daughter's faith was only increased by the introduction of a poor weaver/preacher into his family.

AN EVANGELIST IN TIMES OF AWAKENING

At the age of twenty-four, Elias was becoming a foremost preacher among the Calvinistic Methodists. Such was the extent of the need of the country at large that most of their

preachers in North Wales were compelled to be itinerant evangelists rather than settled pastors. When at home, Elias held
services in the kitchen of their house, or in the surrounding
area, preaching sometimes on a consecutive subject:

> In the year 1800, I received wonderful things from John
> chapter seventeen. I was given wonderful and delightful views
> respecting God's plan of salvation in his sovereign grace, the
> graciousness and stability of the plan of salvation![12]

There was no question of restricting preaching to chapels,
of which at this date there were very few in Anglesey. Elias
would preach at all sorts of locations, whether he was wanted
or unwanted. He was known to invade gatherings convened
on Sundays for anything but the worship of God. One such
event occurred annually in Anglesey on Whit-Sunday, and involved setting fire to nests of ravens on the face of a high and
precipitous rock, *Y gadair* (the chair). Crowds gathered to
watch the cruel excitement, as bundles of gorse and heather
were gathered, set alight, and lowered by metal chains from
above, burning chicks alive in their nests. Such activity was
concluded with other forms of 'revelry'. The tradition was
permanently ended the year Elias interrupted the proceedings
by preaching to those gathered. The same thing happened
at Llanrhuddlad, and at Pentir, where his preaching stopped
Sunday stage plays. 'He would not attack any one form of
sin and immorality', says a biographer, 'but sin in its entirety,
in whatever form it revealed itself.' If he gave special attention to the fourth of the ten commandments, 'Remember
the Sabbath day to keep it holy', it was because the disregard
was so widespread. Elias did not hesitate to oppose whatever
was popular and long established if it were in defiance of the
word of God. He looked not only for changed behaviour, but
inward change, accompanying repentance and faith, without
which no one would 'call the Sabbath a delight' (Isa. 58:13).
'It is very painful to think that the manner of many observing

the Sabbath shews that they have but little delight in Christ, and slender hope of heaven.'[13]

Elias preached for the first time at the Bala Association in 1797. His reputation had also reached South Wales, and it may have been at this date that two men from the South came to Bala to ask that he would visit among their churches. Such an invitation would need the consent of the Association but the request was met with admonition, not approval:

> In heaven's name leave him be, in order to see what the Lord will make of him. In all probability he will rise very high or plummet to the depths. We believe that there is in him the making of a great preacher as long as he is not spoiled at the beginning.[14]

The providence of God was working to keep Elias from that danger. With few exceptions, the condition of society members corresponded to the words of James 2:5, 'Hath not God chosen the poor of this world rich in faith, and heirs of the kingdom which he hath promised to them that love him?' There was no possibility of Elias maintaining a family on such support as he received for preaching, and Llanfechell was hardly a natural site for the millinery shop which carried the name of 'Elizabeth Elias' above its door. With no aid from her prosperous father, for several years the couple struggled with poverty.

> We were the first years after marriage, in adverse and trying circumstances as to worldly matters. My mind was much distressed by fear that we could not pay our creditors, and thereby become guilty of injustice to men, and bring reproach on God's name and cause.

As Elizabeth counted what was in the till of her shop, and considered debts which had to be paid, she sought to keep her worries from her husband. 'My dear wife', he would later say, took 'as much as she could of my burden upon herself, endeavouring as much as possible in great difficulties to carry on the business, that I might have time to go on with the work of the Lord. This troubled me very much; I saw myself placing too heavy a burden on her, especially when she was nursing the children.'[15]

They were given four children, but only two, Phoebe and John, survived. At the birth of one of the others, the doctor in attendance had to decide between the life of the child or the mother. Out of such sorrows Elias counselled others:

> It is well to remember that our Lord's dominion is over all persons, over their lives, faculties, and all their circumstances; and that we have lost all right to every blessing temporal and spiritual. ... He is infinitely wise and good, and carries on all his operations in perfect, wisdom, equity and goodness, Nothing can be made better than God has done it. ... All earthly blessings are only borrowed, and must soon be recalled. But the riches laid up in Christ are our own, and we shall possess and enjoy them for ever and ever. We overcome the world, its troubles and afflictions, as well as in its deceitful smiles, by believing in the Son of God, whether those afflictions have regard to our health, families, prosperity, relations, friends, or reputation. Beholding the glory of him who for our sakes became poor, will make us easy and truly contented.[16]

At a later date, he says, 'God's goodness and mercy' relieved them of the financial trial, but the shop was needed for many years. Elizabeth Elias was clearly an able woman. For her business she was at times as far away as Wrexham to buy items for her stock. There was also cloth to be bought in Liverpool, which was shipped to her by sea. At a later date, when the shop had become better established, they suffered a heavy loss when the *Marchioness of Anglesey*, carrying her goods among its cargo, was wrecked on an Anglesey beach. All was taken by local people acting on the idea that they could claim what arrived in this manner.

Elias speaks of a greater trial, arising not from events or circumstances but from himself. The more his experience of

God, the less he was pleased with himself: 'The discoveries I make in myself, though small in degree, are painful. There is an ocean of sin and misery in me.' 'He favoured me with a measure of his presence. ... But alas, my distance from God is great; this is my constant grief.'[17] He was far from thinking the language of Romans 7 unfitting for a Christian.

No chronological narrative exists of Elias's life as an evangelist. How widespread it became can be judged from the later opinion of his contemporary, Edward Morgan:

> In all my journeys through Wales, I have not heard of any one minister whose preaching has been so universally blessed to the conversion of sinners. In almost every country place, village, or town, you can find some person who will ascribe his conversion to one of his sermons.[18]

But scattered records of particular occasions convey some idea of the effect of his ministry. The texts he took were long to be remembered, none more so than the words he took for a Sunday 'hiring fair' and market at Rhuddlan, Flintshire in the summer of 1802. Harvest time was approaching and some of the roughest in the land were there looking for part-time work; for others it was just a day for pleasure and alcohol. Cautioned by friends against what he proposed, Elias, with a small company of Christians, stood on the steps of the New Inn where he sang, read from Scripture, then began to pray. It was the prayer which arrested the boisterous listeners. He thanked God for holding back his judgments, and then interceded for those present in such a manner that hearts melted. His text followed: 'Six days thou shalt work, but on the seventh thou shalt rest: in earing time and in harvest thou shalt rest' (Exod. 34:21). The words were explained before, with tears on his face and arms outstretched towards the crowd, he summoned them to repentance in the name of God: 'You thieves! You thieves! You thieves! You have stolen my God's Sabbath! You have taken the day of my Lord.' One who was present said the words 'struck the crowd like a thunderbolt'. The sermon not only stopped the event in Rhuddlan, but Sunday fairs were never held again in Flintshire. When some predicted that as an old custom the Ruddlan Fair would recover, Elias responded, 'If anyone will give the least encouragement to its revival, he will be accursed before the Holy Trinity, Father, Son, and Holy Ghost; but blessed be the man that opposes this and every other species of iniquity.'[19] In a comment on that event in Rhuddlan, Tudur Jones has spoken of it as 'a matter of wonder that one preacher, facing a mob bent on pleasure and more than a little drunk, could destroy the institution of the Sunday fair in a whole county with one sermon'.[20]

Certainly the overpowering effect of such preaching was not to be explained in terms of an appreciative crowd. His hearers might be initially careless or even hostile. At a time when spiritual life was ebbing in Caernarvonshire, Elias took for his text the words of Psalm 68:1: 'Let God arise, let his enemies be scattered'. It was an Association meeting in the open-air at Pwllheli, but thousands were there not previously numbered among the Methodists. One report spoke of 3,000 converted that day; another, with more caution, affirmed that the sermon played a large part in the 2,500 who joined the Methodist churches in Caernarvonshire that same year. There could be no certainty over numbers. Two contemporary witnesses of a service in Anglesey disagreed whether the gathering numbered ten or twelve thousand. Even if due allowance is made for exaggeration, the numbers are astonishing.

For forty-six years Elias preached at the annual Bala Association. At the conclusion of the meetings in 1807, Elias and Evan Richardson were both to preach, the older after the younger, at a service which began at 2 pm. It was 2.20 pm when Elias gave out his text, 'That ye may be able to comprehend with all saints what is the breadth and length and depth and height; and to know the love of Christ, which passeth knowledge, that ye may be filled with all the fullness of God'

(Eph. 3:18-19). Standing in the open window of the chapel for those outside to hear, he preached on the love of God until 4 pm. At that point, Richardson was so happy that he got up, not to preach, but simply to say, 'Let us pray.'[21]

In later years, when the numbers attending the preaching services at the Bala Association were yet higher—30,000, some said—the venue had to be the open air on the 'Green'.

Those who heard Elias commented on the style of his preaching. One characteristic was the change which took place in the course of his delivery. At the outset the tone was set by the 'slowly and solemn way' he read the text, nor did he proceed until he had done all he could to fix the text, and its meaning, in the memory of his hearers. In a sermon on 1 John 5:19, 'The Two Families', he quoted the text, in whole or part, six times in the first few minutes.[22] There was nothing of excitement in his manner, only a calm clarification of the biblical words before him. Beforehand he had prayed for utterance suited to speaking the word of God, and a sense of the glory of the truth would take hold of him as he spoke. In the mystery of powerful preaching there is a kind of transmutation that takes place in which the messenger becomes part of the message (Rom. 10:15; Gal. 3:1). This was to be seen in Elias. The look on his face, his tone and gesture corresponded with what he was saying until 'his eyes, mouth, arms, hands, fingers, and even his head and body, all spoke at once'.

When he was speaking on 'the terror of the Lord', people felt that the messenger himself was 'threatening', and they spoke of wanting to hide from his look. When Martyn Lloyd-Jones, a preacher of the same school, was once preaching on the wrath of God, a woman declared, 'He was angry with me.' In such cases the authority of the preaching was such that man and message became one for the hearers. No one could doubt that it was preaching intended to *convince*. 'His solemnity was intense. No sermon of his would ever include a light word or anything that would induce a smile.'[23]

Strong conviction of sin is commonly a mark of true revival, and this is connected with the emphasis of preachers on the sinfulness of sin. But it would be entirely wrong to suppose that these men, such as Elias, preached to awaken hearers rather than to comfort them. They knew that love is at the heart of the gospel appeal. Men felt the compassion of Christ in what Elias preached. Those who heard him have said that he was never more animated than when he was magnifying the love of God. In the words of one eye-witness: 'His face brightens up, softened with holy sympathy. "Mercy" flows in accents of melody from his lips. It is a kind of celestial appeal that captivates every ear and heart.'

In a mid-week sermon in Liverpool, December 19, 1809, Elias's text was Ephesians 2:12: 'At that time ye were without Christ ... having no hope, and without God in the world.' As the sermon proceeded, his words and feelings ran together:

> O the wretchedness of the condition of those men who are without Christ! No tongue can ever tell, and no finite mind can fathom to eternity, the thousandth part of the misery of men without Christ! Bare, without a robe! Ill, with no physician! Hungry, having not the bread of life! Filthy, with no fountain! Guilty, with no righteousness! Lost, with no Saviour! Damned, with no Atonement!

'When he reached this point', we are told, 'he bent forward with his face on the Bible and wept, and the congregation too.' But the preacher was not done. A moment later, raising his head, 'Blessed be God!—Christ is available tonight to those who have hitherto been without him!'[24]

Those who would explain such phenomenon in terms of emotionalism would have said the same about Paul at Ephesus warning 'every one night and day with tears' (Acts 20:31). Why may not God, in any age, give large enduements of his Spirit which move preachers to the depths of their being? A Welshman who was critical of Elias once commented, 'Perhaps he would have been more acceptable to the learned if he had not acted so much.' Tudur Jones, who quotes the criticism, corrects it with the words,

> John Elias's preaching—and that of scores of others of that generation—was accompanied by a divine unction and spiritual consequences in thousands of souls that defy merely historical analysis. God's hand was indeed upon him.[25]

WIDER MINISTRY

Outside of Wales, it was in the cities of Liverpool and London where Elias was heard most. It seems to have been his habit to be in the English capital once every three years. His daughter Phoebe came to live there, and also his friend Daniel Jenkins of the Welsh church in Wilderness Row. Elias stayed with Jenkins and gave advice to his church as it was needed. While he was in London to preach, the city had other attractions for him, including meeting such men as John Newton, and the opportunity to search second-hand book shops for items not to be found in Wales.[26] His London visits also served another purpose. Thomas Charles was in the midst of the great work of providing Welsh Bibles in conjunction with the newly formed British and Foreign Bible Society. As the final stage of the work and the printing had to be done in London, many communications were necessary between Bala and the capital and some were conveyed to and fro by Elias. In 1806 he delivered the corrections for the Welsh New Testament which was published the next year.[27]

When the Bible Society asked Charles for an up-to-date list of the names and addresses of supporters in Wales, he replied: 'John Elias is coming to London and you will have an opportunity of consulting with him. You had better look them all over with him. Some are dead and the place of abode of many is spelt wrong. ... He will explain everything to you and correct the *errata* as far as regards Wales; for he is as well acquainted with the country as I am.'[28] Charles and Elias were often together in Wales and, on at least one occasion, in

London. Apart from their spiritual convictions, the two men differed in age and temperament: Charles was the elder by nineteen years, educated at Oxford, at home in the world of scholarship, and an ordained clergyman of the Church of England, although not serving any church of that denomination. While he would write to his younger friend as 'the Rev. John Elias', it was not in the traditional sense of that title, for the latter, as most of the Calvinistic Methodist preachers, had not been ordained. In recognition of that fact they did not administer baptism or the Lord's supper among the societies; that responsibility was left to the few clergymen among them. But as the numbers in the societies grew, so did a call for the Connexion to become a church in the denominational sense of the word. In allowing men to preach but not to administer the sacraments, the existing situation had the appearance of making sacraments more important than the spoken word. The question of a break with the Church of England was an issue which, for a time, threatened the unity of the Connexion, but in 1810 Elias could write that it has been settled peacefully.[29] In 1811 eight of the leading preachers, including Elias, were ordained and the Calvinistic Methodist Connexion assumed the title 'church', subsequently to be also known as the Presbyterian Church of Wales.

At the death of Charles, aged of 58 in 1814, it must have been apparent that Elias would be their next spiritual leader. In 1815 we find John Davies of Dolgelley writing to Josiah Pratt in London that it is 'the Revd. John Elias who now takes the lead in that body'.[30]

In that role Elias continued until his death. Preaching remained his first work. Other events that stood out in the intervening years were his part in the drawing up of the *Confession of Faith of the Calvinistic Methodists* (1823), his commitment to the work of the Bible Society in Wales, and the death of his much-loved wife in 1829. He re-married in 1830. A fall from a carriage in 1832 affected his health, yet his leadership continued until he preached for the last time at an Association in October 1840.

On February 11, 1841, four months before his death, Elias wrote one of his last letters. The final paragraph gave this brief comment on his life:

> If good has come of my very imperfect labour, it was God that did it. The glory is his, I was nothing. This will be seen in the day when God reveals his mysteries. If God took me as an instrument to bring any sinner, or sinners, to Christ, that has been an infinite privilege.

The epitaph on his grave at Llanfaes, Anglesey, describes him as 'upright, friendly, and affectionate',

Seeking not his own honour, but the good of souls,
And resting all his hope on the Cross of Christ;
In this hope
HE FINALLY TRIUMPHED OVER DEATH,
And slept in Jesus,
On the 8th day of June, 1841;
In the sixty-eighth year of his age.

ELIAS AS A WATCHMAN

The prophet Isaiah speaks of a time when Israel's prophets, appointed as watchmen to warn of approaching danger, were blind, ignorant, and silent, when they should have been speaking (Isa. 56:10). John Elias was a watchman, as well as an evangelist, and warned of dangers of which the succeeding generation failed to regard.

He saw danger in the popular idea that an advance in scholarship would necessarily increase the prestige and influence of the churches. Certainly the nineteenth century brought new knowledge and much progress at the material level: weaving as a cottage industry, and sailing ships wrecked by storms, were to become things of the past. But changes at that level in no way affected the condition of fallen man, without capacity either to know or desire God. 'The carnal mind is enmity against God: for it is not subject to the law of God, neither indeed can be' (Rom. 8:7). So man, without the revelation of God in Scripture, and a new birth to understand it, 'cannot enter into the kingdom of God' (John 3:5).

But the truth that 'the wisdom of God' and the wisdom of the world are contraries (1 Cor. 1:19) did not accord with the spirit of the age. Rather it was felt that, even if the two wisdoms could not be merged, at least there should be more co-operation in theological scholarship between the church and the world. It would take the passage of time to show that this could not be done without reverence for Scripture being diminished.[31]

The very limited education of Elias, and of many of the other early leaders of the Calvinistic Methodists, was thought of by some as a 'handicap' which a more learned ministry would have removed. But if the education of the earlier generation was limited in breadth, it had depth where it was most needed. It produced preachers immersed in Scripture, who reverenced Scripture with the reverence owed to God. Elias knew history too well to depreciate the need for learning in the church, but he saw the peril of making the learning of which the world approves a necessity for heralds of the gospel. If a man is sent by Christ, and has his presence, what the world may call a 'handicap' is no handicap at all.[32] Thus, in commenting on Christ's appointing of his disciples in Matthew 28:19-20, he addressed the idea that Christ would have been better advised to find preachers from Rome or Athens or from the ranks of the rabbis. 'Then the whole world will follow thee', someone would be ready to say. 'Thy disciples are so very weak.' To which Elias represented the Saviour as replying: 'Let that be so. But my strength is made perfect in weakness' (2 Cor. 12:9). 'That the excellency of the power may be of God and not of us' (2 Cor. 4:7).[33]

Among a minority who raised their voices on the same subject in English Nonconformity, were John Angell James and John Campbell. They believed that 'intellectual distinction and academic prestige' were as 'dust in the balance compared with sound theology, fervent piety, and preaching power', and they spoke against the churches adopting the London University degree course in theology. It was their conviction that such alliances were giving rise to 'companies of tutors, rather than evangelists and men "eloquent and mighty in the Scriptures". The churches ask for Preachers, and they are offered BAs, MAs, and LLBs'.[34]

It was noteworthy that the new approach to theological studies gave no importance to confessions of faith. Sometimes this outlook was presented in terms of greater respect for Scripture, and decrying the 'limitations' supposedly imposed by human compositions. But what might sound like praise for the Bible was actually the opposite. It is men devoted to Scripture who are most concerned to be able to state its meaning accurately, and to distinguish the truth from false doctrine. The purpose of confessions is not to replace Scripture but to hinder it being falsified. It is commonly men with little reverence for Scripture who have least sympathy with doctrinal standards being clarified on paper. 'Elias', says Edward Morgan, 'defended the doctrines set forth in the *Confession of Faith* with great firmness and zeal.' He did not do so because he thought the *Confession* had any authority apart from Scripture, or because he believed that confessions in themselves could safeguard orthodoxy. But a confession which preachers collectively own as their personal faith is a public announcement that they hold biblical truth in the same sense. Speaking of the *Confession of the Calvinistic Methodists*, Elias was to say, 'How thankful we should be to God that we have such a bulwark against all heresies that surround us in these days.'[35]

Another area where Elias saw the danger had to do with the necessity of upholding biblical standards of church membership.

It is the desire of every Christian that the numbers belonging to the church should be multiplied. But, however pleasing this prospect is, as soon as numerical success is given a place of first importance a departure from the New Testament is going to follow. The first mark of the New Testament church is her holiness. She stands separate from the world. She is 'the temple of God', to which it is a serious thing to belong: 'If any man defile the temple of God, him shall God destroy; for the temple of God is holy, which temple ye are' (1 Cor. 3:17). It was when the church was a body to which 'durst no man join himself', that God so worked that 'believers were the more added to the Lord' (Acts 5:13, 14).

Early in the spread of the gospel in North Wales we noted the formation of the private societies. There were qualifications for membership, which, as published in 1823, numbered thirty-four items and were named 'Rules for Discipline'. By that means a pattern for church membership and fellowship was established even before the Calvinistic Methodists became a formal church body in 1811. These rules were more than standards of behaviour; they set out the pattern of spiritual life which Scripture expects of the disciples of Christ. While assurance of salvation was not required for society membership, a life consistent with having been born of God was expected. None were to be admitted except:

> Rule 1. That they be, in some measure, convinced of sin by the Holy Ghost, poor in spirit, sorrowing for sin after a godly sort, and seeking to be delivered from it. John 16:8; Acts 2:37, 38; 16:30.
>
> Rule 2. That they be, more or less, convinced of their need of Christ.
>
> Rule 3. That they so hunger and thirst after Christ and his righteousness, as to show all diligence in the right use of the means of grace....

Rule 6. That they be bent upon forsaking all the paths of sin
and shame, which are contrary to the word of God and
mar the beauty of the Christian character.[36]

The rules then move to particulars, including: Members
are not to be married to unbelievers; are to observe family
worship; keep holy the Sabbath day; be

truthful, generous in their judgment of others, and gentle;
remembering that by our words we shall be justified, and by
our words we shall be condemned, inasmuch as our words
are the fruit and index of our hearts: Eph. 5:3, 4; Zeph. 3:9;
Matt. 12:37.

None shall be suffered to remain in church fellowship who
cherish habitual hatred or live at variance with their neigh-
bours. Eph. 5:2; Exod.23:1.

It was a fundamental conviction among the Calvinistic
Methodists that what happens at home, and in private, is the
real index to the state of the church. 'If private prayers were
more frequent and earnest', Elias believed, 'the public ministry
would be more effectual.' Family religion, family government
and right relationships between husband and wife, parents
and children, were all treated as part of the responsibilities of
church members.

Professing Christians today might protest against this kind
of care for church members, and perhaps accuse it of legal-
ism. But the foundation for what was enjoined lay in sound
theology. Regeneration puts a hatred of sin in the heart,
according to the promise, 'I will put my fear in their hearts,
that they shall not depart from me' (Jer. 32:40). For the
person who fears and loves God, the command, 'Be ye holy,
for I am holy', is not grievous. Rather it corresponds with an
inmost desire. Elias writes:

The fear of the Lord is a most valuable treasure in the church:
the dread of sin is in its very nature, and a renunciation of
it is sure to follow it always. 'The fear of the Lord is clean.'
Those that truly fear God, do not allow themselves the things

that others are pleased to indulge in. The true Christian fears grieving and offending him, and bringing reproach on his name and cause here in the world.[37]

How seriously he took the responsibilities of professing Christians is illustrated by an incident in Anglesey when a ship carrying cotton and tobacco was wrecked on rocks near Holyhead. As often happened, much of its cargo was washed ashore and it was reported at the monthly meeting that most, if not all, of the members of the Holyhead church had benefitted from what had been illegally acquired. Elias was sent, with other brethren, to investigate the accusation. After finding that more or less every member was guilty, he 'demonstrated clearly and powerfully to them the sinfulness of their actions', and 'excommunicated the whole church, officers and members, commanding them to leave at once. There was no strength in them to disobey, and all departed.' That night, we go on to read, there was not a Methodist home in Holyhead which would offer John Elias accommodation. At a late hour one family relented and sent their son to find the preacher who was sitting alone in the chapel where he had intended to stay the night.[38] About a month later, on evidence of repentance, all were received back and that was the end of their ever again taking goods washed up by the sea.

I have said Elias did not regard confessions of faith as being in themselves safeguards of orthodoxy. The fundamental safeguard lies in the holiness of a church and its relation to the Holy Spirit: 'That good thing which was committed unto thee keep by the Holy Ghost which dwelleth in us' (2 Tim. 1:14). He knew that if standards of membership are allowed to be relaxed, and worldliness tolerated, then it is only a matter of time before members want a type of elder and preacher suited to their condition. What happened in Jeremiah's time has many repetitions: 'the prophets prophesy falsely, and the priests bear rule by their means; and my people love to have it so' (Jer. 5:31). Such is the consequence when the authority of man replaces the authority of God.

On this subject, as on others, Martyn Lloyd-Jones was a spiritual successor to John Elias. In the context of the need for revival, he said in 1959: 'There is a call today for separation. It is the only distinction in the church which I recognize at all: those who submit to the word of God, and its revelation and teaching, and those who do not.'[39]

With reference to Wales, Emyr Roberts has written:

> The nineteenth century was the age of the preacher, and the 1820s were the mid-morning time of that age, when preaching was strongly in the ascendant. By the high-noon period, the middle of the century, the pulpit and sermon would dominate the life of Wales, even more than sports and politics do today.

This may sound a happy situation, but it brought with it a hidden danger, the near idolizing of good men. The remarkable success of the gospel gave preachers the kind of celebrity status that today is given to 'pop stars and football stars'.[40]

Without any question, amazing things had happened at this period in connection with preaching. Elias saw no less than forty chapels built in Anglesey alone. The thousands who gathered for services, and who bought Bibles, were no dream. But he was alarmed at the way in which an increasing number failed to distinguish between the preacher, as the channel of blessing, and God who is the author. People talked about 'the gifts, manner, delivery, voice, or eloquence of man' as though these were the cause of spiritual results. Many anecdotes about preachers were enjoyed and circulated. Take one typical example. Christmas Evans and Williams of Wern were both leading preachers. One day, the story went, Evans asked Williams, 'Is Elias a greater preacher than you or I?' The answer he got was,

'If he keeps his mouth closed his sermons are no better than ours; but when once he opens his lips, he is as good as twelve of us.' For Elias there was too much danger in such stories to be amusing. His conviction was, 'There is too much of the man in all we do.'

When his younger friend, Henry Rees, appeared likely to be called to Liverpool, Elias expressed his pleasure to the church there while advising them, 'I trust you perceive he is but a conduit pipe, that he cannot be of any use but in the degree in which the true and living water is conveyed through him ... no implicit confidence should be put in us as ministers.'[41]

> Few consider the ministry of the gospel as a means only. The best preacher is but an instrument, and the best sermons but means; they will not answer the end, except God himself will work through them. Alas, how few consider that Paul and Apollos are nothing, and that it is God that does the whole work.[42]

Elias had admirers who heard him deliver such cautions and yet still did not grasp that no preacher can command success. One such admirer asked a friend in later years, 'Did you ever hear John Elias?' 'I heard Mr Elias', was the response, only to be told he ought to have heard 'John Elias in his youth'. The admirer was revealing his own deficiency. If there were times—and there were—when Elias could say, 'multitudes are made willing in the day of Christ's power. I have had the privilege of receiving hundreds into church communion', it was not because of anything in him but 'by the secret and powerful operations of the Spirit'.[43] The youth or age of the preacher is never the explanation of results.

He noted the same lack of discernment in those who could not distinguish between emotionalism and the work of the Spirit. Excitement and tears are no evidence of a work of God. He pressed this point on his son John when the latter spoke of his discouragement that he did not weep under sermons as he saw others do. That was no proof, Elias replied, that he received no benefit, and he continued:

> True religion does not consist in emotions. The passions of many are much excited under sermons, without change of heart! Others may be changed; their hearts broken, conscience tender, sin hated, self loathed, without many tears. There is a great difference in the natural temperament of people, which accounts for the difference in their feelings under the word preached.[44]

CALVINISTIC BELIEF CHALLENGED

In his later years Elias was caught up in the most important doctrinal controversy of his life. Until that time a defence of the theology of the Calvinistic Methodists had played no major part in his ministry. But as the older leaders of the Connexion died, this became his role also, and it was to cast a shadow on his closing years. Until around 1800 Calvinistic belief was almost unchallenged in North Wales, but at that date the Wesleyan Methodist teaching entered and with it the claim that Christ's work of atonement was accomplished for all mankind. This met with little acceptance but, soon after, a more complex variant view of the atonement was published. The source was Edward Williams (1750–1813) who had tutored pastors for the independent churches of Wales before he left for England.[45] Williams thought he saw a middle way between Arminianism and Calvinism: he agreed with the former in saying that Christ died for all and with the latter in saying that his death was particularly for the elect. So it offered the promise of greater evangelical harmony. Still more important, in Williams's mind, it resolved the question which Calvinistic belief did not answer, namely, how could preachers call all to salvation in Christ if Christ had not died for all? How can any trust in Christ if they do not know that he died for them? So here was a proposal for a 'new system', and it involved the claim that to limit the atonement to the elect was to inhibit true evangelism. If Calvinists were evangelists they could only be so if inconsistent with their own principles.

Such was the controversy which was to become by the 1820s and 1830s a dominant issue among the Calvinistic Methodists. In part, this was fuelled by influences from the United States. Edward Williams's teaching had real connections with the so-called 'New Divinity' of New Haven, Connecticut— the divinity which nurtured the evangelist, Charles G. Finney, whose *Lectures on Revivals* were published in 1835. Finney not only taught that Calvinism was an obstacle to evangelism, he did all that he could to prove it. His case was that revivals, and 'how to promote them', depended on the gospel as *he* preached it.[46]

A difficulty over following the controversy in Wales concerns the sources of information. The history of wars is commonly written by the victors, and there is a parallel with respect to this controversy. After the death of Elias, the number of those in sympathy with what he believed dwindled, authors promoted the other side, and their view became the accepted orthodoxy. Among these authors Dr Owen Thomas (1812–91) exercised the greatest influence. In 1874, more than thirty years after the death of Elias, he published, in Welsh, a two-volume biography of a Calvinistic Methodist preacher, *The Life of John Jones of Talsarn*.[47] Jones of Talsarn was an admirer of Edward Williams and on that account, in early ministry, had been in disagreement with Elias. In a long section of his biography of Jones of Talsarn, Owen Thomas treated the whole controversy in Wales over Calvinism and the atonement; it was subsequently published separately under the title *The Atonement Controversy*.[48] His assessment was that while Elias was a great preacher, it was his proneness to hyper-Calvinism which made him critical of the more satisfying and progressive views of younger men. John Aaron, the recent translator of this title, while appreciating the work of Owen Thomas, gives an important caution concerning his treatment of this subject: 'He wishes the "New System" to prevail. ... It must be acknowledged, therefore, that he is not as impartial an observer as we might wish for, nor is his judgement to be followed at all points.'[49] No such warning was to be heard from the admirers of Owen Thomas's book when first published in 1874. The authors of the two volumes *The Calvinistic Methodist Fathers of Wales* (originally in Welsh, 1890, 1897), followed Owen Thomas on the issue in dispute. There thus arose a literature containing a misrepresentation of Elias which was commonly accepted. W. T. Owen, biographer of Edward Williams, wrote of 'hyper-Calvinism' as the 'very formidable obstacle' which formerly 'held Nonconformity in a powerful determinist grip'. He continued: 'In Wales its hold on Nonconformity was especially strong, and it was not until the death of John Elias, its most powerful and influential advocate, that freedom was eventually secured.'[50]

But if Elias was a hyper-Calvinist, so were all the Calvinistic Methodists who were leaders in the revival in Wales. Howel Harris wrote: 'I think we all agree with the good old orthodox Reformers and Puritans; I hold their works in great esteem— We do not think the Baxterian Scheme [of a universal atonement] orthodox.'[51] Sixty years later, in publications accepted throughout the denomination, the *Instructor* (*Hyfforddwr*), and the *Scriptural Dictionary* (*Geiradur Ysgrythyrol*), Thomas Charles answered the question, 'For whom did Christ die?' with the words, 'For his elect people, given to him by the Father'. This was fully stated in a statement of the Bala Association in 1809. Three things, it was written, are involved in redemption:

1. The election and appointing of Christ's own person in the place of those persons (and those only) who were to be purchased...
2. An imputing of their sins (and theirs only) to him...
3. The suffering in his own person for the punishment due for those sins (only) that were thus imputed to him. ... In

> this way he purchased an innumerable number of people,
> by making a full atonement for their sins.[52]

The words, repeated in brackets, lay at the heart of the controversy which was to develop later.

This teaching was not hyper-Calvinism and how it differed from it is very clear. Hyper-Calvinists intruded the doctrine of election into the gospel message in such a way that it comes between the unconverted and faith in Christ.[53] They believed that election limited the appeal preachers are to make to hearers—there should be no invitations addressed to all, no offers by Christ to all, no compassion in Christ to sinners as such. Elias was no such preacher. He could say of himself, 'There is not one Arminian on the face of the earth who would preach Christ to all more freely.' On the words, 'that whosoever believeth in him should not perish', he commented, '*Whosoever!* There is an infinite breadth in this word; whosoever, no matter of what nation, nor matter how wretched or unworthy he might be; whosoever believeth.'

Such language was commonplace for Elias as he summoned thousands to repentance and faith in Christ.

How Elias pointed individuals to Christ is well illustrated by what happened once in his own home. One afternoon, when he had returned from visiting, he was told that a servant girl belonging to the household wanted to speak with him. She was troubled about what she had heard him say at family worship that morning. On his asking what concerned her, the girl looked him in the eye and asked with great seriousness, 'Mr Elias, was it for my sin that Jesus suffered so? ('*Ai am fy meiau i dioddefodd Iesu mawr?*'). It was an enquiry he was delighted to answer, and it prompted him that same day to compose a hymn which put the same question before others:

> And was it for my sin
>   That Jesus suffered so,
> When moved by his all-powerful love
>   He came to earth below?[54]

He had answered the same question many times:

> When we preach generally that Christ is a Saviour to the lost, and persuade everyone that sees his lost estate to flee to him, we do it not under the idea that they are elected or redeemed, but as ruined; *thus* they are to go to him.[55]

> You are not called to believe as elect ones or as redeemed ones. You must believe as a sinner before you can know anything.[56]

> This is the order of things for the Christian as an individual, and it is also the approach we should take with our listeners. Our great purpose should be to get them to believe in the Son of God for salvation.

According to Edward Williams and his followers, Elias was 'narrowing' the gospel, and restricting its influence by answering the question in this way. Williams believed that the preaching of redemption as 'dying for all', and 'sufficient for all', was necessary to present the gospel to the unconverted. So he understood the doctrine of redemption as falling into two parts, one part concerned the salvation of the elect, the other related to the justice of God, which was satisfied, he believed, by an atonement made for all men. The second part, it was argued, provided the basis for the availability of an atonement to be preached to all. According to this thinking, the role of God in the two parts of redemption differed. In the one, he is a 'gracious Sovereign', saving the elect; in the other a 'Moral Governor' providing a general redemption.[57] Corresponding with this distinction was a difference with respect to terms used for Christ. In what Williams called 'actual redemption', Christ is said to be 'the Surety': but in the general redemption he is to be seen as the 'Mediator'.[58]

Elias commented on this teaching that it was inventing distinctions unknown to the New Testament: 'There are no weapons to be found in the realm of orthodox theology to defend their doctrine. That doctrine must be weak and unscriptural, that requires the invention of new phrases to defend and maintain it.'[59]

But he had a more serious objection. The teaching confused the very meaning of what it meant to be redeemed. Redemption has one definite meaning, it signifies the setting free of a captive by the payment of a ransom. 'The Son of man came ... to give his life a ransom for many' (Matt. 20:28). The justice of God had consigned sinners to the service of the devil. Christ died for those for whom he became the substitute and this achieved a change of ownership. Christians are people whom Christ 'purchased with his own blood' (Acts 20:28), 'bought with a price' (1 Cor. 6:20). The saints in heaven sing, 'thou wast slain, and hast redeemed us to God by thy blood' (Rev. 5:9). The teaching plainly indicates a cause and an effect; all for whom a ransom was paid will be set free and will live for God. The *only* redemption is one effected by substitution, and the extent of the substitution governs the extent of the deliverance secured. In the words of Elias, the atonement was 'sufficient, eternally sufficient, on the basis of his substitution, to satisfy justice for all those given to him by the Father.'[60]

Critics of this teaching objected that it narrowed the merit and all-sufficiency of the ransom Christ paid. When the *Confession of Faith of the Calvinistic Methodists* was drawn up, and proposed for acceptance in 1823, they asked that the section on redemption be revised. They disliked the words: 'It was ordained that his Person should stand in the stead of those persons (and those only) who had been given him to redeem.'[61] At that date the number of critics was too small to have the words 'and those only' removed.[62] But insistence grew that in addition to the redemption of the elect there was need for the proclamation of a general redemption. Would it not be more hopeful and wherein lay any danger?

Elias answered the question, although all did not want to hear him. He saw what was proposed as a redemption which did not carry within it any certainty of success. In one sense 'Christ died for the elect', and in another, Christ provided a redemption that did not contain a certainty of salvation for any. This was the same teaching which had provoked John Owen to ask its promoters,

> what exaltation is given to the death of Christ, what encouragement to sinners in the things of God, by maintaining that our Saviour ... died for the redemption of millions for whom he purchased not one dram of saving grace?[63]

Once the error of a universal redemption gains acceptance, Owen argued, it makes way 'for the troop that follows'.

This is precisely what happened with the New Divinity. The doctrines of original sin and of regeneration, as the work of God, had to be revised to make a receiving of the benefits of a general redemption dependent upon the human will. Finney had arrived at that conclusion by the 1830s. He taught that the new birth is not by a supernatural intervention, rather it occurs through 'the natural principles of the human mind'. People were no longer to think that saving faith was something beyond their ability. Let them hear the truth, said Finney, and there is no place for supernatural intervention before they can believe.[64] Only let them act on what they hear and their salvation is bound to follow. 'The atonement of itself', Finney wrote, 'does not secure the salvation of any.' Its application rests in the human decision. 'When a sinner repents that state of feeling makes it proper for God to forgive him.'[65]

For Elias, this teaching, instead of magnifying the Saviour, was introducing false teaching on redemption. It altered the truth of redemption so that it meant only the availability of forgiveness for those willing to accept Christ. But what is contained in the biblical word is of far greater magnitude. Those purchased by Christ receive, not a part of redemption, but everything necessary to bring them to eternal glory (see, for instance, Rom. 5:10; 8:32; Titus 2:14). In the light of Scripture, the *Confession of Calvinistic Methodists* could say of the redeemed:

all things—that is, grace and glory—are obtained for them through the Redeemer, and through the redemption which is in Christ Jesus. Thus the redemption ensures their calling, justification, sanctification, perseverance, adoption, and glorification.[66]

The teaching is the same in the *Westminster Confession of Faith* (VIII.5): 'The Lord Jesus ... purchased, not only reconciliation, but an everlasting inheritance in the kingdom of heaven, for all those whom the Father hath given unto him.'

The New System in reducing the content of redemption was passing over the extent of the need. The sinner needs a new nature, a new life, a new standing before God. The supposition that there is a potential redemption, dependent on the human acceptance, is contrary to all that Scripture says on the condition of fallen man. Such a limited redemption falls far short of what Christ secured by his sufferings. In the words of Elias:

> Man, under the fall, is as incapable of applying salvation to himself, as of planning and accomplishing it. There is as much need of the Spirit to apply salvation, as of the Mediator to work it out, though he became the Author of eternal salvation unto all them that obey him (Hebrews 5:9), yet no one will or can obey him, except the Spirit, in his infinite and overcoming power, works in him. The grace of God appears as clear in turning man, giving faith and repentance to him, as in redeeming him on the cross.[67]

It is evident that the two sides in this controversy read the proposed new teaching in a very different way. Elias viewed the change being promoted with the utmost seriousness. Contrary to the view of those who wanted the words 'and those only' removed from the redemption statement of 1823, he declared, 'I would prefer to lose my right arm, than to lose these words from our *Confession of Faith*.'[68] In 1831 he wrote to a friend,

> I am amazed, if these are powerful awakenings from above on the English in America as stated, that the doctrines of divines there are so confused and carnal. The truths of the Bible respecting the covenants, the fall of man, original sin, the suretyship of Christ, his substitution in the place of his people, the imputation of their sins to Christ and of his right-eousness to them, are all darkened by these writers![69]

In another reference to the new teaching, supported by the claimed revivals in America, he wrote:

> In heaven's name, dear brethren, let us avoid this ground. Our neighbours' houses are on fire, and some of the sparks are fall-ing on our own roof. Never imagine that any amount of light, however strong, falling on the mind, will change the nature of the heart. For all I know, the light of an angel shines in Satan's mind, but he has the heart of a devil nevertheless.[70]

The other side regarded such words as alarmist. The authors of the *Fathers of Wales*, reporting the disagreement between Elias and Jones of Talsarn, were of the opinion, 'there was no great difference except that they were considering matters from different perspectives'.[71] This was the judgment of Owen Thomas who ended his biography of Jones of Talsarn with the opinion that all had settled down in 'mutual tolerance and peace. Both sides began to realize that the differences between them were small, unimportant and superficial.'

But that there was a serious difference between the old and the new voices is not to be denied. Certainly, in some respects, both were influenced by the same consideration. By the 1820s and 1830s the general awakening of earlier days had passed. Both sides noted this with concern, but whereas dis-ciples of Edward Williams and supporters of Jones of Talsarn connected the ebb with deficiencies in the prevailing theology, Elias believed that the change they proposed was calculated to do the very opposite of what was desired. One of his reasons for so thinking was the willingness of the critics of Calvinistic belief to be concessive to 'rational' thinking—to allow a modification of Scripture in order to reduce its offence to the natural man.[72] Thus the argument that the gospel invitation could not be delivered consistently to all if redemption was only accomplished for a certain number. But it was enough for Elias that truth beyond our understanding was upheld by Christ. As Edward Morgan writes:

> It is quite remarkable that some of the most tender and all-embracing of our great Saviour's invitations to sinners are found in direct connection with the most clear, definite statements of the divine intention, in his sovereignty and grace, to bring a particular number to eternal life. This shows that there is no inconsistency in these matters in his own infinite mind.

Elias believed in divine sovereignty. If no revivals were taking place it was not because the gospel was not being made 'wider' and more appealing. It was not the message which led sinners to see no attraction in Christ, it was the absence of their knowing their need of him. Let Christ be held up where the Spirit has done his work of convicting of sin and there will be no lack of response. In the words of Thomas Charles, 'Everything in the councils of heaven favours a *returning sinner*—election, particular redemption, vocation, justification, etc, all, all are in his favour.'[73]

The controversy here summarized needs to be judged by Scripture. But it is not without significance that the belief which was to prevail after the death of Elias would ultimately sadly disappoint what had been hoped for it.

For a time the new system appeared a success. In 1861, Thomas Rees in his *History of Protestant Nonconformity in Wales*, could speak of the beliefs of John Roberts (disciple of Edward Williams), for which some men were 'much slandered forty years ago', as 'now so generally received, that hardly a minister of any note in the Principality would publicly oppose them'.[74]

In 1873, Owen Thomas believed, 'The preachers among us now feel quite free and unfettered, within the confines of revelation, and not bound by any system.'[75] Two years later, the General Assembly of the Connexion added an amendment to the confessional statement on redemption which a minority had questioned in 1823. It read: 'While we do not wish to make any alteration in what is stated in this Article concerning the substitution of the Person of the Mediator in the stead of those who were given him by the Father, we think it necessary to call attention to the opposite truth concerning the infinite sufficiency of the atonement.'[76] Those who still used the name of Calvinistic Methodists would quietly let the *Confession* of 1823 pass out of sight. The anti-confessional party had won.

In the after-glow of what had been a great evangelical era, the tendency of the new system was recognized by few. But as John Aaron, a recent close student of the period has written, the changed teaching 'proved to be the first steps in a rapidly accelerating journey that would eventually more or less eliminate Calvinistic thinking in the land'.[77] Similarly Tudur Jones, the Welsh church historian, has written of the thought which Elias opposed:

> It was the beginning, also, of the disparagement of theology: the subjection of theology to being the handmaid of morality; the repudiation of doctrine in favour of exhortation, a process which in time led to the doctrinal vacuum of our day.[78]

The verdict of W. T. Owen, biographer of Edward Williams in 1963, is very significant. He writes that Williams, setting out to be a reformer of evangelical theology, and a promoter of evangelism and unity, did not foresee the consequences of the changes he had set in motion. In a comment on why his subject should be 'practically unknown' today, he thought

> The key to the solution of this mystery is supplied by Dale when he speaks thus of Moderate Calvinists: 'They thought ... they could modify some of the Calvinistic doctrines which

in their rigid form had become incredible to them. But they were attempting an impossible task.'

W. T. Owen proceeds:

> Another writer has in a similar strain expressed the opinion that the historical significance of 'modified Calvinism' is that it was a 'polite dismissal of Calvinism'. Williams failed to forsee this event. ... The moderating process was carried on much further than Williams ever intended it to go; his standpoint was left behind and even forgotten, as Congregationalists become increasingly broader and more liberal in their theology. Eventually it was taken to a point where Calvinism was virtually abandoned altogether. ... It was moderate Calvinism that paved the way for the political and theological liberalism of the second half of the last century. In the process it lost its identity and was forgotten.[79]

It was not only Calvinism but the Bible itself which was to be forgotten. In the 1880s Congregationalists in England were at the forefront of what Spurgeon designated the 'downgrade controversy'. Deploring the change which was taking place, he commented, 'We used to debate particular redemption, now the question is whether there is any redemption at all.'[80]

The attempt to gain more influence and unity through a 'modified' gospel was a tragic failure in England and Wales. The effects of error may be slow but they are sure. The old judgment came again, 'I will send a famine in the land, not a famine of bread, nor a thirst for water, but of hearing the words of the LORD' (Amos 8:11). In many parts of Britain, the only memory of what had once been is large church buildings, now silent and empty, or disused and sold.

Geoffrey Williams was right to urge the study of Elias for light on the meaning of a revival. His ministry demonstrates

Jonathan Edwards' conviction that, while Christ is ever present with his church, his greatest work is done by 'remarkable effusions of the Spirit at special seasons of mercy'. The characteristic of such seasons is ever the same, it is in the power and authority with which the word of God is preached. It might be thought that this power is uniformly present wherever the word is preached, for is not the gospel always 'the power of God unto salvation'? To think thus is a serious mistake. Orthodox teaching may exist with little or no evidence of power. Truth may be preached 'in word only', and where it is there will be no such awakening as Paul tells us occurred at Thessalonica. That idol-worshipping city was so shaken that it could be said, 'the word of the Lord' sounded forth 'not only in Macedonia and Achaia, but also in every place your faith to God-ward is spread abroad'. The explanation was, 'Our gospel came not unto you in word only, but also in power, and in the Holy Ghost, and in much assurance' (1 Thess. 1:5). The same was true in North Wales in the lifetime of John Elias. The only explanation of it is the one to be found in the New Testament. When men speak with 'great power' it is connected with prayer and being filled with the Holy Spirit (Acts 4:31-33). Not all preaching is in 'demonstration of the Spirit and of power' (1 Cor. 2:4).

The Spirit of Christ is a living, divine Person, to be honoured and obeyed. He may be grieved and displeased. We may lose his help and power. In such times Christ's presence may be assumed and his absence unnoticed, as happened in the church at Laodicea. Then an experience akin to that of Samson may be repeated, when 'he awoke out of his sleep, and said, I will go out as at other times and shake myself. And he wist not that the LORD was departed from him' (Judg. 16:20).

In the latter period of his ministry Elias grieved that 'the divine light and power, once known and felt, do not accompany the ministry in these days!' He thought there was more than one cause of this situation. One was a lowered standard of personal holiness, and he urged, 'We ought to renounce everything in us, or amongst us, that we think gives any occasion to the Lord to hide his face from us.' Another cause was the declining commitment to the truths deemed Calvinistic. A heartfelt understanding of those truths, he believed, always brought its possessors to a low view of themselves. The preachers whom he remembered much owned of the Lord, were men who

> used to go into the pulpit as poor, needy and trembling creatures; their dependence for everything was on the Lord. They were very anxious that the people should be benefitted and eternally saved.

In contrast, he saw a different situation developing in which people could not tell the difference between a sermon delivered in the power of the Holy Spirit and one delivered only in the gifts and ability of the preacher:

> I hear that unsound and slight thoughts of the work of the Holy Spirit are entertained by many in these days, and that he is grieved thereby. I heard a man this week assert in a speech that 'Influences are inseparably connected with all truths, so that if the truth be set forth sufficiently clear, accompanied with strong reasons and earnest persuasions, it will prevail with all.' If so, nothing more is wanted but that we be strong and eloquent speakers, persuasive, impressive, and clever; and then we shall overcome the world. Is there not here a want of perceiving the corruption, obstinacy, and spiritual deadness of man, and the consequent necessity of the Almighty Spirit to enlighten and overcome him?[81]

Elias concurred with the words of Thomas Charles:

> I am persuaded that unless we are favoured with frequent revivals, and a strong, powerful work of the Spirit of God, we shall, in great degree, degenerate and have only a 'name to live'; religion will lose its vigour; the ministry will hardly retain its lustre and glory; and iniquity will, of consequence, abound.[82]

Thomas Charles and John Elias were of one mind on the remedy for this. It is not speaking more about revival or the Holy Spirit, but renewed faith and renewed communion with the Lord Jesus Christ. The Spirit is given to glorify him, and the Spirit leads to personal fellowship with the Saviour himself. Power is not a commodity to be sought. It belongs with communion with Christ and the resolution:

> I count all things but loss for the excellency of the knowledge of Christ my Lord ... that I may know him, and the power of his resurrection, and the fellowship of his sufferings, being made conformable unto his death (Phil. 3:8, 10).[83]

Sad although Elias was over the decline which he saw in its early stages, his faith was fed from a higher source than contemporary circumstances. He looked to the one who has all authority in heaven and earth, and in whom the final victory is assured. He believed that the success of Christ's kingdom has been determined before the world began. 'He shall not fail nor be discouraged, till he have set judgment in the earth' (Isa. 42:4). 'He shall be great ... and of his kingdom there shall be no end' (Luke 1:32, 33). 'The zeal of the LORD of hosts will perform this' (Isa. 9:7). The Calvinistic Methodists of Wales had cause to be a singing people. A hymn by a predecessor, 'Onward march, all-conquering Jesus', expresses the vision with which John Elias left this world:

> How my raptured soul rejoices
> That the jubilee is near;
> Every word will be accomplished,
> Spoken by our Saviour here.
> North and South, in countless myriads,
> From earth's darkest ends shall come,
> With the dance and gladsome music,
> Into heaven's eternal home.[84]

2

Andrew A. Bonar:
Fellowship with Christ

'"Holiness," said William Hewitson, "is a habit of mind—a setting of the Lord continually before one's eyes, a constant walking with God as one with whom we are agreed." And in the attainment and maintenance of unbroken communion, "Prayer is amongst duties, as faith is amongst graces." Richard Sibbes reminds us that "Prayer exercises all the graces of the Spirit," and Flavel confirms the sentence: "You must strive", he writes, "to excel in this, forasmuch as no grace within or service without can thrive without it".... Holiness is conformity to Christ, and this is secured by growing intimacy with Him.'

D. M. M'Intyre [son-in-law of Andrew Bonar],
The Hidden Life of Prayer, pp. 78-79.

IT was while I was in the British army in Malaya, some sixty years ago, that I first bought a book by Andrew A. Bonar. The decision was hardly my own, for I was urged to buy it by a Canadian missionary in a Singapore Christian bookshop. The book was a milestone for me as a young Christian, but I was soon surprised to find that others were as ignorant of it as I had been. When I told the Scots Presbyterian chaplain of our battalion of Cameronians that I was reading Bonar's life of Robert Murray M'Cheyne, he responded, 'Ah, yes, he was a saintly old man'—a surprising comment about one who died at the age of twenty-nine! On a visit to Glasgow after returning home, I sought out Bonar's grave in Sighthill Cemetery. It seemed to be having few visitors. In the years since that date, I have taken up Bonar's writings from time to time, but only recently to read him again with more thoroughness. It has been a challenging experience, and it has convicted me of the negligence I thought I saw in others half a century ago. When Andrew Bonar's *Diary and Letters* were published in 1894, William Robertson Nicoll, editor of the *British Weekly*, wrote of it as 'perhaps the most impressive Scottish religious biography that has appeared since Dr Bonar's own *Life of M'Cheyne* was published' fifty years earlier.[1] If we could get these books studied today, I am certain they would make a deep impression again. It is hard to think of any reading which would be more challenging and convicting.

'But', perhaps someone says, 'Is it relevant?' That can be answered by another question, 'Is revival relevant?' If it is, then the Bonar books take us to a period of history well able to help us today. Bonar and M'Cheyne were at the centre of a group of a dozen or more likeminded young ministers (mostly from the Divinity College in Edinburgh), which arose in the Church of Scotland in the 1830s. Marked by their close friendship with each other, by their preaching of Christ, and their love for their people, they were prominent instruments in a remarkable era of evangelism and revival. They have been called 'a school of saints',[2] and while they would have repudiated any such description, we can understand why it was used. Less favourably, some referred to them disparagingly as 'the Evangelical Light Infantry';[3] but James Stalker, with personal knowledge, could write that they 'were all, or nearly all, highly cultivated men, though they sank their culture in something better, and therefore sometimes received less credit for it than they deserved'.[4]

But our interest is not so much in these men as men; it is rather in what made them what they were. If the principles which governed their lives had been well tried in our day, and with little benefit to the churches, there could be reason to question their relevance in the twenty-first century. Instead of that being the case, to read Bonar is to be convinced that there are great biblical lessons which we are not taking seriously enough.

THE YEARS OF PREPARATION

The Bonars were something like a 'tribe' of ministers, of which Andew, born in 1810, was the youngest. His uncle was minister at Cramond; a cousin served the parish of Larbert, and he had two older brothers, John and Horatius, who were lifelong preachers of the gospel.[5] Educated in Edinburgh, Andrew did not enter the Divinity Hall until he had assurance of salvation. At the Hall, then led by Thomas Chalmers, the lives of a future generation of ministers were moulded in study, prayer, and visitation among the city's poor. Of the group of men who left the Hall about the same time, Andrew was one of the last to be settled in a charge. Licensed in 1835, for nearly four years he was to work as a probationer, first at Jedburgh, then in Edinburgh. M'Cheyne, three years his junior, was settled in

St Peter's, Dundee, in 1836, and he urged Andrew to believe that his opportunity for greater usefulness was coming. In the event it was through M'Cheyne that Bonar's settlement came. The evangelical patron of the parish of Collace, Perthshire, sought to take M'Cheyne away from Dundee. The latter declined but with the words, 'I will tell you of a much better man', and he named his friend.

Thus Andrew Bonar was settled at Collace in 1838. It was a parish made up of three small villages,[6] situated some eight miles from Perth and fourteen from Dundee. The location beneath the hill of Dunsinnane was beautiful; the spiritual situation, in contrast, was more like a desert. Bonar was ordained as colleague to a senior minister who had been there nearly fifty years, during which time it is said that only one person had ever received any benefit from him. It was thought that 'there were perhaps not more than half a dozen living Christians in the place'. The old minister wanted no 'new doctrines' to disturb the peace, and a member of his family was to ask the new preacher, 'Do all young men preach that it is necessary for people to be converted, or is it just yourself?' To which Bonar replied, 'Oh, every one of us preaches what the word says—that it is needful for all to be born again.' It is hardly surprising that Bonar was not liked by the majority on his arrival, and when he declined to drink whisky while visiting homes, the word went round that he was 'a proud man'.

A number of other young ministers were similarly settled in parishes in parts of Perthshire and Angus at this time, and they became a brotherhood in their help to one another. Together they shared the conviction once expressed by the New England Puritan, John Eliot, 'Prayers and pains through faith in Christ Jesus will do anything.'[7] M'Cheyne, their natural leader, urged patience and counselled that they were not yet ready for revival. They learned that there is a divine order with regard to revivals, and that their first business was to prepare themselves. 'Revivals begin with God's own people;

the Holy Spirit touches their heart anew, and gives them new fervour and compassion, and zeal, new light and life.'[8] In his first years at Collace, Bonar settled into the habits of study and prayer that became the pattern of a lifetime. A favourite place for prayer was the wood of Dunsinnane. In allusion to words in 1 Samuel 23:14-15, he came to call it 'the "Wood of Ziph", where God has often strengthened my hands, my divine Jonathan meeting me there'.

Bonar's Perthshire location was remote by nineteenth-century standards, and he was to spend eighteen years there. For the most part they were years of quietness and seclusion, but there were exceptions. One day in March 1839 a farmer met him leaving Collace on his white pony. He greeted the minister with the words, 'You'll be gaun to Pairth the daay, Mister Bonar'—more easily read as, 'You'll be going to Perth today, Mr Bonar.' To the man's astonishment, Bonar replied, 'No, I am on my way to Jerusalem.' He meant it literally. The Church of Scotland had appointed a deputation of four ministers to go to Palestine to examine the state of the Jewish people with a view to initiating missionary work among them. One of the ministers appointed was M'Cheyne, chosen it is said for the good of his health. Bonar's ability in Hebrew, and his affection for the Jewish people, must have contributed to his inclusion in the deputation. The 'Mission of Inquiry', as it was called, lasted from April to November, and included ten days in Jerusalem itself. It led to the publication of a book of over 500 pages, much of it written by Bonar, with some drawings supplied by M'Cheyne.[9] The experiences of these fascinating months—still in print today—deepened Bonar's concern for the Jewish people and, it is said, 'gave a colour to all his future ministry'.

Another major exception to the quiet years at Collace occurred soon after the return of the deputation from Israel. In the seven months they had been away revival had begun that was to affect various parts of the land. At St Peter's, M'Cheyne came back to see remarkable evidence of multiplied conversions, and spoke of 'an awful and breathless stillness pervading the assembly'. When Andrew visited his brother Horatius at Kelso, he noted the same change, 'a solemnity and stillness which I almost never saw before anywhere'.[10] For a time the people of Collace continued in their slumber but it was not to last. On February 26, 1840, Bonar noted in his *Diary*, 'I think God is about to bless us.' He was right. At the end of a prayer meeting in April, 'many waited behind in distress'. A confession of their unconverted state became common among the people, and Bonar found it no easy matter to know how to relieve them. On June 26 he wrote, 'There is a general anxiety throughout the whole parish and much fear.' And on October 12, 'Still the appearances of revival are not withdrawn.'

Especially noted at Collace was the depth of conviction of sin, and the clear understanding of the way of salvation that usually followed. The conversions seem to have begun among 'the older people'. One elderly woman who had been converted said, 'I canna say much, but my heart's like a burning coal.' But the young also were reached. Such was the hunger for the word of God that numbers walked many miles to services. A group of factory girls used to come seven miles on foot, crossing the Tay in order to do so. One night after a service they were so late in getting back to the ferry that there was no boat to take them over and so they slept cheerfully among bushes beside the river until the morning.[11]

'The great revival', as it was called, affected many areas and inevitably led Bonar to help in other parishes. As well as regular visits to Dundee and Perth, he was also preaching in Edinburgh, Huntly (where he found 'droppings of the Spirit throughout the whole region of Strathbogie'), Rattray, Kelso, and other places. He noted at the end of 1840:

> Through the past year, God has shown me new things indeed: a revival, a shower of the Spirit in my own parish, a thing I had longed for, and reckoned among the highest blessings I could ever receive. ... More vexation and more opposition,

too, this year than ever before. I have been permitted to visit and preach in many more places than before.[12]

There were many permanent results from these years of revival. In Collace the face of the parish 'began to assume a different aspect'. Family worship came to be practised in nearly every household and a public house was closed. In the wider scene the surge of new life played a vital part in the numbers of ministers and people who shared in the Disruption of May 1843 that brought the Free Church of Scotland into being. Bonar came back from the Disruption day in Edinburgh to preach in the open air to about five hundred people. Thereafter a large tent was used until a new church could be built. The revival had brought a close fellowship of Christians into being, and at the Collace communion season in June 1843 many were present from other churches. Long to be remembered were Bonar's words in his closing address at the Lord's table from the words, 'Until the day break, and the shadows flee away.'

Comment on Bonar's preaching at this period is to be found in a rare document, the diary of M'Cheyne's close friend, Jessie Thain. After hearing him in Dundee she noted: 'Mr Bonar's exposition of Psalm 102 was precious, and his sermon on Phil. 2:1-2, "If there be any consolation in Christ", was rich and full. He spoke of resting on the mercies of God as on a pillow.' Again in her hometown of Blairgowrie: 'In the evening Mr Andrew Bonar gave us a very fine discourse on the Paschal Lamb, as typical of Jesus our Passover who was sacrificed for us. It was full of rich matter, offering nourishment to the hungry soul. On the Saturday ... Mr Andrew Bonar's sermon in the evening was very good indeed. He showed in it very plainly our poverty by nature, and that even after believing in Jesus, we possess nothing in ourselves, but must to the very end draw all our riches from the treasures that are in Christ.'[13]

One particular convert in these revival years was to be the means of changing Bonar's life: she was Isabella Dickson of

Edinburgh. Perhaps it was through her brother, William Dickson, that Bonar came to know her; certainly the outcome was of God's planning. Not everyone in Collace, however, was so persuaded. Bonar had been a bachelor for ten years among them and when one old woman heard that their minister was to change his single state, she told him plainly, 'Weel, sir, I hope it's a'richt, but we women are awful cheats!'[14]

The marriage took place in April 1848 and there followed, at the temporal level, the happiest years of his life. A new manse was built for them on the edge of Dunsinnane wood, and over the door Bonar had the words engraved, 'He that winneth souls is wise', and, 'For yet a little while, and he that shall come will come and will not tarry.' These texts had a bearing on a growing sense of unease that came to him. In his peaceful country retreat, he could not forget the thousands in British cities who heard no gospel. He wondered if London might be calling him, but it was the need of Glasgow that most persistently came into his thoughts. For five years from 1852, the 'perishing multitudes' of that city were often before him. Thus when a call came to him in 1856, to establish a mission church among the poor in the west end of Glasgow, he knew what he was to do. On August 24, 1856, he wrote in his *Diary*: 'Today announced my conviction to my people that if I did not go to Glasgow I feared I would be acting the part of Jonah.'[15]

Yet he was loath to leave. He felt there had been much left undone through the previous eighteen years, and the place was twined round his affections: 'Every road in this neighbourhood, every house in this place, almost every tree I have passed, might witness some mercy. ... Happy years have passed here, very happy; but we are pilgrims.' To a friend he wrote: 'To leave Collace I had always thought would be like Abraham leaving Ur of the Chaldees—that is, nothing but the clear call of the God of glory would effect it.'

THE GLASGOW MINISTRY, 1856–1892

The only physical description of Andrew Bonar that I have seen comes from the time when his Glasgow ministry began. He is described as a 'tall, straight, and somewhat spare man, about forty-five years of age, with hair just tinged with gray'. At this date, although he had acquired something of a reputation as a writer, he was little known as a preacher, and there was no excitement over his arrival in the city. The nucleus of his congregation, only ten or twelve people, came from Free St Matthew's, and included the loan of three elders, one of whom became permanent. They met in a new church building in Finnieston Street, and while curiosity brought a large attendance on his first Sunday in December 1856, 'for many a day after there was only a sprinkling of people in the church'. Robertson Nicoll, commenting on the perception people had of Bonar at this period, wrote,

> He had a scattered but enthusiastic band of admirers. ... But we believe it is true that he was not valued at anything like his worth. His intellectual power was underrated. Even when at last he went to Glasgow, it was to one of the smallest of mission churches.[16]

Bonar was not dismayed at the situation he found. He had anticipated that, entering a largely non church-going area, he would, as a missionary, have to 'dig the wretched people out of the wynds' [back alleys]. He saw his future congregation among 'the indifferent, the drunken, the lazy, the ignorant, the practical atheists'. The first need was to 'learn their language and habits', and to seek openings among them. In this he was gifted with the ability of getting alongside all kinds of people. It was said of him, 'He never launched an appeal to saint or sinner from a distance, if it was ever possible to step forward and put arm within arm.'[17] His memory for names and faces helped to win attention. A young girl was one of many who were surprised to be addressed by name on the street. She went home with the message, 'Mither, he kens me.'

How the situation changed during thirty-six years in Glasgow would make a lengthy story in itself, and cannot be told here. Suffice it to say that, aided by earnest Christian helpers, the congregation finally outgrew its building. In 1878 a larger building had to be built near West End Park, and by the 1890s over a thousand made up the congregation. By that date Bonar had become something of a legend in the city. On the birthday that began his eightieth year, he reminded the company at breakfast 'that when Moses entered on his eightieth year he was only beginning his best work'. That was his ambition, and his weekly routine seems to have continued much as it ever was. 'Latterly', his daughter records, 'when overwhelmed by work—visits, letters, interruptions, engagements of every kind—it was his rule to devote two hours every day, before going out, to prayer and meditation on God's word.' Every afternoon from Monday to Thursday went to visitation until 5 pm. Fridays and Saturdays were for sermon preparation. Once a month, he sought to give the best part of a day to prayer, frequently with fasting. Sundays began with an elders' prayer meeting at 10.30 am, and did not close till 9 pm. There were two regular services of public worship, morning and afternoon, and he generally attended a prayer meeting which took place in the interval between; at 5.30 pm he led the young men's Bible class; then visited the Sabbath school, and commonly preached a third time either in the church or at a mission hall.[18]

It was not until September 1891, fifteen months before his death, that he began to share the ministry with a colleague, D. M. M'Intyre. Bonar believed that a Christian should need no special preparation for death, and he once anticipated how he would like to die in these words: 'I shall preach on Sabbath, take the Prayer-Meeting on Wednesday, and on Thursday night people will be going about saying, "Do you know that Dr Bonar is dead?"' In the event the fulfilment was very close to his wish. He preached a Christmas sermon on Sunday,

December 25, 1892; the next Wednesday he was at the Prayer-Meeting as usual; Thursday he began with a chill that took him to his bed, where he was occupied with thoughts of the parish and the work of the next Sunday. But he became too weak to rise. Family worship was held round his bed on the Saturday night, and he led in prayer with a clear and distinct voice. Then without any 'good bye' or reference to death, he said 'good-night' to each of his children, asked for the lights to be put out, and at 10.30 pm 'fell asleep so quietly that those round the bed hardly knew when life was gone'.[19]

At his burial on January 4, 1893, men, women and little children followed through the snow to his burial. Numbers of Glasgow shops had his picture displayed in their windows. More than a dozen tributes were written by men of almost all denominations. The Rev. W. M. M'Gregor spoke of him as 'probably the most obliging and unsparing worker in Glasgow in any profession; no labour was ever refused by him, and everything was done with a zest and lightness of heart'.[20] Robertson Nicoll contrasted the little-noticed beginnings of Bonar's years in Glasgow with his subsequent stature as 'one of the most powerful religious forces in the city. ... His existence came to be at last in the great, busy city of the West like the witness of a church spire pointing to God.' Another contemporary wrote:

> He was one of the mightiest spiritual forces in this great city, unnoticed by most men, just as the great engines that drive the dynamos are out of sight, yet but for them there would be no illumination, soft or brilliant, in shop or street.[21]

The most abiding influence of Bonar's life has still to be noted. It began, while he was at Collace, with the book *Narrative of a Mission of Inquiry to the Jews from the Church of Scotland in 1839*, for which he wrote a large part. While still in Perthshire he wrote seven books. He was also writing volumes in shorthand that he never intended for publication and which he continued through sixty-four years. These were his diaries, and for the Christian church they were to become the most valuable of all that he left. They would be abridged and published by his daughter after his death, as already noted. In their pages we see him as a man before God, and as one aspiring to greater love and holiness. Nowhere is there a hint of praise for himself.

I will give three episodes which stand out for me in the *Diary*.

M'CHEYNE DIES AND THE BIOGRAPHY LIVES

About five o'clock on the afternoon of Saturday, March 25, 1843, a message came to Bonar at Collace with the news that one of his closest friends had died. It was startling news, for M'Cheyne had only missed the previous Sunday from his pulpit at St Peter's. In pastoral visitations he had caught the typhus fever then present in Dundee and, after only a few days' delirium, he was gone at the age of 29.

Bonar reached St Peter's by nine that same Saturday night and found himself, he noted, in such a scene of sorrow as 'has not often been witnessed in Scotland. It was like the weeping for King Josiah.' The main part of the church was full of people, and 'Every heart seemed bursting with grief.' Despite his own tears, Bonar addressed the people from Revelation 21:1-6, and again the next morning from Paul's words at the end of Romans 8, beginning, 'For I am persuaded, that neither death nor life … shall be able to separate us from the love of God, which is in Christ Jesus our Lord' (Rom. 8:38, 39).

Struggling to overcome his own emotion, Bonar would note in his *Diary* afterwards, 'I had too much feeling of the event, too little care for God's glory in it.'

A few days after M'Cheyne's death, Bonar wrote this of him in a new Preface to the third edition of the *Mission of Inquiry*, the book they had authored together:

Those who knew him most loved him best. … During the six short years of his ministry, he was the instrument of saving more souls than many true servants of God have done during half a century. But as in our journey to Jerusalem, he hastened before us all to get a sight of the city of the Great King, so now he has got the start of us all in seeing the New Jerusalem that is to come out of heaven from God.

It was the closeness of the two men which brought Bonar to write the book which was to make their names known throughout the Christian world. In September 1843 he began to write Robert M'Cheyne's *Memoir*. By December 22 of the same year it was finished, and from that day to this it continues to be read. Those who wonder why unemotional Scots should have been so distressed by one young man's death find the answer in Bonar's pages. In its converting and sanctifying influence very few biographies are its equal. Forty years later, Spurgeon would say of it, 'This is one of the best and most profitable volumes ever published. Every minister should read it often.'[22]

There is a sense in which Bonar himself never got over the death of M'Cheyne. His portrait was in his study; he dreamed of him; and in his *Diary* there are such recurring notes as one on Saturday, March 25, 1871, 'I well remember twenty-eight years ago this day the messenger came to my house in Collace to tell me that Robert M'Cheyne was taken from us.'

TIMES OF REVIVAL

The pages in the *Diary* that deal with the times of revival in Bonar's lifetime are especially noteworthy. There were three or four such periods. The first, of the years 1840–41, has already been mentioned. The second was in 1859, a year of great awakening in Ulster. Reflecting on the situation in the Finnieston district of Glasgow, he wrote in his *Diary* for July 3, 1859:

> I have come to this again and again these two years: that unless the Lord pour out his Spirit upon the district, nothing

will bring them out to hear and attend; and now we hear that this is the very thing which God is doing in the towns of Ireland. O my God, come over to Scotland, and help us. O my Lord and Saviour, do like things among us in this city!

Others were so praying in Scotland and the prayer was answered. The next month he writes on August 10:

This has been a remarkable week: every day I have heard of some soul saved among us; one on Sabbath morning struck, and now in Christ. Several on Monday under deep concern. On Wednesday several spoke at the close of the meeting. Last night again, where I found one of my class awakened that morning.

As in 1840, Bonar's help was now sought in a number of places. He finds himself asked to preach mid-week to a hundred men in Thomson's Foundry, Glasgow; twice he is invited to Ferryden in Angus and finds that there 'the Lord is working wonderfully. The souls of men here are everywhere melted down.' On the last night of 1859 he can write, 'O what a year this has been for conversions in many places!' Yet such was Bonar's self-scrutiny that we see that these days of revival also brought some pain to him. He had to struggle with the sins of jealousy and envy as he saw others being more widely used than he was. 'Lord, undo this corruption', he prays. Revival times are not heaven: 'One thing I find this year, we must expect always to eat bitter herbs with Passover food.'[23]

From 1859 to 1874 the work of God went on with nothing exceptional, then days of unusual blessing returned and conversions were again multiplied in the land. This was the occasion of D. L. Moody's first visit to Scotland. First Edinburgh was profoundly stirred; then the evangelist came to Glasgow in February 1874. Bonar had long been a student of histories of revival. He believed every Christian ought to be, and quoted Psalm 111:2 in that connection, 'The works of the Lord are great, sought out of all that have pleasure in them.' He was therefore not prepared to credit any religious excitement as 'revival'. He had been unsparing in his criticism of C. G. Finney,[24] and knew the difference between a well-organised evangelistic campaign and a powerful work of the Spirit of God. In his mind there was no doubt what they saw in Glasgow in 1874 was revival, and it is to his pen that we owe probably the fullest record of those remarkable days. It can be found in his biography of James Scott,[25] and in the *Narrative of Messrs. Moody and Sankey's Labours in Scotland and Ireland*.[26]

It will be sufficient here to give some of Bonar's *Diary* entries which were not written for publication:

> Tuesday, Feb. 10th. This city has been at last visited; Moody and Sankey, sent by the Lord, as when 'He sent them two and two to every place whither he himself would come.'

> Saturday, 21st. The work goes on. Not a few have been brought to Christ this week, among the rest several anxious among my people.

> Sabbath, March 1st. The past week has been a time of great blessing to souls among us. Every day I have met with some who have been blessed.

> Sabbath, 15th. This morning, at nine o'clock, a gathering of three thousand young men, and the lecture on Daniel was most memorable.

> Saturday, 28th. Many among us are receiving blessing. I have a communicants' class of fifty-two. Most of them very distinct in their account of their conversion.

Two months later he could note in his *Diary*: 'In our Sabbath school there have been not less than one hundred awakened, and most them very hopeful.'

True revivals are ever accompanied by a stronger fear of God. Bonar describes a private meeting of about thirty Christians, at which he was present, as a 'Most solemn scene, never to be forgotten.' At some of the public meetings we read of people so awe-struck that they had to hide their face in their hands.

In a letter written in 1879 Dr Cuyler of New York reported:

I asked our friend Moody who rendered him the most assistance in Great Britain. He answered: 'The Lord Chancellor and Dr A. A. Bonar,—the first one by attending our London meetings and giving me his powerful influence, and Dr A. A. Bonar by helping me to a deeper knowledge of the word, and by his letters and counsels.'[27]

After Moody had spent another five months in Britain in 1882, Bonar noted in his *Diary*:

It seems to me plain that the Lord uses his sovereignty in making that man a vessel through which the converting power of God may be poured out on various classes of men. The drunkards have had their 'day of visitation', and many others of the working men especially.

Moody's work in Scotland was unhappily regarded by some as marked by wrong teaching and superficial excitement, and this opinion has remained in some quarters. If it were true it would be hard to explain why so many ministers of Calvinistic convictions were supportive. That number included men of the M'Cheyne circle, such as Moody-Stuart, Alexander Somerville, and Andrew's brother, Horatius. Whereas Finney had criticised preachers of that stamp, Moody endorsed them and their ministries:

Do not let young converts get it into their heads that the minister or pastor is not an important man. I consider that there is no man in the world more important than a good pastor. ... I believe the dearest thing to the heart of the Son of God on this earth is the church. You talk about the success of our meetings here. What would they have been if your pastors had not been sowing the seed here for years? And when the seed is once sown, you may rest satisfied a reaping time is sure to come. If you have any regard for the truth that has been a blessing to you, stand right behind the church of God.[28]

Concerning the substance of Moody's teaching, Bonar believed, 'There was no novelty; the great truths taught in the *Shorter Catechism* were enforced and applied.'[29]

ISABELLA BONAR

Nothing is more moving in the *Diary* than Bonar's references to his wife. They came from Collace with three children, and two more were born before 1864, one of whom, Andrew, was to die at the age of two. That sorrow was in part met by the birth of another daughter, Mary Elizabeth, in September 1864. Mother and baby were apparently doing well until less than a month later, when he wrote:

> O what a wound! Last night most suddenly, after three hours' sinking, my dear, dear Isabella was taken from me. Lord, pour in comfort, for I cannot. Lord, what innumerable kindnesses thou gavest me through her: a true wife, a true mother, a true friend. She passed away so gently that, till I held her and touched her cheek, I could scarcely believe she was dead.

In the words of their long-serving family servant, Isabella Bonar 'slipt into glory'. Through seventeen years she had been 'the light of the home' for her husband. The eldest children, Isabella and Marjory, were aged only fourteen and nine. The father, his boy James staying close beside him, with baby Mary often in his arms, felt bewildered at the suddenness of the change. 'How dreary, how truly empty, everything seemed on the side of earth. A constant want was what I felt at home and in every corner.'[30] Twenty-eight years alone were to be ahead, yet while the sense of loss never left him, his testimony was to be, 'The Lord has led me on, and has quietly taken the place of all, by his own blessed presence and fellowship.' His children were also made a comfort to him.

GODLINESS AND USEFULNESS

The life of Andrew Bonar shows us how closely the usefulness of servants of Christ is related to the holiness of their lives. Certainly it is true that from time to time men of outstanding natural gifts are given to the churches but, even in their case, their gifts are not *the key* to their usefulness. Bonar certainly had gifts, but they did not include a natural eloquence of speech and an appealing voice. He was not what is commonly called 'a popular preacher'. That was his own assessment: 'I am not, and never was, a great or popular preacher', and it seems to have been the opinion of others.[31] How then did he build and sustain a large congregation through many years? The answer is because what a preacher is *as a Christian* is of greater consequence than his natural gifts. In the words of M'Cheyne: 'It is not great talents God blesses so much as great likeness to Jesus. A holy minister is an awful weapon in the hand of God.'[32]

This being surely true, it must lead to the question, What is holiness in personal life? That is the question which compels consideration in Bonar's *Diary*, and the answer there provided is surely the true one: the essence of holiness is communion with God, it is Christ in us—'Truly our fellowship is with the Father, and with his Son Jesus Christ.' This is the thread that ran through Bonar's life as a Christian:

> [Aged 33:] 'I see plainly that *fellowship with God is not means to an end*, but is to be *the end itself*. I am not to use it as a preparation for study or for Sabbath labour; but as my chief end, the likest thing to heaven.'

> [Aged 34:] 'Close walking with God, daily, if not hourly, taste of the sweetness of Christ ... O to be as Enoch till I die!'

> [Aged 55:] 'Some nearness and enjoyment in spending some hours alone with the Father, Son, and Spirit. It was basking in the beams of grace.'

[Aged 60:] 'My heart's desire is to be a temple of the Holy Ghost, full of Christ.'

[Aged 64:] 'Christ is more than ever precious to me in his atonement, righteousness, merit, heart. ... Nothing else satisfies me. I only yearn to know him better, and preach him more fully.'

[Aged 72:] 'I sometimes get moments when I seem to realise myself as face to face with Christ within the veil, walking with him .... Still distressed at the fact that my fellowship with the Lord is so broken, instead of being constant and continuous.'

[Aged 79:] 'All forenoon spent in special prayer, that my latter days may be days of rapid progress in the knowledge of Christ.'

[Aged 80:] 'I am struck to the heart often with wonder that I have so little communion with Christ.'

Bonar knew the perplexities and uncertainties all Christians face, but on how communion with God is to be maintained he had no doubts whatever. It is by the ministry of the Holy Spirit on God's part, and by prayer on our own. His *Diary* shows he regarded prayer as his main work, and among his prayers the most frequent was for the Holy Spirit to make the person and glory of Christ more real to him. He advised believers to follow the pattern of Paul's fifteen prayers recorded in the New Testament; and it is noteworthy how his own petitions were closely tied to Scripture. Perhaps the prayer that appears most frequently in his *Diary* is that of Ephesians 3:16-19:

That he would grant you, according to the riches of his glory, to be strengthened with might by his Spirit in the inner man; that Christ may dwell in your hearts by faith; that ye, being rooted and grounded in love, may be able to comprehend with all saints what is the breadth and length, and depth and height, and to know the love of Christ that passeth knowledge, that ye might be filled with all the fullness of God.

WHAT FOLLOWS FROM COMMUNION WITH GOD

1. Communion with God brings resemblance to Christ. 'But we all, with open face beholding as in a glass the glory of the Lord, are changed into the same image from glory to glory' (2 Cor. 3:18). The first thing people noted about Bonar was not so much what he said, or did, but what he was. 'If you were not carried away by the man's teaching, which was as likely as not, yet were you infallibly carried away by the man himself.' 'He had a charm which is difficult to describe.' 'He was in touch with God.' 'You felt at once that the man was acquainted with Jesus Christ, he had lived in his company.'[33] The happiness of the man was a feature particularly noted by numbers. Bishop Moule said of him, 'He was one of the very sunniest Christians I ever met.'[34] But the leading feature of his character was love, the love of God in him. He not only prayed the words of Ephesians chapter 3, but the prayer was answered. His life became an example of the words, 'God is love; and he that dwelleth in love dwelleth in God, and God in him' (1 John 4:16).

This showed itself in his tender, urgent concern for the unconverted. We read in the Gospels that Christ was so taken up with the needs of the multitude that eating was forgotten, and his friends said, 'He is beside himself' (Mark 3:20, 21). To live near to Christ has to be to know something of that same compassion and compulsion. A servant girl described M'Cheyne as 'deein to hae folk converted'. This whole brotherhood of ministers believed that the conversion of men, women and children ought to be an uppermost concern. Bonar's entry in his *Diary* for his 49th birthday, after his coming to Glasgow, reads:

> Felt in the evening most bitter grief over the apathy of the district. They are perishing, they are perishing, and yet they will not consider. I lay awake thinking over it, and crying to the Lord in broken groans.

Approaching twenty years later, when his church is now well filled, he is far from content. He writes on December 30, 1876:

> I fear much I have been sliding into easy-minded contentment with the truth and the work going on without seeing souls added every day. Delight in the word read and preached is not the same thing as light shining upon the dark world.

This same spirit showed itself in his pastoral work among his people. His daughter Marjory writes:

> His acts of loving ministry were countless. He would toil up long flights of stairs to take a remedy to someone in pain, or to find lodgings for one who was friendless and homeless. He would carry a bottle of beef tea in his pocket to a sickly woman, or a picture book to while away the hours of a child's sickness. ... No service was too small for him to do for any of Christ's little ones. 'Love is the *motive* for working', he used to say, 'joy is the *strength* for working.'[35]

2. Communion with God will make a man humble. It was when Isaiah saw Christ's glory that he cried, 'Woe is me! for I am undone ... for mine eyes have seen the King, the LORD of hosts!' (Isa. 6:5). The knowledge of God brings true knowledge of self. Listen to what Bonar wrote about himself in the presence of God:

> I am ashamed of my shallowness in knowledge, feeling and desire. Most humbling.

> I want some discovery today of my inexpressible worthlessness, impotence, weakness. That God has used me is nothing else than the merest sovereign grace.[36]

> It is this day exactly forty-seven years since I was ordained. My ministry has appeared to me to be wanting in so many ways, that I can only say of it, *indescribably inadequate.*

> Imperfection stamped on everything I ever undertook; omission running through my life. My place is under the shadow of the Righteous One.

> Sometimes, as this morning, I get most painful discoveries of my soul's barrenness and coldness, when I awake and find myself without any real compassion for souls; without any real burning zeal for God's glory; with very shallow and poor apprehension of the doctrines I preach.
>
> So very much of self has been in my ministry, so very little of Christ's compassion for souls.

Bonar believed that such self-knowledge was necessary for all Christians, and that one reason why indwelling sin remains is 'to keep us from leaning on our personal holiness'.[37]

He also reflects in his *Diary* on his duty to 'know his place'. Once when he was commended for his work in later life, he replied, 'I never thought I did more than draw the water and let the flock drink.' From time to time he likened himself to the sons of Merari among the Levites, whose work in the wilderness was to carry such little things as the pins of the Tabernacle. Here is a typical reference from a day in Collace, when he was sitting reading the life of Thomas Chalmers. He has recorded what happened next:

> A man came in to ask me to go with him to settle a quarrel between him and his wife. The Lord does not use me, like his servant, Dr Chalmers, for great things, but my way of serving the Lord is walking three or four miles to quiet a family dispute! The Lord shows me that he wishes me to be one of the common Levites who carry the pins.[38]

3. Communion with God will save us from losing time on religious futilities. Christ has not promised to make all we do of lasting benefit to ourselves or to others. There is a qualification: 'He that abideth in me, and I in him, the same bringeth forth much fruit: for without me ye can do nothing' (John 15:5)—that is, nothing of eternal value, nothing glorifying to God. As Bonar faced the work in Glasgow in 1856 he wrote: 'Unless I go forth among them, filled with the Holy Spirit, I see that all will be vain.'[39] Again in 1871: 'More and more do I learn that continual watchfulness unto prayer is essential to right preaching, right visiting, right conversation, right reading of the word.'[40] He embodied this principle in his sayings: 'If we are filled with the Spirit, God will bless everything about us, the tones of our voice, even the putting out of our hand.' 'The best part of all Christian work is that part which only God sees.'[41]

The truth is that there is no mechanical benefit in the fulfilment of biblical duties. It is only by Christ working through us that there is fruitfulness. Our own busy-ness can accomplish nothing. The temptation of the devil is to make us think that we have so many duties that we cannot afford the time to stop and wait on God. The opposite is the truth. We waste time when we do not pray. Above the fireplace in Bonar's study a card read: 'He who has truly prayed has completed the half of his study.' Robertson Nicoll has his finger on this truth when he writes: 'His prayerfulness did not diminish—it greatly increased Dr Bonar's activity, which was of the most amazing kind.'[42] Yet Bonar's own regret was the conviction he would have done more good had he lived closer to Christ. 'The Spirit has put a full cup of blessing to my lips; but scarcely ever have I done more than merely take a sip. O what I have lost! O what I have lost!'[43]

4. *Communion with God will directly affect a man's preaching.* The further we get in fellowship with Christ the more prominent he will be in our preaching. There is surely an inevitability about this. In Bonar's words, 'Acquaintance with the personal Saviour and constant fellowship with him imparts fresh life and unction to ... preaching.'[44] 'Saw today', he notes again, 'the blessed effects of preaching Christ distinctly, fully, fervently, and that it is praying much that makes preaching felt.'[45] To preach Christ is much more than quoting him and making reference to him. The preacher is to stand in the place of Christ, and to use such language as this: 'we are ambassadors for Christ, God making his appeal through us. We implore

you on behalf of Christ, be reconciled to God' (2 Cor. 5:20). How can this be unless we come from his presence with something of his heart and spirit? How else can we be possessed with great and high thoughts of Christ? It can only be as the Holy Spirit reveals him to us. How can we speak of Christ's love, and of how he satisfies every need, unless we ourselves have fresh experience of these realities?

Bonar was certain that the more he was filled with the Holy Spirit the more fully would he preach Christ. And the paradox is that the more a preacher has of the Spirit's anointing, the more pitifully feeble his sermons appear to him compared with the greatness of the Saviour.

As I have already said, high views of Christ are always accompanied by low views of self. Bonar's daughter wrote of her father: 'The person and work of the Lord Jesus Christ occupied him at all times.' But that is not how he saw himself. He wrote of how he lacked sermons 'full of Christ'. To the very last year of his life his ambition was the same, 'O that I might preach a hundred times more fully and gladly concerning Christ himself.'[46]

Does this not lead us to an answer to the question, what is unction in preaching? It is related to the inner and secret life of the preacher; there is a mysterious overflow *from* the man, and yet it is not *of* the man; it is from heaven and it brings an awareness to hearers that what is being spoken is from Christ himself.[47] And the more a preacher has of Christ's Spirit the less he thinks of himself: 'Self-forgetting work is heavenly work.'

There is also a practical point here which is particularly relevant to preaching at the present time. It has become customary in many places for preachers to think that the only way to preach is to expound a passage or a book of Scripture consecutively from week to week. It is worthy of notice that this was not the view of Bonar or his friends. Their most common method of preaching was to take distinct and separate texts.

How is that to be explained? The explanation cannot be that Bonar had a defective view of the need to teach Scripture, or that he was lacking the skill of an exegete. He produced two commentaries on books of Scripture (Leviticus and Psalms) and never preached on a text, from Old or New Testaments, without examining it in the original languages. Nor was he unfamiliar with the practice of consecutive exposition which was called a 'lecture' in Scotland; indeed he used it himself at times.

There is more than one reason to account for the older practice of taking individual texts; I will only mention the one that is connected with our main theme. M'Cheyne charged a young minister with these words, 'Get your texts from God.'[48] Extracts from Bonar's *Diary* will make clear what this means:

> I see that I should get my texts directly from the Lord, and never preach without having got something that shows me his counsel in the matter.

> I have been much impressed with the sin of choosing my text without special direction from the Lord. This is like running without being sent, no message being given me. I ought to feel, 'This I am sent to tell you, my people.'

> This I see, but have been long of learning, that I should be like David seeking counsel, every time I sit down to select a text. … I have often chosen texts, resolved on what I should do, etc., and then asked blessing; when I should have asked the Lord to direct me in the choice.[49]

The modern tendency is to treat this thinking as akin to mysticism. I doubt if Bonar would have understood such an objection. He would have asked, is not God wonderfully interested in our lives and work? Is he not willing to direct us? As we pray, study the needs of our hearers, and consider God's providential dealings, can he not cause texts to take hold of us and 'grip us by the hand'? Before we decry Bonar's practice we need to remember it has the sanction of not a few leading preachers, such as C. H. Spurgeon, whose phrase I have just quoted. They all believed there was a difference between preachers taking a message from the Bible, and taking it *from* God through the Bible.

Of course, this is not to argue that God does not bless the consecutive method, or that preachers cannot be led of God if they follow that practice. Referring to these two different methods of preaching, Charles Bridges said wisely, 'It is far better to combine the advantages of both, than to set either plan in opposition to the other, or to adopt either exclusively.'[50] All I am arguing is that the single-text method ought to be taken far more seriously than is often done today. And one added reason for that method is that commonly it lends itself better to direct evangelistic preaching. All Scripture is given by inspiration of God, but not all Scripture is equally applicable to the conviction and conversion of sinners. There are great, pointed and searching texts that have been repeatedly used of God and they need to be a staple part of effective preaching.

5. *Communion with God will make a man expectant.* Our contentment with little personal growth, and few if any conversions, is surely to be traced to our small experience of God. It is Paul's prayer for the conscious indwelling of Christ that leads to the doxology, 'Now unto him who is able to do exceeding abundantly above all that we ask or think, according to the power that worketh in us' (Eph. 3:20). Bonar notes how the more there is of the Spirit's work in the church the greater will be the spirit of expectation. Referring to a time of the outpouring of the Spirit in Glasgow, he noted: 'One marked effect upon ministers here has been the state of expectation in which they now are, looking for real results of their work.'[51] It was the same in his own life. In the revival times of 1840, instead of being content, he writes to his brother Horatius: 'There have been some interesting cases of conversion. But when is the heaven to become black with clouds and winds, and the rain to fall in a Carmel flood?' In his first difficult

years in Glasgow, a man met him on the street and asked, 'How are things doing with you? How are you getting on?' 'Oh', Bonar replied, 'we are looking for great things.' 'You must not expect too much', said his friend. To which Bonar instantly responded, 'We can never hope for too much.'[52]

A spirit of expectancy governed his life. He lived looking for more love, more zeal, more conformity to Christ. The prayer of M'Cheyne was equally his own: 'I long for love without any coldness, light without dimness, and purity without spot or wrinkle.'[53] Ultimately these men were expecting a perfection not to be gained in this scene of time. They knew that. They were 'looking for that blessed hope, and the glorious appearing of the great God and our Saviour Jesus Christ' (Titus 2:13). Two texts were ever before Bonar, even inscribed on the walls of his study: 'Behold, I come quickly', and 'Even so, come, Lord Jesus.' It is as Christians enjoy something of the heaven of Christ's presence here that they look for that which is to come. 'Resurrection is coming soon'—he would often tell his people—'and he who is the Resurrection is coming. O my people, you won't know your minister on that day. It will be ecstasy to have made this attainment—to love the Lord our God with all our heart and soul, and strength and mind.'[54] No wonder he insisted, 'The prospect on before is very bright—the sadness is all in looking back.'[55]

WHY ARE WE IMPOVERISHED?

I was once at a ministers' conference in Scotland where silence descended on the meeting when the speaker pressed the questioned why, given our numbers, did we not make a deeper impression in the land. The answer is surely with the above theme.

Another witness to the same truth is Daniel Lamont, a professor at New College, Edinburgh, in the 1930s. In a book of that period, Lamont expressed the conviction that 'our church life has largely lost its zest. The gospel has a mighty potency to move men and we should therefore expect all our churches to be filled with eager worshippers. The church is not alive enough. Why is this?' The answer he gave was this:

> The secret of the church's comparative failure lies in the eclipse of the individual prayer life. It is to be feared that a host of people who still give formal assent to the truth of Christianity do not cultivate an inner life with God. ... Prayer is the chief avenue to communion with God. All other avenues lead to, or from, this one.[56]

This testimony is true. Yet despite many other calls to prayer since the 1930s, the decline has not been arrested. Evidently something more is essential, something even more foundational. Prayer will never retain the place it has in Scripture, if the trustworthiness of Scripture itself becomes a matter of doubt. If the author of Scripture is also the author of true prayer, how can his aid remain once 'all Scripture is given by inspiration of God' (2 Tim. 3:16) is questioned? Since the Holy Spirit is given 'to them that obey him' (Acts 5:32), how can men be mighty in prayer who do not honour his word? Can the gospel advance where we do not regard 'prayer and Scripture as twins'? 'Praying always with all prayer and supplication in the Spirit', belongs with taking 'the sword of the Spirit, which is the word of God' (Eph. 6:17, 18; Acts 6:4).

Scotland's spiritual decay in the twentieth century was the direct result of the failure of many evangelicals a generation earlier to see the danger introduced into the churches in the name of 'scholarship'. The issue was whether Christ could be surely believed, and the gospel advanced, without commitment to *all* Scripture. Bonar was among a minority who believed it could not. He refused to allow a wedge to be driven between commitment to Christ and commitment to Scripture. Without such commitment, Jesus had taught him, prayer would die: 'If ye abide in me and my words abide in you, ye shall ask what ye will, and it shall be done unto you' (John 15:7).

Of course, in Bonar's day the attack was not on the words of Christ but on the Old Testament, and some supposed that the best defence was a retreat to the New Testament. Bonar saw that such a proposal was contrary to the witness of the New Testament itself. To concede to the claims of rationalism over one part of the Bible would undermine the unity and authority of the whole. 'Every line in this inspired Bible is wet with the dew of the Spirit's love.' 'My heart has been distracted and worn out by most dangerous error in the Church at large and within the bounds of our own presbytery', he wrote in 1877.[57] Again, on May 20, 1880: 'I spoke with God as a blood-washed sinner warranted to come to him. I spread out the sad facts: no revival; our church tainted with rationalism.'

Bonar teaches us that the true living of a devotional life means more than being a mild peacemaker. It was not the placid who turned the world upside down in the apostolic age, and that was not Bonar's spirit in the face of error and unbelief. 'Old obstinate', was the nickname some gave to him. 'If our father's life was modelled on that of another', wrote his daughter, 'it was on the life of the Reformers and Covenanters.' But while he revered history, the motivation for his life came from a higher source, and his hope lay in the future, not in the past. His wish was to be found with those of whom it is written: 'They overcame him by the blood of the Lamb, and by the word of their testimony; and they loved not their lives unto the death' (Rev. 12:11).

We must go to the Saviour, as Andrew Bonar did, and say, 'Lord, teach us to pray.'

3

The Rediscovery of Archie Brown

'Cast upon the power of the Holy Ghost, it becomes us to recognize his glorious might, to render him the homage due unto his name, and to act in practical dependence upon him. Our reliance is not upon the truth itself; for light alone cannot cause the blind to see. Much less may we depend upon attractive speech, cogent argument, or profound learning. The highest mental powers will be mere idols if we trust in them. As to attempts to spread the Redeemer's kingdom by amusements, by the arts and sciences, by music and sensuous display, let this be far from us. The Holy Ghost must be met on his own ground; and we fear that very much of the work which is done by the church at this present moment is not upon a plane sufficiently elevated to be recognized by the Holy Ghost. If all the power to create faith must come of the Holy Spirit, those who would propagate truth must be careful to go to work in *his* way.

Our religion is either supernatural or it is an imposture; and it must be spread by supernatural means or not at all. Every advance that is made by Christianity, other than that which comes distinctly from the Holy Ghost, is a step backward. The enlightened reader of church history will not need to look long before he will perceive that this is the case.'

C. H. Spurgeon, 'A Word for the Hour',
The Sword and the Trowel, 1886, p. 154.

ON the cold morning of Thursday, February 11, 1892 it is said that 100,000 people stood still in South London as a funeral procession made its way to the cemetery in Norwood. Spurgeon was dead. The service at the grave side was taken by a man described as his 'closest friend'. He was Archibald Brown, at that time a household name in the East End of London, where he had seen some 2,500 people joining the church he served. Beyond London, Brown's sermons were read across the world so that when his congregation needed a new building, gifts came in from India, Japan, and America. Certainly no one was more suited to preside at the burial of his friend than Archibald Brown. It is therefore surprising to us that his ministry would largely pass from the memory of later generations until it became almost unknown. But Spurgeon would not have been so surprised and he gives us the reason for why his friend would be forgotten. Ten years before Spurgeon's death, he had said with sorrow, 'Few men are like-minded with Mr Brown—a brother tried and proved.' They both stood for convictions which were already a minority position in the religious world of 1892. A general departure from biblical Christianity was occurring in Britain. Ten years after Spurgeon's death, his son Thomas said of his father, 'There are very few who think he was right.'[1] By the time Brown died in 1922 he belonged to a remnant. But it was a remnant which shared the conviction Spurgeon expressed in the words, 'I am quite willing to be eaten of dogs for the next fifty years, but the more distant future shall vindicate me.'[2] Today there is hope that we are seeing both Spurgeon and Brown rediscovered.

It might be asked, if Archibald Brown's sermons were so widely read in his day, why have they so long disappeared from the shelves of second-hand bookshops? Those of us who search for old books have puzzled over this. But there is a simple answer. While his sermons were in constant publication for forty years, for the most part they did not appear in fine buck-ram-bound volumes but in plain paper as 'penny sermons'—to be read, passed on, re-read and finally just worn out. When people hunger for bread, they do not care much about how it is packaged. So it was with the thousands who read Brown's sermons.

CALLED TO CHRIST AND TO PREACH

The Browns were originally Scots who settled in London. Grandfather and father were successful businessmen. Archie, the eldest son in family of four sisters and two brothers, was born on July 18, 1844. His parents were Christians of Baptist persuasion and admirers of Spurgeon's ministry. As a youngster Archie often heard Spurgeon, but by his teen-age years he had lost an earlier spiritual interest. On finishing schooling at sixteen, he headed for a business career, becoming an apprentice in the lucrative tea trade. Along with his family he was still churchgoing, and at the age of sixteen he belonged to the Sunday School at Union Congregational Church which was close to their home in Brixton. There is no record that he benefitted from the Sunday School until one very definite Sunday. The date was April 15, 1861, and the benefit came entirely unexpectedly. Among the teachers was an attractive young Christian, a few years older than Archie, whom he had admired from afar although they had not spoken. On this particular Sunday, he later wrote:

> Annie Bigg said to me, without knowing me at all, 'Are you a Christian?' Though I hated the question, yet I could not help honouring in my heart the one that had the moral courage to put it. The next question was, 'Will you go and hear Mr Blackwood preach on Monday?' Before I knew exactly where I was, I found that I had given my word.[3]

The next day the two went to the home of S. Arthur Black-wood, a young civil servant who had been converted after serving with the Grenadier Guards in the Crimean War. It proved to be a crowded evangelistic meeting, and afterwards Blackwood said to the newcomer:

> 'Young man, you are a stranger here. Are you a Christian?' I confessed at once that I was not, and had no great desire to be. I think I can now hear him answering, 'How sad!' The question hooked itself into my heart. For two days I had no rest.

If we knew the history of all conversions we might well find that prayer precedes them in every case. Brown was the special subject of his mother's prayers and they were now answered. In his own words in later years:

> I was convinced of sin one Monday night, and I know all Tuesday it was hell within. I remember how I spent one whole night, alternately praying and swearing. One moment down on my knees asking God for mercy, and the next cursing myself for being such a fool. I shall never forget that night. And it was about eleven o'clock on the following morning, under an oak in the Palace Road, Tulse Hill, while reading a little book by Dr Newman Hall's father, called *The Sinner's Friend*, that I leaped into peace. Oh, the joy that came into my soul as I caught a little cap I was wearing and flung it up into the air, and shouted, 'Who would have thought it?' Why, the very first thing I had to do as a Christian was to climb up that oak-tree to get my cap, for it was caught in the branches.

At once he went to tell Blackwood, who very soon guided him into Christian work and witness.

The revolution in his interests was so complete, that the tea-trade apprenticeship suffered. After real hesitation his father allowed him to give it up and, the next year, at the age of eighteen he became the youngest student in Spurgeon's College. That college, still in its first years, was challenging the current system of training for the ministry. Instead of accepting all who wished to study, evidence was first sought that the applicant was called and gifted for the gospel ministry. The curriculum also differed from the usual. While there was little attention to contemporary theology, the men were trained to appreciate the best literature in a large heritage, including titles, such as Elisha Coles on *Divine Sovereignty*, long disused elsewhere. To know the kind of thing which gave Brown a life-long appreciation of books one has only to pick up Spurgeon's, *Commenting and Commentaries*, which began as Friday afternoon addresses to his students.

A further difference in the curriculum was the evangelistic work that the students were expected to continue while still at the college. Spurgeon personally directed Brown to serve a handful of Christians seeking to start a witness in Bromley. When his two college years were over, Brown married Annie Bigg and continued as the pastor of what had now become an established Baptist church in the town. It was due to the recommendation of Spurgeon that Brown, still only 22, was called to Stepney Green Tabernacle, in a densely populated area of London. On his first Sunday, January 6, 1867, his text was, 'And I, brethren, when I came to you, came not with excellency of speech or wisdom, declaring unto you the testimony of God.'

The Stepney Green Tabernacle, at the heart of the East End of London, could seat 800 but in 1867, with only 76 members, the congregation looked 'a handful'. Brown had begun preaching there before a meeting could be arranged to mark his formal installation on Tuesday, February 26, 1867. This event was to be overshadowed by another of far greater significance. At the Stepney Green Tabernacle there was a tradition of an annual Sunday evening sermon especially for young men and the date for it had been fixed for February 10. Brown would later remind his people of what happened that evening:

> There are not a few present who can remember this Sabbath
> evening six years ago—that time when, if ever this church held
> a prayer meeting, it held it then—that wondrous time that we

went down to the school room, when, as it seemed to us, a very tempest of prayers rose up to God,—that time when we all seemed bowed together before the throne, when all our desires joined in one; and a great—I might say an agonized cry—rose up from the throng, 'Lord, in the sanctuary above, save souls this night.' We shall never forget being literally swept up into the sanctuary that evening, not merely physically, but as it seemed to us, carried right on to the platform by an irresistible power of prayer. And what was the result? We have not yet forgotten how God marched through our midst—how there were almost as many conversions as there were pews in the place.

One striking fact about the night was that the sermon Brown preached was the same as the one which he had delivered without any observable effect at Bromley, from the text, 'Young man, I say unto thee, Arise' (Luke 7:14).[4] But on this second occasion, 'God brought in seventy souls at one sweep of mercy.' The preacher had no doubt about how this was to be understood; it was a lesson he never forgot. New life is neither from the preacher nor from the words he speaks.

> It is not the means used, but the Lord's blessing on them. The teacher may teach Jesus and him only, and that with tears; but unless the Divine Master of both place his hands upon the blind, no miracle of grace will be effected.

THE AWAKENING AT STEPNEY

The Spirit of God was working in their midst in reviving power, and what began in the early months of 1867 was to continue through several successive years. Brown could say to his people: 'For five years you have flocked to the prayer meetings, as the world does its pleasures. Let everything else go rather than the meetings for pleading with God.' The change that occurred at Stepney Green Tabernacle has characterised communities in every revival. As at Pentecost, Brown told his people:

The blessing spread far and wide. If it commenced with the disciples it did not end with them. From the upper room it soon flew along the streets of Jerusalem like an electric current. The crowds gather—they surge around the building—curiosity is aroused and all cry, 'What meaneth this?' Peter preaches. The power goes abroad. Three thousand find out what a revival means. O, Sirs, there is no telling where the influence of a revival in a church may spread. It finds its way where nothing else will. It creeps into homes shut against the tract distributor. It glides into darkest places of vice. It penetrates the whole neighbourhood. A revived church will be certain to draw the multitude together. Let but a revival come and the dreary waste of empty pews to be seen in many a sanctuary will be gone. This is the secret of getting at the masses. Our churches do not want cleverer or better ministers but *revived* ones. A revived church has magnetic power. The people *must* come to it.

By the end of that first year, 294 new members had been added to the church. A year later, preaching on December 6, 1868, Brown said:

I cannot but look back through the two years so nearly gone with wonder and thankfulness that defy language. God has been pleased to give us as a church such prosperity as is given to few, he has permitted us to reap with one hand while we have sown with the other. The converts are not numbered by tens only but by hundreds. In no spirit of pride do we say this; for what have we that we have not received? It is his work and his only.

In May 1869 he noted in a letter to 'our hearers':

The numbers desirous of hearing the word are far more than we can by any means accommodate. Every Sunday evening some four hundred more than the place was built to hold, are crowded in, whilst large numbers are necessarily denied admittance.

Times of revival always show the same characteristics, and foremost among them, is *prayerfulness*. Those who would later look back on this period drew attention to this feature. One member recalled: 'At 7 o'clock on Sunday morning there were hundreds met for prayer. Rain, hail or snow made no difference. They were all in dead earnest.' Another spoke of witnessing 'many memorable scenes—none, perhaps, more remarkable than the great Saturday evening prayer meetings, which formed a fitting prelude to Sundays of grace and power.'

'The fruit of Spirit is love', and when the Spirit is given in larger measure, *love* will show itself in a working church. Brown could speak of a thousand 'of brethren and sisters' who 'visit 2,900 families every Sunday afternoon'. There were others who took a special interest in the infirm and the distressed. Such a church needs little organization. Love leads to spontaneous action. In a sermon entitled, 'Supreme Devotion', Brown said, 'Just as Mary found her own service in the ointment she poured on Christ, so love will always find a way to work.' Literature was one agency and he could refer to '14,000 tracts and 16,000 sermons' circulated in the district in one year. In the same sermon on Mary, he said:

> Mary came to the conclusion that there was no reason why she should not find out for herself a way of doing good. Oh, if only God's church were filled with love, what wonders we should behold! … O, my Lord, let me be swayed by love, ruled by love, inspired by love, until I come like Mary, with my all in my hands, and break every alabaster box I possess that thy dear head be anointed.[5]

Inevitably a new building was needed. Capable of holding some 3,000 people, it was opened on Thursday, February 22, 1872, and named the East London Tabernacle. Support for the large building had come in 2,300 separate donations, including a generous one from his father. Some wondered if it could only be filled by drawing people from other churches, but at the opening Brown pointed out that of the 650 received into membership since 1867, 500 'came direct from the world'.

Spurgeon was the preacher that day. He reminded the congregation what they had seen:

> lions are turned into lambs, ravens into doves, and the most unlikely spots in East London that were deserts, salt lands not inhabited, that looked as if they were cursed of God, have been made to rejoice and blossom like the rose.

DEATHS AND SORROWS

All Christians have trials, 'whom the Lord loves he chastens', and when preachers are unusually honoured by God great trials may be a necessary part of their lives. Such was the case with the apostle Paul, and so it was with Brown in whose case the trial was that of repeated family bereavements. Only two years after the opening of the East London Tabernacle, he preached at the funeral of his wife Annie, telling his people:

> October, 1865, we were married. Only eight years and a half have passed by since then, and I thank God that I can bear testimony in his presence that a happier life was never lived, and a happier home was never found in this East-end of London … for the last three years and a half she suffered with intermittent agony, which came on more constantly as time progressed, until at last there came three months of anguish almost without a pause. If ever one went a rough road to glory; if ever one passed through a burning furnace into heaven, she did. But now she is at rest. As I marked the anguish that she suffered, I often felt, 'Lord, though it will make an unutterable blank, and though it means the breaking up of the happiest home that mortal man ever had, yet I could thank thee if thou wouldst take her into thine arms, and ease her of her frightful agonies.' She fell asleep in Jesus, as you know, at half-past-four on Tuesday morning, the 5th of May [1874]. Well do I remember her last words to me as, coming to consciousness at half-past ten on Monday night—after you had been praying for her—and

taking me by the hand, she said, 'Well, Archie, we have had a happy life, haven't we?

> I have no cares, O blessed Lord,
> For all my cares are thine.'

I marvelled, as I saw not only the conflict, but the complete victory. No cares! Leaving six little ones, and the youngest but seven weeks' old, and yet no cares? None! For he whom she had loved many a year had come and put all cares to flight. So there fell asleep in Jesus, the gentlest, the most loving and most self-denying character that I believe the Lord ever called home.

Over a year later Brown was given a second 'help-meet', and mother for the children, in the person of Sarah D. Hargreaves of Liverpool. He was now 31 and she was 25. With her there came a new joy into the home but it was short-lived. Sarah died in childbirth, with the baby, on September 20, 1876. At a meeting of the London Baptist Association on September 26, 1876, Spurgeon sadly told the brethren that Brown could not be present 'as he was that afternoon attending the funeral of his wife and still-born baby daughter'.

Brown was overwhelmed by this sudden sorrow. There was no question now of his preaching a funeral sermon. His mother took all six children into her care and Archie was desolate. After four days, as he later wrote,

> Broken with sore grief, I went over to the Metropolitan Tabernacle. I could not preach but I thought I could worship, and how amazed I was to find that he had prepared a sermon on purpose for me. That sermon can be found among his volumes, entitled, 'Why the Heavenly Robes Are White.'[5]

Several weeks of profound grief were, however, to follow before he could resume his work. Before going to bed one night, he tells us, his eye fell on the words of Revelation 22:16, 'I Jesus have sent mine angel to testify these things in the churches.'

The text came to me the other day, or rather, I should say, the other night, in a deep depression that I cannot describe. I was sitting alone in a house that has been stripped of everything that made life bright—sitting utterly alone, in a deep depression, as I say, I cannot describe in words. I sat in a stupor till past the midnight hour, thinking about the past, and, about one o'clock in the morning, I mechanically took this Testament in my hand and opened it without a thought. It opened on this 22nd chapter of Revelation and my eye fell on the two words, 'I, Jesus'. They were enough. The darkness vanished. The thought which flashed like a ray of morning light through my soul was the one I have tried to give you this evening—*that Jesus is still alive*.

Though children die, though wives be cut down, though husbands go to the grave, though fortunes break, though all depart, yet in the darkness, and through the storm, there comes a voice, and it says, 'I, Jesus, live still.'

Brown was given a third wife, Edith, and they had happy years together before she also died when he was only fifty years of age in 1895.

Had Brown been asked to name the greatest trial of his life, it may be he would have pointed in another direction. He shared with Spurgeon in the Downgrade Controversy of the late 1880s, and together they were profoundly moved as so many in the churches ceased to regard all Scripture as God-given revelation. They saw faith failing in many and even Christians 'dazed and reeling'. His own testimony was: 'Nothing short of the power of God could have maintained faith during the years of trial through which hundreds of us have passed.'

This is not the place to speak of the apostasy which was entering the churches at that period. It was a sifting time for Christians and a great grief to Brown. Yet these same trials enriched him and led him to say, 'What should we be if we had no trials to drive us to prayer?' They led to closer dependence on God and, from his greater experience of God's love, there came blessing for others also. Such is the design of God 'who comforteth us in all our tribulation, that we may be able to comfort them which are in any trouble, by the comfort wherewith we ourselves are comforted of God' (2 Cor. 1:4).

This was certainly true for Archibald Brown. As one contemporary wrote: 'Mr Brown has been taught much by books, more by men, and most by sanctified affliction.'

THE ENLARGED WORK

A sympathy for others was given him which enabled him to take on seemingly impossible burdens. Thus, to the extensive pastoral cares which he was carrying in the 1870s, the hard winter of 1879-80 impelled him to new endeavours. Situated as he was in one of the neediest parts of London, close to thousands in poverty, illness, and unemployment, he believed that more had to be done than they had yet attempted. So he established a full-time mission and employed two missionaries. The number was increased in the following years to six, and then to nine, including both men and women. An intensive system of visitation was begun that first winter, covering 8,000 houses, the inhabitants of which included 1,800 sick and dying. Road by road, districts were surveyed, with all kinds and conditions of people and few Christians to be found among them. To spread accurate information Brown began in 1880 to publish an annual *Record of Service* which commonly ran to more than fifty pages. In this document he wrote:

> This work has been quite a revelation to us. Being brought into almost daily contact with the poorest of neighbourhoods, we have become acquainted with a mass of misery, want, vice, and filth we had previously failed to comprehend. None can conceive it until they try practically to deal with it. The degrees of poverty and sorrow seem endless.
>
> Sheer want has in many cases stripped the houses as well as the little furniture once in them. Our missionaries have entered homes where banisters have been pulled down for firing, and then the iron stove sold for bread. Men and women

who have been worsted in the battle of life, after every effort to retrieve the day; men who walk from morning to night 'seeking a job', until, wet through, they return to a supperless room, sleep in their drenched garments and then lie down for weary weeks racked with rheumatic pains; women who, with their husband in the infirmary, toil at the wash-tub or ply the needle for a wretched pittance, from dawn to midnight; widows who wage heroic battle against overwhelming trouble and pinch themselves to give their fatherless bread. Such cases as these we know by hundreds. Want is the short history of thousands. Their lives consist in 'not having'. The hands want work, the heart wants sympathy, the body wants bread, the mind wants light, the face wants a smile, the spirit wants hope, the nerves want rest, the conscience wants peace, the soul wants Christ.

How this need was addressed is too large a story for these pages. Suffice it to say that within a few years London's *Daily Telegraph* could speak of Brown as 'a man who has a larger practical acquaintance with the homes, the misery, the overcrowding, and the social horrors of the foulest corners of the East of London than anyone who could well be cited.'

Brown was by no means the first into philanthropic work in the East End,[7] and there were other agencies in the field. Brown encouraged them all: 'No body of workers can afford to despise others, or arrogate to themselves the "patent" for removing the evil.' While physical needs were addressed, and included in 1884 1,000 pounds weight of tea, over 9,000 loaves, many hundred pounds' weight of meat, and quantities of potatoes and rice, his primary emphasis was on the gospel:

> The people are wrong as well as their houses and circumstances, and nothing can put them right but Christ in the heart. Change a man's nature, and he will alter his own environment; but if you change his surroundings it does not follow that you will effect a change in him. ... Deeper than all their other needs is their need of Christ and his salvation. Let any man be saved from his sins, and he will be saved from dirt into the bargain.

A saved soul includes a saved character, and that leads to new tastes and fresh aspirations. Let no social reformer despise Christian work. While he is busy erecting clean houses, the Christian is busy finding him clean tenants.

By the time he was fifty-two years old, Brown was worn out after thirty years of constant labour in the East End. To the great sorrow of the people he resigned from the East London Tabernacle in 1897, and had thoughts of a 'little cottage on the cliff, where he might retire and peacefully end his days'. But there were soon calls for his help which he could not resist, and after a smaller charge at Chatsworth Road, South London, his final pastorate was to be at the Metropolitan Tabernacle (1907–10).[8] Even then, however, his work was not done. He preached in the West Indies, travelled to New Zealand and Tasmania, and gave several years to South Africa where he spoke in every Baptist church in the land.

He returned to England from South Africa in 1919, and after a few years as an invalid, on April 2, 1922 he died at 'Rock Cottage' in the country village of Easton on the Hill, Northamptonshire. With his fourth wife, Hannah, he had enjoyed the longest period of marital happiness. She was to pre-decease him by only nine days.

THE MAN AND THE MESSAGE

It is the work of the Holy Spirit to put the message Christians believe into the life which they live. For a preacher to be 'filled with the Spirit' means that message and character are blended together. Brown could tell his people, 'You who worship here will, I know, bear me witness that my general theme is the love of God', and it was his theme because it was his life. His hearers saw love in the man.[9] No appeals for help ever came to him in vain if he could possibly give it. A dying young woman pleads with Brown to care for her six-year-old boy so that he should not go to a workhouse. A mother, hearing he was going to Denver, Colorado, asked that he should carry a wreath to lay on the grave of her runaway son. All such pleas were answered. He carried the wreath, about a foot-and-a-half in diameter, 5,000 miles and eventually found the cemetery where, he says, 'with tears in my eyes, I laid the wreath on his grave in the name of his mother who had followed him to the end'.

When Brown told his congregation, 'I would that I could take the whole of this congregation in my arms, and never drop one until all of you were safely carried to the kingdom', the people knew that he meant it. He knew, 'There is a way of handling men and women, and the art is acquired through intense love.'[10] It is no wonder that when he visited an East End street people soon came out to gather round him.

When he preached in Australia, the *Australian Baptist* wrote:

It is the sheer lovableness of the man that is irresistible. ... One can listen long to Mr Brown because of the ring in the message he utters. Perhaps, this is why he appeals to so many. The one who can feel and sympathise cannot speak to unheeding ears. It is a splendid thing to compel respect, to compel admiration; but to compel love, this is surely the greatest power God has put into man's hands.

This being true, it can be a surprise to us to read Brown's sermons and find an element which is far from common today. We are victims more than we realise of the effects of the apostasy which was beginning in his day. With that change the opinion entered the churches that it is not 'loving' to speak of guilt and wrath and judgment to come. The popular belief became that it is inconsistent with the character of God to warn people of hell. As Brown put it, there has arisen 'the fiercest onslaught upon the doctrine of the severity of God against sin'. For Brown, silence on this subject was not because of more love, it came from unbelief and the lack of love. If a preacher is truly concerned for his hearers, he believed, he will make people see that they are sinners, and that sin is not some small, easily excusable thing, but an offence against the

Creator of heaven and earth whose holy law they have broken and despised.

> It is when a man loves another intensely, that he will dare even to offend him. We must not mind the feelings of a friend receiving somewhat of a shock; it will do them no harm, and far better to be awakened from a pleasing dream *now*, than by the icy hand of death, when it is too late. He will never win many souls who keeps in the background all that is calculated to alarm them. The first step towards being saved is when the sinner feels himself lost; and it is when he feels himself within a step of hell that he is just putting his foot on the road to heaven. The beauties of the Saviour will only be seen when that which he saves *from* has been in some measure understood by the soul. The sinner's danger *must* be shown him.[11]

For an example I give a few words from his sermon on the text, 'The Lord is known by the judgment which he executes: the wicked is snared in the work of his own hands. Higgaion' (Psa. 9:16).[12] 'Higgaion' was the title of the sermon. He believed the word means, 'Stop! Pause! Meditate! Think about this!' The text says God is to be known by events in history. Catastrophes and disasters are not random accidents; they make God known. God spoke in the flood which once destroyed the old world, 'God spared not the old world, but saved Noah', just eight persons saved, 'Higgaion!' Think about it, take it in. Brown went on to speak about the Dead Sea, 'the sea of death', beneath which are the remains of once great cities. God abhorred their sexual immorality: 'He turned the cities of Sodom and Gomorrha into ashes.' 'The Lord is know by the judgment he executes ... Higgaion!'

There followed a succession of biblical texts showing how God deals with unbelieving sinners, and after each instance the command, 'Higgaion, Meditate!' like a warning bell. To the objection, 'We live in New Testament days', he replied that Herod was smitten in a moment for allowing himself to be called a god:

Ananias tells a lie—he falls a corpse. Sapphira, his wife, endorses the lie, and the young men returning from carrying him out, are just in time to bear away her body. The Lord is known by the judgment he executes. Higgaion. ... Do you still doubt the existence of any present judgment whereby the Lord is known? Then have one other tremendous truth— THERE IS HELL TONIGHT. Its fires have not gone out nor burned down.

Oh, will you doubt God's vengeance against sin when there is a hell burning at this moment? Ah, you may turn away and say, 'This is a hack subject when preachers are hard up and know not what to talk about.' Say what you like—God knows the thought is agony to me—but there the fact remains. There is a hell *somewhere* tonight, and that hell ought to say to every soul in this tabernacle, 'Higgaion, Meditate!'

Lastly, I would speak to some of you here who have been impressed. I know you have. I have seen the tear in your eye, and I have marked the way you have listened. Well, dear friend, remember that impression is not conversion, and the mere shedding of a tear is not coming to Christ; nor is the feeling uncomfortable under a sermon, a change of heart. To the most impressed I say 'Higgaion'.

There was gospel in this sermon, too, but its burden was for the awakening of the careless. Such preaching is no longer heard from many pulpits. Yet Paul makes 'warning every man' a mark of gospel preaching (Col. 1:28). He could say to his hearers, 'I kept back nothing that was profitable unto you' (Acts 20:20). Such preaching is not optional. Where the fear of God and conviction of sin are missing there is good reason to believe that something is absent from the message.

Calvary, preached as forgiveness apart from the holiness and justice of God, ceases to be the gospel. Christ bore the curse of the law for all who turn to him in repentance and faith, but who will turn before they learn the seriousness of their condition? To offer a Saviour to the man who is ignorant of his sinnership, is to offer him that which he cannot possibly appreciate. Christ to him is a mere useless addendum. To talk of pardon to one who has never seen himself condemned, is to talk of that which cannot possibly excite any thrilling emotion in the soul.

The more the Holy Spirit makes the presence of God real to the individual the more there will be of real humility. Here, too, Brown's character resonated with his message. Humility is born in knowing that one's salvation is entirely of God. Brown was only once in the United States and we have record of only one sermon that he preached. It was delivered at the Southern Baptist Theological Seminary, Louisville, Kentucky, and, if the subject was unusual for a visitor, it was characteristic of the man: 'For who maketh thee to differ from another? and what hast thou that thou didst not receive? now if thou didst receive it, why dost thou glory, as if thou hadst not received it?' (1 Cor. 4:7) One of Brown's hearers that day was Dr A. T. Robertson, professor of homiletics, and years later, in his book, *The Glory of the Ministry*, he wrote: 'I shall never forget a masterly address delivered to the students of the Southern Baptist Theological Seminary many years ago by Archibald G. Brown from this text.'[14]

Brown regarded a sense of unworthiness, and a dependence on grace, as the lifelong marks of a Christian. He would tell his hearers: 'If God only forgives sins committed before conversion, I am an undone man. Every hour of every day there is need of pardon.' He professed as a Christian to have attained to no 'higher life', and he hoped that none of his hearers supposed they had advanced to it.[14] While fully pardoned, he did not cease to be a sinner. Paul, many years an apostle, said that of sinners 'I *am* chief'. Not, 'I *was*'. Thirty years after Brown first knew Christ, he said, 'If God says to me, "What is thy name?" I have to say from the very depth of my heart, "My sinful name is Archibald Brown."' It is such self-knowledge that finds rest in the sovereignty of God's love:

There are times when I would not for all the world be without the doctrine of God's electing love. Oh, if you have never done business on the great waters of soul depression, I can understand some of you sneering at it; but if you had known what it is to be wiped right out, and to feel what an unutterable sinner you are, you will thank God, that when he loves, he finds the reason of his love in himself and not in you.[15]

Brown had to be a humble man. As he entered a London shop on one occasion, a confused assistant addressed him as 'Colonel Grey'; Brown instantly corrected him with, 'No, I am Private Brown'! He was not averse to humour as illustrated on another occasion when he was on a boat crossing to Ireland. The captain had been a hearer at Brown's church on a few occasions, but having sat far back in the crowded church, he did not recognise the preacher when they came face to face on the ship. On learning that Brown came from London's East End, he proceeded to ask him, 'Did you ever hear Brown of the East London Tabernacle?' 'Oh, several times', was the reply, 'in fact I question if he has preached half a dozen sermons that I have not heard.' 'Well, what do you think of him?' was the next question. 'In what way do you mean?' Brown quizzed. 'Well, he's a very clever man, don't you think?' 'No, I don't think he is. I shouldn't say he is at all.' This brought the captain to a pause, and then the further question, 'Don't you think that he means what he says?' 'Yes', says Brown, 'I can answer for that.' Before they parted Brown gave him his card and invited him to visit the church again!

THE PLACE OF THE HOLY SPIRIT

The key to Brown as a Christian and a preacher was the teaching of the Holy Spirit on the person and glory of Christ. The effect of that teaching brought the ambition that Christ alone should be magnified. 'I am humbled to the dust', he wrote at the close of one of his pastorates. He knew, as Paul, 'it was not I, but the grace of God which was with me' (1 Cor. 15:10).

When the Holy Spirit is in a man's ministry there will be some resemblance to the testimony of the first disciples, 'And we are his witnesses to these things, and so is the Holy Spirit, whom God has given to them that obey him' (Acts 5:32); and something like the last verse in that same chapter will be repeated, 'And daily ... they ceased not to teach and preach Jesus Christ.' This was Archibald Brown's theme through a lifetime of preaching. For him Christianity was all centred in a person. 'All your religion, if it is worth anything', he would say, 'will just be centred in a living, personal Jesus.' Without Christ, there is no message to preach. 'A living Christ is the warrant for preaching; an ascended Christ is the inspiration for preaching; the gospel must be the matter for preaching; the Lord co-working is the power of preaching.'

It was in this connection that Brown, as Spurgeon before him, identified what he regarded as a dangerous development in evangelicalism. Activity and work were going on, but there was declining emphasis on God directing all things by his Spirit and by his word:

> One may take a merely business-like view of God's work until the supernatural becomes all but eliminated. I am inclined to think that in the present day there is an unholy lust after mere visible success ... we are responsible, as workers, not for success, but for faithfulness.

This change he saw as the explanation of the readiness to appeal to the world by the use of means which have no authorisation from the Holy Spirit. Gaining influence and not following Scripture was becoming the priority. Brown was the last man to condemn originality, but it pained him to see long-established patterns of evangelical work and worship being laid aside on the grounds of being 'up-to-date'. He did not believe the cry that church life and worship 'must be contemporary' to achieve 'success'.

> God, in his sovereignty, has been pleased to make preaching his greatest power for the ingathering of souls. I do not read

that they went forth lecturing, or band playing, or amusement providing; but they went forth *preaching*. The church
has in great measure lost her faith in this mighty weapon, I
do not wonder at it, for the church today is losing faith in
her Lord, and it follows that she should lose faith also in the
Lord's selected instrumentality. ... We are living in grievous
times. The church of God is not staking her all upon the
power of spiritual weapons. Gymnastics take the place of
prayer meetings, concerts in the place of testimony, laughter
the place of pleading, and the spirit of the age the place of
the Holy Ghost.[16]

By the twentieth century such beliefs were a minority
opinion but Brown was certain they were true, as he told the
congregation at the Metropolitan Tabernacle towards the conclusion of his ministry there. Answering the question, 'What
meaneth this?' asked by the multitude on the day of Pentecost,
he replied:

It means that all instrumentality is nothing without the Holy
Ghost, but that the instrumentality with the Spirit is mighty
enough to accomplish anything. Alas, what an amount of
powerless machinery we have in the so-called 'religious world'.
Powerless because it had no unction. Powerless because it
is the work of man, not the working of God through man.
Powerless, because it is dry and official. Powerless, because
it is done by men who have never 'tarried until they were
endued with power from on high'.

On another occasion on the same subject he spoke on the
words, 'Suddenly there came a sound from heaven' (Acts 2:2),
and said:

When the sound is heard from heaven, and the next revival
comes, there will be nothing said from the pulpit or platform
about 'up-to-date' or 'social subject', or the clap trap that is
popular today: it will be Bible! Bible! Bible! And the people
clamouring, 'Let us have the word of God.' The gospel was
preached [at Pentecost], and what followed? Conviction!

'They were pricked in their heart.' They said to Peter, 'Men and brethren, what shall we do?' 'But', says someone, 'do you imagine such a thing could ever happen today?' Yes, indeed I do. I have seen it! Every week for years, men and women coming and saying, 'What shall we do?' May the Spirit of God return again in power to his church! But brethren, do not be looking here and there for revival; do not say, 'Oh, if we could only get Mr So-and-so, we should be sure to get a blessing! The only revival worth having is the revival that is inaugurated by a sound from heaven.

Given the change in the spiritual conditions, one could suppose that reference to past days would have figured largely in Brown's later ministry. But it was not so. Rather the emphasis fell on the *present ministry* of Christ. To the living Saviour belongs 'all power in heaven and on earth'. In his life the believer is now sharing: 'I live, yet not I but Christ liveth in me' (Gal. 2:20). The Christian, sustained by union with the Son of God, depends not for his comfort on the times in which he lives.

This was a lesson about which Brown and Spurgeon once talked at Mentone, on the south coast of France. It was an area that Spurgeon loved and, in showing his younger friend round, they walked up the hill, behind the hotel Beau Rivage, to a garden from which there was a fine view out across the Mediterranean. Visible at times in the midst of the blue water below was a fountain, springing up out of the sea, and although the sea is salt the fountain gave fresh water that could be drunk. The secret was an underground passage from the mountain and under the sea. The only thing that could stop the flow of that fresh water would be if the mountain was sunk lower than the sea. As long as the mountain is there the water must flow. Brown was later to repeat the lesson of that scene to his congregation back in London:

The mountain's height is the guarantee of the sea's fountain. The only thing that can be the destruction of the saint is

Christ vacating his throne on high. Whilst Christ is Christ, and whilst the incarnate God sits on yonder height, there is a guarantee for the continuance of the believer's life. Your life is secure as long as Christ himself shall live. 'The water that I shall give him shall be in him.' 'Springing', then, it is ever fresh, 'unto everlasting life.'

The present exaltation of Christ is the church's great assurance for the future. To him we give thanks that the ministry of one of his faithful servants is being rediscovered today, and let us unite in prayer that he will send another generation of preachers filled with the Holy Spirit and with fire!

NOTE: C. H. SPURGEON ON HOW TO OBTAIN AND RETAIN THE ATTENTION OF HEARERS

We ought to interest all the audience, from the eldest to the youngest. We ought to make even children attentive. We want all eyes fixed upon us and all ears open to us.

You must secure your people's undistracted thoughts, turning them out of the channel in which they have been running six days into one suitable for the Sabbath.

Frequently it is very difficult for congregations to attend, because of the place and the atmosphere.

The next best thing to the grace of God for a preacher is oxygen. Pray that the windows of heaven may be opened, but begin by opening the windows of your meeting-house.

Bad air makes me dull, and my hearers dull too. A gust of fresh air through the building might be to the people the next best thing to the gospel itself, at least it would put them in a fit frame of mind to receive the truth.

What next? *In order to get attention, the first golden rule is, always say something worth hearing.* Most persons possess an instinct which leads them to desire to hear a good thing.

Give your hearers something which they can treasure up and remember; something likely to be useful to them, the best matter from the best of places, solid doctrine from the divine word. Do it, brethren. Do it continually, and you will have all the attention you can desire.

Let the good matter which you give them be very clearly arranged. Be sure, moreover, to speak plainly; because however excellent your matter, if a man does not comprehend it, it can be of no use to him. Go down to his level if he is a poor man; go up to his understanding if he is an educated person.

Let your hearts indite a good matter, clearly arranged and plainly put, and you are pretty sure to gain the ear, and so the heart.

Attend also to your manner of address: aim in that at the promotion of attention. And here I should say, *as a rule do not read your sermons*. If you must read, mind that you do it to *perfection*. Be the very *best* of readers, and you have need to be if you would secure attention.

In order to get attention, make your manner as *pleasing* as it can possibly be. Do not, for instance, indulge in monotones. *Vary your voice continually*. Vary your speed as well—dash as rapidly as a lightning flash, and anon, travel forward in quiet majesty. Shift your accent, move your emphasis, and avoid sing-song. Vary the tone; use the bass sometimes, and let the *thunders roll* within; at other times speak as you ought to generally—from the lips, and let your *speech be conversational*. Anything for a change. Human natures craves for variety, and God grants it in nature, providence, and grace; let us have it in sermons also.

As a rule, *do not make the introduction* TOO LONG. It is always a pity to build a great porch to a little house. The introduction should have something striking in it. It is well to fire a startling shot as a signal gun to clear the decks for action.

If you want to have the attention of your people—to have it thoroughly and always, *it can only be accomplished by their being led by the Spirit of God into an elevated and devout state of mind.*

Be interested yourself, and you will interest others. And then when your hearers see that the topic has engrossed you, it will by degrees engross them.

Do you wonder that people do not attend to a man who does not feel that he has anything important to say? Have something to say, and say it earnestly, and the congregation will be at your feet.

It may be superfluous to remark that for the mass of our people it is well that *there should be a goodly number of illustrations in our discourses*. We have the example of our Lord for that: and most of the greatest preachers have abounded in similes, metaphors, allegories, and *anecdotes*. But beware of overdoing this business.

In your sermons *cultivate what Father Taylor calls 'the surprise power.'* There is a great deal of force in that for winning attention. Do not say what everybody expected you would say. Brethren, take them at unawares. Let your thunderbolt drop out of a clear sky. When all is calm and bright let the tempest rush up, and by contrast make its terrors all the greater.

A very useful help in securing attention is *a pause*.

On a sultry summer's day, if nothing will keep off the drowsy feeling, be very short, sing more than usual.

Again, we must *make the people feel that they have an interest in what we are saying to them*.

Preach upon practical themes, pressing present, personal matters, and you will secure an earnest hearing.

I will now give you a diamond rule, and conclude.

Be yourself clothed with the Spirit of God.

You have golden chains in your mouth which will hold them fast.

'He that hath ears to hear, let him hear.'

4

Kenneth A. MacRae:
Preacher and Pastor

'There were in the Church men of greater note in her councils, and more useful in arranging the framework of the tabernacle. There were men too of greater gifts, and some, perhaps, of greater grace, but none more highly honoured by his Master in the post assigned to him in His work. The preacher is above the counsellor. The latter arranges the tabernacle, the former conducts into it and reveals the glories that are to be seen within the veil. The outer court is the place of the one, the inner is the station of the other. The one is charged with the covering, the other with the treasure. There were and are men of more splendid talent, but none who devoted his gifts more unreservedly to the service of Christ. The Lord honoured him in having set him in the honourable post of which Paul speaks when he says that he was separated unto the Gospel. This is what Christ esteems the chief post of honour.'

John Kennedy of Dingwall, April 30, 1849,
preaching after the death of John MacDonald of Ferintosh.
Words applicable to Kenneth MacRae.

EVERY Christian life is made up of unexpected providential direction. One of the most memorable in my own experience was how I came to know Kenneth MacRae when he was minister in Stornoway, on the Isle of Lewis. Situated in the Outer Hebrides, off the north-west coast of Scotland, the town is one of the most remote in the British Isles. But when the little magazine I edited, *The Banner of Truth*, was launched in 1955, it was from Mr MacRae and his congregation that some of the earliest support came. The following years, when I was serving as assistant to Dr Lloyd-Jones in London, I learned how Christians from Stornoway, coming to London for work, found Westminster Chapel a spiritual home. It was an invitation from one of these friends which took us to Lewis for a family holiday in 1958. That led to the beginning of a friendship with Kenneth MacRae who was then seventy-four and I twenty-seven. Subsequent correspondence with him played a part in the early years of the Banner of Truth Trust, but I was only able to be with him once again, in 1962, before his death in 1964.

LESSONS FROM THE DIARIES OF FIFTY YEARS

It was after his death that I came to know him much more closely. From 1912 to 1963 he kept diaries containing a careful and often full journal of his life. These forty diaries were not destroyed, as they might have been, for they were never intended for publication. Instead his widow, Catherine MacRae, loaned most of them to me, and, intermittently, for fourteen years I lived with them, slowly preparing the large selection which was published as *Diary of Kenneth MacRae* in 1980.[1] In the diaries I felt entrusted with entrance to an inner sanctum, and to sharing in someone else's life in a way I was not to experience again. Although coming to 516 pages, the material eventually published was far less than the originals. My aim had been to arrive at a balance in my selection. To select entries so as to impress readers would have been utterly abhorrent to him. But I am thankful that when the published *Diary* came into the hands of others it spoke to them as the originals had spoken to me. MacRae's friend, the Rev. Kenneth Macleay, minister at Beauly, Ross-shire, wrote to me: 'As you know I always thought highly of him, but by reading these pages I now realise how far short my estimate of him was. The Lord knew his worth and I am sure he is reaping his reward in heaven.'[2]

Although the *Diary of Kenneth MacRae* has introduced him to others,[3] he still remains comparatively unknown, and, living as he did in an age and a culture widely different from our own, the question may arise why include him in these pages. I have two reasons.

First, MacRae's life gives us a *high view of what the life of a preacher and pastor ought to be.* He was a man possessed with a number of natural abilities, and once in the ministry he could have exercised his gifts in various directions. He might have been an author, a churchman, a busy committee man, or a professor of church history. Instead his view of preaching and of pastoring a congregation compelled him to give all his attention to that one calling. His study, his notebooks, his discipline of time, were all organised with the pulpit and his people in view. He knew nothing of comparable importance to preaching. To be used as a messenger of God was his dominating ambition. His diaries contain such words as the following:

> I would not wish to live a day longer in the world if I were able no more to preach the gospel. May the day never come when I shall be of a different mind!

> My eyes have seen the beauty of the King. My heart is once more fired with the desire to make Christ known to perishing sinners.

I realise there is no work like preaching. I can honestly say that, apart from the work of the ministry, I have no interest in life, and would not wish to live unless I could get to preach Christ to sinners.[4]

This remained his life work. When asked to give addresses at the Leicester Ministers' Conference in England in 1962, he accepted the invitation, but with the proviso that he could not give lectures, he 'could only preach'. This he continued to do in Stornoway until the month before his eightieth birthday. His last sermon there, on 27 October 1963, was evangelistic from Genesis 7:1, 'And the Lord said unto Noah, Come thou and all thy house into the ark; for thee I have seen righteous before me in this generation.' The next month with reference to his thirty-three years in that charge, he wrote to a friend, 'I have been mostly skimming the surface and my flock are only half fed. I am therefore amazed as well as humbled that anyone outside my own circle should take any notice of my ministry.'

Second, there is benefit to be gained not only from Mac-Rae's individual example, but *from the way he introduces us to a school of thought on preaching which is a richly rewarding study*. He was himself representative of a tradition of preaching which had been used of God to make once wild areas of the Scottish Highlands and Islands fragrant with evangelical belief and godliness. To confess that this was a tradition which has largely passed away, would be enough for many to suppose it has little instruction for us. Such an assessment would be a great mistake. Nothing in the Bible leads us to believe that the latest views are always the best. Certainly, every era has distinctive and passing circumstances but, where a generation of preachers has been used of God to change the course of history, we may expect to find lessons exemplified which are unchanging. Such was the conviction which led Lloyd-Jones as a young preacher to check his practice by the writings of the Calvinistic Methodists of the eighteenth century, and the same conviction led MacRae to break with an apparently successful contemporary model of preaching and find his mentors in an older school, believing that it gave guidance which resonated more closely with Scripture. That school of preachers did not want to know what gave preachers favour with their hearers, or whether their style appealed to their times. They looked for unction and its life-changing consequences. In their definition of that word both MacRae and Lloyd-Jones would have agreed with R. L. Dabney, another 'old-school' man:

> *Unction*—This term is suggested by that scriptural trope which so frequently represents the effusion of the Holy Ghost as an anointing from God. It expresses that temperature of thought and elocution which the Spirit of all grace sheds upon the heart possessed by the blessed truths of the gospel. It is not identical with animation. Every passion in the preacher does not constitute unction. While it does not expel intellectual activity, authority and will, it superfuses these elements of force with the love, the pity, the tenderness, the pure zeal, the seriousness, which the topics of redemption should shed upon the soul of a ransomed and sanctified sinner.[5]

THE PREPARATION

1. That Kenneth MacRae owed much to his parents and home is beyond question. He was born on November 4, 1883, at Dingwall, Ross-shire, the third son in a family of four sons and two daughters. His father at that date was serving as a Recruiting Sergeant in the Seaforth Highlanders. Probably it was with that famous regiment that Kenneth's love of history began, and certainly from his father, Murdo MacRae, and from the Seaforths, he inherited the order and personal discipline which would mark his life. His father's retirement in 1892 took the family south to Edinburgh. Here Kenneth completed his education at Sciennes School before starting a career in telegraphy at the General Post Office. Of his mother he would later say, 'A nobler mother man never had.'[6] It was a religious, church-going family, and as a teenager, like numbers of other young people at the time, Kenneth attended the special evangelistic meetings which were then popular. At one of these he professed his faith in Christ.

He was a happy, carefree youth—athletic, humorous and, among other leisure activities, belonged to the kilted Royal Scots Territorials. Then, in his early twenties, his world fell apart when his fiancée broke off their engagement. He was plunged into profound and prolonged distress. It was what Scripture calls 'the sorrow of the world', the sorrow of self-regard and self-pity, 'which works death'. His later testimony was, 'I was in extremity, but instead of calling upon God I was only railing against him.' In this condition he came to the awakening that, whatever religious change he had known, it was not from death to life. He had never been a Christian at all. How long this lasted is not recorded, but it ended decisively when he was twenty-five. He tells us that August 9, 1909, was the day when God changed 'my will, my affections, my mind,—the whole outlook of my life'.[7] At the age of twenty-six he started to study for the Christian ministry, at Edinburgh University and at the theological college of the Free Church of Scotland.

It is possible to get into the ministry with an orthodox message without there being any personal fellowship with Christ. Some men have only come to a saving knowledge of Christ after being in the ministry without it. Others, Christ gives us reason to believe, remain in that office without ever questioning whether the experience described by him could become their own, 'Many will say to me in that day, Lord, Lord, have we not prophesied in thy name? ... And then will I profess unto them, I never knew you: depart from me' (Matt. 7:22, 23). A sound conversion has to be at the beginning for a gospel ministry.

2. The next stage in his preparation involved his introduction to the school of preachers already mentioned. It had a few representatives in Edinburgh belonging to the Free Church of Scotland, but most of its people were to be found in its churches in the Scottish Highlands and on the west-coast islands. These churches, it could be said, were the survivors of a spiritual awakening which had come to the north of Scotland from the mid-eighteenth century, and was at its height in the early nineteenth. Before that period there had been church buildings in the region but generally with lifeless preachers and congregations. The new era brought a great change. A people once indifferent to preaching would now walk long distances to be hearers; Gaelic New Testaments and Bibles were eagerly sought; and services connected with the administration of the Lord's Supper had to be held in the open air on account of the hundreds, and sometimes thousands, who gathered. While school teachers and catechists were involved in this movement, the leaders were a succession of men such as those we read of in the Acts of the Apostles, 'full of faith and of the Holy Spirit'. One was John Kennedy of Dingwall (1819–84), who was described by Spurgeon 'as every inch a man of God' whose 'death was a loss to the Highlands greater than could have befallen by the death of any other hundred men'.[8] Kennedy died the year after MacRae was born, and by the time the latter was training for the ministry there were comparatively few of the old type left. A transformation in preaching had been taking place. For the majority it was a move to a more up-to-date form of Christianity and constituted 'progress', but for MacRae the changed times were like the sunset at the end of a summer's day. A glow in the sky was almost all that was left. He loved the company of older men who had known something of the day in its brightness. He also studied the literature on which the former generation had fed and which expressed their convictions. From this source he learned lessons which were to guide him all his life.

The books revered by these preachers of the Scottish Highlands were not simply by men of their own school.[9] Their manse libraries were often extensive and included the writings of Church of England men from Charles Simeon and Richard Cecil to J. C. Ryle and H. C. G. Moule. While leading Scots authors of the seventeenth and eighteenth centuries were prized, the first place as instructors was given to the English Puritans. Dr Kennedy wrote, 'Among British theologians John Owen is *facile princeps*' [easily first], and in a Preface to *Owen on Communion with God*, he said, 'Highlanders, if you would retain what the best of your fathers enjoyed and commended, read and study with much prayer this precious book.'[10]

Spurgeon commended not only the *Life of John Kennedy* but the whole school of Highland preachers to which the latter belonged. On leaving Glasgow for London, after a visit to Scotland in 1865, Spurgeon had been given the biography of Kennedy's predecessor, John MacDonald of Ferintosh. He found it had 'a marvellous power in shortening the journey', and gave it an extensive review in his monthly magazine, *The Sword and the Trowel*.[11] One of the last reviews he ever wrote, a quarter of a century later, was on a book that came from the same source, *Ministers and Men of the Far North* by Alexander Auld. Spurgeon acknowledged that the title, first printed in 1869, would have no interest for those who favoured 'the modern movement' in the churches: 'According to them, there are no Calvinists now alive with the exception of some half a dozen fools', but he was confident that the spiritually minded would 'welcome the memorials of happy days when gospel truth was to the front'.[12]

One of the old-school remnant that was left early in the last century was the Rev. George MacKay of the Free Church of Scotland. He spent most of his life on the Isle of Lewis and then in the parish of Fearn in Easter Ross. One might wonder what good such a man could do if he were transplanted out of his culture and put down in modern Australia. Happily we do not need to wonder, for this actually happened in 1927, when MacKay came to supply the congregation of St George's

(Presbyterian Church of Eastern Australia), Sydney, for a period. There were several notable preachers in Sydney at that date, but when a young student for the ministry, Marcus L. Loane, went to hear MacKay it was a new experience for him. So strong was the impact that Loane was himself drawn to the ministry of the Free Church of Scotland. MacKay dissuaded him, but the future Archbishop and Primate of Australia had learned something about preaching which he would never forget.[13] It illustrates the point that the principles which underlie a powerful ministry are not determined by time or place.

3. Kenneth MacRae's preparation for preaching did not end when he was ordained to his first charge at Lochgilphead, Argyllshire in 1915. It was to go on through several years and this leads me to mention a primary truth. No matter what he reads, or who he meets, it is not simply by such means that a preacher comes close to being what he needs to be. For usefulness, it is the life of the man himself that matters most, and no one has ever become a true guide to others without a personal preparation at the hands of God. A few men spring to early success as preachers, but in many instances it is the experience of difficulty and of comparative failure which is the way to greater usefulness.[14]

Lochgilphead was a difficult first charge. The beautiful surroundings on the shore of Loch Gilp contrasted with the spiritual coldness for which Argyll was known. It was an area, it seemed, little touched by revivals formerly experienced. The congregation had 223 adherents, but only 66 members, that is people who professed faith and came to the Lord's table. To them he had to preach in both English and Gaelic, the latter a language which he was still struggling to learn. In that connexion, as in so many others, he was to be helped by his Gaelic-speaking bride, Catherine Matheson, whom he married and brought to Lochgilphead in 1916.[15]

In addition to his own congregation, he had the responsibility for three other churches at a distance from his own, where he preached regularly. There were encouragements and praying people, but in his diary he noted how the carelessness in church attendance vexed him. At times he felt, 'the worldliness and materialism of Argyll is strangling me'. A minority party developed in the Lochgilphead congregation who quietly opposed him where they could. Some of these persons may have sympathised with criticism in the local press when he declined to co-operate with all the other denominations in the town, Protestant and Catholic, who were engaged in a 'Mission of National Re-dedication'. He had told those who invited him that what was needed first was 'sincere repentance in the ministry for sins of frivolity and heresy'. But another criticism in the press hurt him more deeply. The Great War at this point was being waged in France, and thousands had gone to the front from the Highlands of Scotland, including his two brothers. Military instincts were in his genes and it was only the call to the ministry which kept him preaching. But all around him were homes without younger men, and in 1917 the local newspaper attacked him for staying where he was. They did not know how he wrestled with the issue or that he had, that same year, sought his denomination's agreement for a release from Lochgilphead so that he could take a chaplaincy in France. But in his case the denomination refused, pointing out that they were already short of five ministers in the area where he was. This was a profound trial for him, the more so as both his brothers, serving in the Scottish infantry, were wounded, the eldest dying from those wounds. His wife had only one brother, John, and he was killed at the front. Out of such ordeals the prayer and the desire grew 'to try to be a loving minister'. The horror of the war also taught him that belief in a personal devil is no theory.

There were conversions and blessings in the Lochgilphead ministry and the heartaches proved to be preparations for greater usefulness. In 1919 he was called to his second charge, no longer on the mainland but on the Isle of Skye, a' the care of the three joint charges of Kilmuir, Kilmaluag, and Staffin. His work there finished in 1931, when, at the age of 47, he removed to the place where his ministry would be best remembered. The Free Church of Scotland in Stornoway, on the Isle of Lewis, had been strong for many years. At the time of MacRae's settlement Stornoway was a town of 3,644 people; more than half that number were connected with his congregation in some 650 homes. Part of the congregation was also found in six outlying country districts. Depending on the weather, families would walk in from these districts to the main church building in the town which could contain 1,600. In addition there were mission halls in each district where weekly prayer meetings were held, so that the minister had between ten and fifteen services under his supervision, with two Gaelic and one English on Sundays. There was a central prayer meeting on Thursday nights, and the mission hall meetings maintained with the assistance of lay preachers. The Sunday morning congregation consisted of about 500, the evening could approach twice that number.[16]

GOVERNING PRINCIPLES OF MINISTRY

1. Live and speak under the authority of the word of God. Without that authority MacRae believed a minister had no business doing anything in the name of Christ, who commanded, 'teaching them to observe all things whatsoever I have commanded you'. He was living at a time when this principle had been relaxed and eaten away in many parts of the Presbyterian churches in Scotland. Concessions were being made to the world in the expectation that a more culturally-acceptable Christianity would be more successful.

For MacRae the divine authority of Scripture was not simply a belief to be held, it was to be lived out in daily life and practice. He believed this with the greatest seriousness. Church work and the teaching must be Scripture-proof or it will be found as 'wood, hay and stubble' in the day that Christ will judge all. One consequence of that conviction was the practices maintained in his ministry which are little seen today. For example, the book of Psalms were sung, the Christian Sabbath was kept holy, family worship was expected in all Christian homes, and fasting was an occasional duty—not because these things were part of Presbyterian tradition but because they were all authorised by the word of God.

This foundational principle had a twofold effect in his ministry. First, it kept him from following many who moved with the times. He believed that all that is of first importance for the life and prosperity of the church is already laid down in the word of God. This is a liberating principle. In all ages many new formulas for building the church have continually been presented with the promise of success. How are these formulas to be tested? Not by their alleged results, not by the personalities of their advocates, but by the question, has Christ commanded them? Today we live in a time when changes take place at a giddy rate. All kinds of new ideas and practices are in the air. 'To the law and to the testimony: if they speak not according to this word, it is because there is no light in them' (Isa. 8:20).

In a rare comment by way of self-analysis, Kenneth MacRae was to say when he was eighty:

> There is only one thing I know I can do well. I cannot lead, but I can truthfully say that I am able to hang on. It may arise from natural stubbornness, but I know that popular religious movements which, despite their lack of scriptural support, carry away so many good people, leave me entirely unaffected. I believe that I can set my teeth and hold on, but that is all I am good for.[17]

This foundational principle leads to another vital consequence. If anyone has to live by faith it is the gospel minister. He needs the assurance and the expectation of success when, to all appearances, it seems improbable. But for the preacher to be governed by the things that are seen, and to preach without faith, is to achieve nothing.

This was a lesson brought home to him in his early ministry at Lochgilphead. In a notebook of that period which he headed, 'Self Admonitions', he listed the sins besetting his preaching. He believed they were, 'pride, lightness and lack of solemnity, fear of man, and the greatest of the lot, unbelief. This sin robs me of all present expectation.' He noted that an expectation of better things in the future, rather than the present, was something he could entertain, but this, he came to see, was a snare—'an ideal, a mirage'—likely to come to nothing as far as his ministry was concerned. 'Despite all these golden future expectations, I never come to the church expecting conversions during or as the outcome of the service. What unbelief won't let me do is to look for this hope in the present, to remember the promises of the Lord and to plead with him to fulfil them *now*.' In other words, the promise, 'lo, I am with you always', goes with the command, 'teaching them to observe all things whatsoever I have commanded you'. 'Above all, taking the shield of faith' (Eph. 6:16) speaks to present duty.

Yet he also knew that faith will be honoured in God's time and way, and that it is faithfulness to Christ, not results, which needs to be the preacher's primary concern. In encouraging younger ministers, he would often refer to words addressed to him when he was a student for the ministry. He had been preaching in Dr Kennedy's congregation in Dingwall and, after the evening service, was troubled and downcast at how poorly he felt he had done. The church officer, rightly understanding the situation, said to him, 'Never you mind, my boy, it is not "Well done, good, and successful servant" but "Well done, good and faithful servant."'

2. Always give attention to the young. According to contemporary ideas a ministry such as MacRae's might be helpful to mature and older Christians but he was surely far too straight and strict to have any appeal to the young. So it might seem, but the opposite was the truth. The young heard him, in many cases followed him, indeed, loved him.[18] When he was sixty-four years of age, and feeling the heavy demands of the Stornoway charge, he had a call to the quiet mainland parish of Ferintosh, a place to which he had strong attachments. His initial inclination was to accept the call, but five deputations of young people from the Stornoway congregation begged him not to leave them. When he wrote to the people at Ferintosh to explain why he could not come, he told them it was the affection of the young people which had overcome his judgment.

In 1960 there was a discussion in the columns of the *Scotsman*, a national newspaper, about the state of preaching and declining church attendance. MacRae contributed with the claim that it was only Reformed doctrine which could bring back the people. When this was challenged by a subsequent correspondent, MacRae replied further and, in passing, included this statement: 'In this town any favourable Sabbath evening I can count on a congregation of up to 1,000—and sometimes over—80 per cent of whom are young people.'

His bond with the young goes back again to a biblical principle. He was totally against the modern idea that children are best taken out of a worship service for separate classes in a Sunday School. Behind that practice was the supposition that children cannot profit from sermons and, if made to listen, are put off the practice of church attendance in later life. Not so! The Bible knows nothing of congregations being divided by age groups. Little children can also be fed and prepared for life by preaching. The habit of church attendance springs from childhood.

It has to be said that MacRae had an advantage which ministers today may not have, namely, the children in his congregation came from homes where the *Shorter Catechism* was commonly taught. It was also taught in the Stornoway public school, so the words of Scripture and of Christian doctrine were familiar from childhood. But history shows that children who never benefitted from such an environment have also profited from early attendance at public worship.

The main reason for MacRae's success with children and young people was his care for them which they knew and felt. They were not ignored in public worship. He could speak to their understanding, and their needs were ever included in public prayer. When he gave counsel to the lay preachers, who served in the congregation, he would exhort them to 'remember the infants. Give them fundamental doctrines—the pure milk of the word. But don't spend all the time in the nursery.'

3. Closer fellowship with Christ is the primary need. Love for Christ is *the* qualification for speaking in his name and the maintenance of that love and personal devotion needs life-long attention. Depending on Christ alone for peace with God, re-alising his presence, acting by faith in the strength he gives, are lessons that have to be learned again and again. 'That I might know him', is for ever a desire awaiting a greater fulfil-ment. References to this theme recur throughout MacRae's life. In the earlier years of his ministry he wrote:

> My method has been all wrong and must be changed. More prayer, more personal soul exercise, more retirement, must be my method henceforth, and then haply I may look for more fruit in my public ministrations.

> My freedom in public does not depend on my thoroughness in preparation but upon the spirituality of my mind. Is it not then my wisdom to give more attention to the preparation of the heart before services?

When he was fifty years old he suffered several months of serious illness, and he wrote afterwards:

> I saw how utterly foolish I had been in my ministry, working at high pressure all the time, and forgetting that all my efforts

would be vanity were they not blessed of the Holy Spirit. This is what troubled me more than anything else in my illness. I longed that I might work aright, learning to take the Lord with me in every sermon. One sermon preached in the power of the Holy Spirit is better than 100 without. If I learn to work less and plead more, I will be able to accomplish much more.

He would have said that he never learned this lesson as he desired to do, but without doubt the usefulness of his ministry was bound up with a deepening fellowship with Christ. His diaries contain such sentences as: 'Got a sweet sense of Christ's favour going down the brae tonight.' 'Spoke on the three figures on the crosses of Calvary. My cup seemed just to overflow and I got lovely views of the glory of Christ.'

It was Christ in him which gave him the yearning to see conversions. It was Christ who made preaching the joyful thing it ought to be. It was Christ, not self, that made him what he was. 'Beware of self, beware of self.' In November 1957, when he suffered an illness from which there was concern that he might not recover, he dictated the following words to his wife:

I hereby testify that I have lived a long, satisfying and happy life, and now that I come to die I pass on trusting in the merits of my adorable Redeemer who has taken away the shadows of alienation and filled my cup to overflowing with an unspeakably sweet sense of his love. To him be all the glory!

'Let all the earth his glory fill,
Amen, so let it be.'

THE PREPARATION OF SERMONS

Very few of MacRae's sermons were published, in part because he never wrote them in full, and there were no recorders or short-hand writers to take them down. But we have at least two valuable sources to trace what he thought about preaching.

The first is in his diaries. From these it appears that only slowly did he establish what became his normal pattern for sermon preparation. He settled on what he called 'Whitefield's method' which he described

> as being the most effective plan, i.e., sketching out the plan carefully and then preaching more or less extempore upon it. I have come to that conclusion on former occasions, but in order to adhere to this method without coming to grief I require (1) to live close to the Lord and (2) to act in faith in dependence upon him in every service.

The second source of information is in the fifteen lectures on preaching which he gave from time to time to lay preachers who preached at the smaller country services and prayer meetings around Stornoway. In these addresses we can hear him expressing what he had learned:

A first rule he gave them was, 'Be natural. Don't imitate any other speaker. Be yourself. You were meant to be.'

In his own case as a preacher he started a sermon calmly, giving out the text very distinctly, and speaking slowly and deliberately. 'Don't be hurried. Don't pour out your sentences in a torrent. Speak in a natural tone.' Animation should come as the subject develops, and it should never be imitated. 'Avoid unnecessary noise. Don't bang the Bible.' In his diary he records hearing preachers who confused noise with power, as in this instance from the year 1940:

> Mr ___ said a great deal, but very little of it, except what bore on the last clause, had any relation to his text. It was quite evident that he had not tried to get at the meaning of his text nor to study it. He shouted and banged, however, to such an extent that he seemed to get the better of the nerves of some of the country girls. Fortunately they were able to control themselves, but I felt very displeased.

Some gestures should be used in preaching but they should be appropriate and not distracting for the hearers. To stand like a wooden doll, and with a heavy listless delivery is not preaching. Yet gestures fitting to one man may not be so to another. 'Be careful in their use', he would say.

Nothing in preaching should draw attention to the speaker himself. 'Preach in humility, wondering at the condescension which would use such an unworthy creature.' He would commend the example of a Highland minister who said, 'Never did I truly preach the gospel but while I felt that I myself was the greatest sinner in the congregation.'[19]

Another high priority for him was the need for the preacher to get into sympathy with his hearers. 'Remember they have immortal souls and feel for them. Be faithful to them—but never roughly, the tender reproof goes deeper. Courtesy and consideration will win respect.' He agreed with Spurgeon's dictum that to catch fish you need bait, and the best bait for the preacher is love. For MacRae there was little possibility of a preacher having a bond with his hearers unless he looked directly to them and spoke to their faces. For a preacher to read a sermon should therefore be out of the question. How a congregation should not be addressed is well stated in a book which MacRae valued:

> There are some who preach *before* their people, like actors on the stage. There are others who preach *over* their people. Studying for the highest instead of speaking for the lowest in intelligence—learned treatises which float like a mist over the heads of their hearers. There are some who preach *past* their people. Directing their praise or their censure to intangible abstractions, they never take aim at the views and the conduct of the hearers before them. There are others who preach *at* their hearers, seemingly possessed with the idea that the transgressor can be scolded out of the ways of iniquity. There are some who preach *towards* their people. They aim well, but they are weak. Their eye is along the arrow towards the hearts of their hearers, but their arm is too feeble to send it to the mark. Superficial in their experience and in their knowledge, they reach not the cases of God's people by their doctrine, and they strike with no vigour at the consciences of the ungodly.

Powerful preachers, the same author urged, are of a different type, they preach to the individual directly, 'with authority, unction, wisdom, fervour and love'.[20]

For MacRae, a true sympathy for hearers is closely related to the practice of constant pastoral visitation. When care for people is expressed only to a congregation from a pulpit, it falls far short of what is needed. The large congregation in Stornoway might have provided a plausible excuse for his not being often in the homes of the people, but for any such excuse he had contempt. One of the reasons he got so much done was that he was highly disciplined and systematic, and part of his discipline was to keep a record of every house visit. Their number was remarkable. In his first year at Stornoway he made 1,103 home visits, the next year it increased to 1,250, and this was the kind of routine he kept up. Towards the close of his ministry he was still commonly visiting three hours every day, five days a week.[21] People who have this kind of care from their pastor are far more likely to believe that affection expressed from the pulpit is genuine.

In his rules for preaching he gave a high place to what he called 'orderliness', that is to say, that the contents of a sermon should not be thrown together in haphazard form, but be planned and logically arranged. A sermon needs to have divisions to it, or 'heads', which the hearers can follow as the sermon progresses. As someone has put it, the different heads of a sermon can be likened to blocks of granite, one laid on top of the other, but each block red hot, so that they merge together.

Definite heads within a sermon are vital. Because they are 'of great assistance to your memory'. Not everything the preacher has thought to say in his preparation is likely to be recalled, but heads and divisions *can* and *must be*, or there will be confusion. Without them not only will the preacher be confused but his hearers also. A sermon without clear structure is little likely to be understood, and still less remembered. A good sermon should both 'strike and stick'.

So the question is where does the preacher get his 'heads'? This leads to another question, Is the text for the sermon to be one or two verses, or part of a more extended passage which is being continued through consecutive Sundays? In other words, is the sermon to be complete in itself, or is it one of a series in a chapter or book of Scripture. This has already been discussed in earlier pages. The Scottish tradition knew both types of preaching, but the second, the consecutive exposition, was called—not in any derogatory sense—the 'lecture'. This might be given at one service on the Sunday, with the 'sermon' delivered at the other. Any discussion of which of these methods is the more scriptural is likely to be unprofitable, for it depends on *how* each method is used and done.

In his lectures MacRae dealt with the danger of taking single texts, in no consecutive order, from week to week. In that practice a preacher may too easily revert to the type of text which suits his cast of mind. Or he may lose much time in trying to determine the text he should take. But there are remedies for these dangers,[22] and speaking from a single text was MacRae's normal, though not invariable, habit.[23] I believe there are good reasons why this method has usually been the most popular in Christian history.

So, coming back to the question where does the preacher get his heads, the answer has to be, whether it is an individual sermon or part of a series, he should get them *out of the text* he has announced. He must therefore first be sure of its meaning, 'soak himself in the text', then arrive at 'heads' for his main points, and order them into a plan. 'To handle several points at once is only to distract the attention and dissipates the effect.' The object is to set out the meaning as clearly and convincingly as possible. Referring to this, one author says,

> Many a text seems to have a new force and brightness after a preacher has opened it up. It sticks in the conscience and to the heart, and sometimes becomes the kindling spark of a new

life in the soul. It recurs again and again to such a hearer amid the manifold changes and trials of life.[24]

The fact that the heads and plan of a sermon are the most difficult part of sermon preparation is borne out by MacRae's lectures on preaching.[25] In the fifteen lectures he gave to his helpers, no less than five are on 'The Plan of the Sermon'. Those who heard him weekly in church were aware of the care he took in that respect. But while they saw the result, they did not know of the two stages through which his sermons passed. First, he prepared and typed a full outline on two sides of a sheet of paper of uniform size, 10 by 8 inches; second, he transferred this in abridged form, handwritten, to a card, only 5 by 3½ inches, which he took with him to the pulpit for reference.

Thus the fuller version of a sermon on 28 October, 1962, 'the Great Division', reads as follows: The text was, 'Then shall ye return, and discern between the righteous and the wicked, between him that serveth God and him that serveth him not' (Mal. 3:18).[26]

INTRODUCTION

A dark day is here described. The conduct of the Lord's people in it is indicated in Malachi 3:16. A day is foretold when they shall be delivered and acknowledged—v. 17; that is, the end of the world. Then it is that looking back they will be able to make a competent judgment concerning matters which at the time were so hard to understand.

I. THE CONFUSED SCENE

1. *The Lord's people and the children of this world live together; they are inextricably mixed.* The former try to remain *separate* but there is infiltration everywhere. When Christ was *deserted* by most of his followers (John 6:66-71) Judas *remained* with him.

2. *There is no pure church upon earth.* A church may be pure in *doctrine* but no church is pure in *personnel* or *practice*.

3. *This is in accordance with God's scheme to let both grow together.*

4. *The lessons which this should teach us:—*

    1. That it is wrong to break away from a church pure in doctrine for any reason less than unfaithfulness in doctrine.

    2. Not to lose heart when we see one reputed to be sound in the Faith depart from it.

    3. Not to be discouraged because many say—v. 14.

    4. Not to be confused when wicked men prosper and are exalted and the righteous are visited with calamities.

    5. That judgment pertains to the Lord.

        1. It is not for us to judge our neighbour's state before God.

        2. We should realise that we cannot see the end, that God is working according to his own plan, and that although all is confused now, yet the end will be to the glory of his name.

    6. That we should see to it that we ourselves bear the marks of those who truly are the Lord's.

II. THE DIVISION THAT SHALL BE MADE

1. *Although all is so confused—hypocrites and formalists in the church and saints in Caesar's household—yet the Lord will have no difficulty in dividing them.*

2. *A great secret dividing process is going on under the gospel but that division is known only to God.*

3. *But he will make a final and open division on the Great Last Day; and the Great White Throne shall divide them.*

4. *We should realise that despite all the differences among the children of men, yet in God's sight there are but the two great classes—the righteous and the wicked.*

5. *It follows then that if you are not in one class you must be in the other.*

6. *It should therefore be your serious concern to ascertain in which class you are.*

7. *For in the Great Day there is to be an eternal division, the righteous to go into eternal blessedness and the wicked into outer darkness.*

8. *And this duty is all the more necessary because many think they are among the righteous who shall yet find themselves among the wicked.*

9. *I shall give only two marks of the righteous, only one is mentioned here but both are essential:*

    1. The righteous have all been born again.

    2. They serve God.

III. THE BASIS OF THIS DIVISION

1. *The basis is as to whether or not they serve God.*

2. *Only the born again are admitted to God's service.*

    1. A man may serve the church who has never been born again, he is no servant of God.

    2. They serve God wherever he has placed them. Be content then with your field of service and be faithful in it.

    3. Go on serving God there until he remove you to another field; but when you do remove be sure it is the Lord who is removing you and not worldly ambition.

3. *How can you serve him?*

    1. By living a life of dependence upon him on the earth.

There is little of this nowadays.

2. By doing for him what he puts in your power to do. Look about you, and you will see much that you can do for his glory.

3. By standing firm by his testimony in a day of backsliding. God is glorified by faithful witness; e.g., Daniel.

4. By seeking to advance the cause. His is not a lost cause. Advance against the enemy.

CONCLUSION

1. *Do not seek for comfort in this world. Such would only make you drowsy. You will get your comfort in a better world.*

2. *You may reckon yourself an unprofitable servant, but it is the Lord who will assess the value of your service.*

3. *Those who serve him not will be cast out. They may be acclaimed by the world for their wonderful service in the field of science, scholarship or statesmanship, but Christ will not acknowledge them. They did not serve him.*

4. *The world may honour and praise their great ecclesiastics but Christ will not acknowledge them, for they did not serve him.*

5. *And how can you who obviously live for self and the world think to pass this scrutiny?*

6. *Oh come to realise your sin in neglecting the Lord and his salvation, and repent before it is too late.*

In preaching no numbers were announced in his divisions. The numbers in the sub-heads, and the sub-sub-heads, were purely for the benefit of his own clarity of thought and aid of memory. That he put down Scripture references, not the words of texts in his notes, did not mean he meant the people to turn to them. He simply quoted the Scripture, and often from memory. The main text of the sermon was repeated several times in the course of its delivery.

This type of preaching differed widely from what was becoming fashionable in Scotland. In numbers of the well-known city pulpits, sermons had become akin to well-composed essays, written in admirable literary style and ready, perhaps intended, for publication. No place was left for extempore delivery. In contrast, MacRae believed that thoughts are more important than words, and that freedom in delivery was far better than reading from a manuscript. In the words of J. W. Alexander:

> Public eloquence and pulpit power are both compromised if literary ingenuity replaces impassioned, extemporaneous speech true to a man's nature and individual personality. True eloquence must be natural and not artificial. It is marked by simplicity of style, sincere conviction, and purposeful pronouncement.[27]

MacRae believed that no man should be in the ministry who cannot discipline himself to hard work and to be much alone for study. This he found no easy matter. His early ministry contained such diary notes as, 'Oh to live nearer to him and to be less called away by multitudinous duties eating away all my time![28] A cold pulpit is the natural fruit of it.' In his settled routine he became virtually unobtainable during morning hours. Only something of the greatest urgency would take him out of his study at that time. Failure here, he believed, accounted for much ineffective ministry. 'We live in a day when many ministers are extremely busy about trifles, and the thing they like least is the hard work of the closet, of the study, and the homes of the people.'

One thing sure to discourage hard study is self-satisfaction. To avoid that, he urged his church 'agents' (as he called his lay-preaching helpers), always to be critical of their work and to be open for comment. 'If you are satisfied with yourself no improvement is possible. Perhaps the audience is not so satisfied with such a preacher.' 'Don't be above taking advice from a friend who is qualified to give it.' He practised what he taught and in his diary there are many notes by way of self-criticism. To quote a few entries at random:

> It is in the lack of the element of love in my preaching that I come short.

> If I rebuke sin, my nature is such that I become roused and pugnacious and that drives away the gentle influences of the Spirit; if I don't, my conscience reproves me.

> I long to be able to preach Christ more fully.

> Have been somewhat impressed by reading Shedd on the place of fear as a motive to vital religion.[29] I am afraid I have somewhat overlooked this in recent years. I have found it difficult to preach the sterner aspects of the truth in love, or without being myself more hardened in the process, and I have tended more and more to neglect such subjects. But I am convinced that I have been in the wrong. I fear the deceitful heart prefers both to preach and to hear 'smooth things'.

> Jonathan Edwards's sermon on the Justice of God revealed to me today how much I have neglected the duty of bearing in upon the individual the guilt of his various sins and the amazing power that lies in this type of preaching.

After preaching on Romans 9:25, he noted, 'I am afraid my discourse lacked logical connection and point, that, in fact, it wandered unduly from the text.' After another sermon, on Acts 13:38, 39, he recorded that he had spoken to 580 people 'with measure of liberty and much confused thought. Must be completely recast before it can be used again.'

Occasionally the criticism registered came from his much-loved wife. 'I am given to understand', his diary noted,

> that my delivery has become monotonous, mournful and slow. I believe this is the result of my relaxing—as it were—in the pulpit under the impression that the Lord would help me.

I see the danger of this—that it has the tendency to make me heavy and drowsy. I remember how sleepy and dull Mr ___'s delivery used to be, and how I wished he would wake up; and here I have drifted into the same fault, and were it not for my faithful wife I might have been allowed to remain in it until it had become a confirmed habit. I must not spare myself, but preach with energy and force.

On another occasion he summed up his feelings about himself in the words, 'I fear I am a poor failure both as a minister and as an ordinary Christian.'

THE HOLY SPIRIT IN PREACHING

If it be asked how a man can be convinced of his utter insufficiency as a preacher, and yet be enabled to preach with power and authority, the only answer is by the ministry of the Holy Spirit. Far from the sense of inability being a hindrance to spiritual usefulness, it is the essential pre-condition. 'Who is sufficient for these things?' says the apostle, and answers, 'Our sufficiency is of God; who also hath made us able ministers of the new testament' (2 Cor. 2:16; 3:5). Was there any lesson given by our Lord more fully to the disciples, on the night before his death, than the truth that another was to be with them to make his glory known to sinners: 'I will send unto you from the Father, even the Spirit of truth ... he shall testify of me: and ye also shall bear witness' (John 15:26, 27)? Here is a conjunction of human incapacity and divine strength. The disciples were called to convict men of sin, and righteousness and judgment, but they were not to do it alone, 'And when he is come, he will reprove the world of sin, and of righteousness, and of judgment' (John 16:8).

What was present in the earthly ministry of Christ was to be seen multiplied in his servants. He was anointed with the Holy Spirit, and those he sends to speak in his name he baptizes with the Holy Spirit. This was the credential Paul claimed for the gospel ministry. Preaching with the Holy

Spirit is New Testament preaching (2 Cor. 3:1-6; Gal. 3:2; 1 Thess. 1:5).

I can only summarise some of the practical consequences of this truth for MacRae.

1. He looked for the Holy Spirit in the preparation of a sermon and there were occasions when his guidance was marked. He was in the midst of working on a sermon in December 1918 when there came news of the death of a friend. 'I was constrained', he wrote, 'to put it aside and seek out another subject. The text which I took was "This is my comfort in my affliction."' The following Lord's Day one of his hearers happened to be a sad stranger from Oban, a young woman who had lost her brother and her fiancée in the war, together with another brother whose war service had left him in an asylum. 'The sermon met her case and on her own confession made a great impression upon her. How wonderful are the ways of the Lord!'

But the preacher also receives help in the delivery of the sermon. He did not believe that preaching means delivering simply what was in his notes beforehand. 'Leave room for the Spirit' was his counsel to others. The Spirit of God can give a man liberty in the very exercise of preaching, and help him to say more than he intended to say. So a preacher should never go into a pulpit depending on his preparation. God is involved in preaching, and in a real sense it is his work rather than the preacher's. This is the antidote to our feeling overwhelmed in facing the difficulties which belong to preaching.[30]

2. While high place is to be given to the making of a sermon, the preparation of the preacher himself must come first. Words spoken may instruct the mind, but unless there is an enduement of the Spirit there will be no speaking to the heart. He it is who gives fire and warmth. MacRae noted the words of David Brainerd that it is men filled with the Spirit who can address the conscience.[31]

For MacRae, and the whole school of men to which he belonged, it was a serious error to think there was no need for a continued receiving of the Holy Spirit. Certainly, every true Christian is permanently indwelt by the Spirit of God, but that is not in conflict with New Testament direction for believers to pray for the Holy Spirit. George Smeaton called 'the modern notion' an error that 'believers are not to pray for the Holy Spirit, because he was once for all given on the day of Pentecost', and asserted, 'The history of the apostles shows that not once, but on many occasions, they were made partakers of the baptism of the Spirit and fire.'[32]

The command to be 'filled with the Spirit', is for the receiving of new measures of the Spirit's grace and influence. The Spirit is not a static gift but a living person. There is a sovereignty and mystery about his work, far more than we can understand, but Christ deliberately connects the giving of the Spirit to prayer, 'How much more shall your heavenly Father give the Holy Spirit to them that ask him?' (Luke 11:13).[33]

3. *The more we know of the Spirit's enabling the less we will think of ourselves.* MacRae wrote: 'So far as I can see, the more a man is filled with the Spirit the more he will be aware of and mourn over the vileness of his own heart.' This coincides with the answer Lloyd-Jones gave to a preacher who asked, 'How do you know if the Holy Spirit is working in your ministry?' He replied: 'That is very easy. If you are preaching in the energy of the flesh, you will feel exalted and lifted up. If you are preaching in the power of the Spirit, you will feel awe and humility.'[34]

4. *Disbelief in the agency of the Holy Spirit is the great hindrance to fresh and energetic gospel work.* Faith means dependence on God and his word; unbelief dishonours him, and brings spiritual stagnation. 'And he did not many mighty works there because of their unbelief' (Matt. 13:58). Mac-Rae became convinced that the receding tide of blessing in Scotland was related to this failure. It is true the Holy Spirit is not in our hands; we do not direct his operations; he works sovereignly, but, 'the rule of the kingdom is that we shall have

according to our faith, "According to your faith be it unto you" (Matt. 9:29).' MacRae noted that at the times and in the places when there was particular blessing and numbers converted, there was an expectancy of faith among the people. And he saw it as a vital part of the ministry so to preach that faith in God's promises is strengthened.

Revival always begins among the people of God. MacRae regarded it as an important aid to the quickening of a congregation that they should hear mid-week addresses on the history of revivals from time to time.[35] Let them listen to evidence that times of awakening are not theories but realities. Sinners are then brought to repentance and faith in large numbers. This entered largely into MacRae's thinking, and at different points in his life he saw something of the Spirit in reviving power.[36] He was certain that the life of the church does not proceed on one uniform level through the ages. There are interventions and enduements of the Holy Spirit which may affect not one congregation only, but sometimes whole communities, bringing a new epoch. A great change in situations is possible. One of his favourite texts was the promise, 'A little one shall become a thousand, and a small one a strong nation' (Isa. 60:22).

It grieved MacRae that, in the light of God's promises, and the evidence of history, there should be a decline of expectancy in the Highlands of Scotland. Instead a passive acceptance of conditions had come in.[37] Preachers continued to do their duty; they preached three times a week; and people went to church, but in declining numbers. Formality was taking the place of life. 'What ails our Church', he wrote at one point, 'is that our orthodoxy is a dead one.'[38] 'We seem so bound up in formality that it appears almost impossible to get rid of it. Oh to be awake myself!'[39] 'If only some East Coast ministers were a little less hidebound by custom and tradition, and if only they realised our day calls for exceptional measures, they would not have to complain so much of the rising generation

drifting away.'[40] Opposed though he was to modern evangelistic methods, he approved churches having an occasional
series of evangelistic services.

Kenneth MacRae preached to within seven months of his
death on May 6, 1964. Two days later, Stornoway saw the
sight of a Christian funeral such as is not often seen in this
world, and which these pages cannot convey. The life of the
town stopped still that Friday afternoon. All was silent save
for the sound of the feet of the thousand men who walked
behind the simple wooden bier. Their procession, three-
quarters of a mile long, moved on streets lined with 'hundreds
of women, many of them weeping, past the manse and
the school where the children lined the playground, to the
cemetery beside Sandwick Bay.' The multitude felt what *The
North Star* reported, 'No man in the Free Church was so much
loved by the people.' A prophetic ministry which had spoken
for God had come to an end. A watchman whose authority
had held back the inroads of unbelief had been taken away.
The loss to the whole community was more than could be put
into words.

His final message, sent to his congregation, had been, 'Be
ye faithful unto death, let no man take your crown', and he
prayed, 'Bless my dear people. Give them a man after thine
own heart. Bless my young people.' At the last, before lapsing
into a coma, he said in the presence of 'Cath, my darling', who
was beside him,

> Christ's finished work is perfect. He has made *all* perfect. If
> I had opportunity to speak I would emphasise the excellency
> of his work. Into thine hands I commit my spirit, Lord Jesus.

5

Understanding
Martyn Lloyd-Jones

'Today our essential trouble is that we are content with a very superficial and preliminary knowledge of God, his being and his cause.... Our supreme need, and our only need, is to know God, the living God, and the power of his might.'

D. M. Lloyd-Jones, *Revival*, pp. 90, 127.

'To me, Calvinism means the placing of the eternal God at the head of all things. I look at everything through its relation to God's glory. I see God first, and man far down the list. We think too much of God to please this present age; but we are not ashamed. Man has a will, and oh, how they cry it up! But, sirs, has not God a will too? What do you attribute to that will? Have you nothing to say about its omnipotence? Is God to have no choice, no purpose, no sovereignty over His own gifts? Brethren, if we live in sympathy with God, we delight to hear Him say, "I am God, and there is none else".'

C. H. Spurgeon, *An All-round Ministry*, p. 337.

After Dr Lloyd-Jones had been a preacher for over fifty years, his health failed and it was evident he would not preach again. A visitor who came to see him after that time sought to express sympathy by saying, 'It must be a disappointment for you that you are no longer able to preach.' He promptly replied, 'Not at all, I did not live for preaching.' The statement, 'I did not live for preaching' is fundamental. To ignore it, and to go straight to considering him as a preacher, is to miss the key both to his preaching and to his life. He meant, of course, that there is something greater than preaching. What that is, comes out in his words, 'A life spent in communion with God is the only life worth living.' To be reconciled to God, to live in his presence, is a far higher thing than simply working for him. To disciples who thought too much of their service, Jesus said, 'in this rejoice not, that the spirits are subject unto you; but rather rejoice, because your names are written in heaven' (Luke 10:20). To know God is 'life eternal'. Lloyd-Jones felt the weight of the warning that he gave to others, 'You may spend fifty years of a very busy life in preaching the gospel, or in organising this or that, and you may know God no better at the end of the fifty years than you did at the beginning.'

START WITH THEOLOGY

To start with God is to start with theology. Theology means, literally, speech about God. There is a quotation from Lloyd-Jones which has often been repeated: 'Preaching is theology coming through a man who is on fire.'[1] Too often, however, interest has centred on 'man' and 'fire' rather than 'theology'. A recent book about him has very little to say on his theology except that the reader is cautioned that Lloyd-Jones read history with 'a firm Calvinistic bias'.[2] This was thrown in as an aside, with no question how Calvinistic belief relates to Scripture, or whether it is belief which ought to 'bias' a Christian. But the starting point for preaching should be the truth men are called to deliver. The message is more important than the messenger. The faith believed is the biblical priority. Thus when once asked on television, 'What makes a successful preacher?' Lloyd-Jones at once told his interviewer that he was asking the wrong question.

When Lloyd-Jones was a medical student he learned a principle that would stay with him all his life; it was that a patient should be looked at as a whole before attention is given to any particular part: 'Always look at the general before the particular', was the maxim. 'Look first at the big thing.' This applies equally to an understanding of the life of Lloyd-Jones. How he prepared his sermons, how he got his sermons, and such like, are details. The big thing for him was theology, what he believed about God. His most serious criticism of modern evangelicalism was that it is weak at the foundation:

> We are living in an age when definitions are at a discount, an age which dislikes thought and hates theology and doctrine and dogma. It is an age characterized by a love of ease and compromise ... It dislikes a man who knows what he believes and really believes it.[3]

The Bible is truth about God, and he believed that truth should control every sermon preached. God is working all things for his own glory, and that glory is revealed supremely in the salvation of sinners. God has planned it. God has determined its success. It is about the giving of eternal life 'which God, that cannot lie, promised before the world began' (Titus 1:2). This is the big thing. Lloyd-Jones writes,

> The sovereignty of God and God's glory, is where we must start and everything else issues from here. If it were not for God's grace, there would be no hope for the world. Man is a fallen creature, with his mind in a state of enmity towards God.

He is totally unable to save himself and to reunite himself with God. Everyone would be lost if God had not elected some for salvation, and that unconditionally. It is only through Christ's death that it is possible for these people to be saved, and they would not see or accept that salvation if God through his irresistible grace in the Holy Spirit had not opened their eyes and persuaded them (not forced them) to accept the offer. Even after that, it is God who sustains them and keeps them from falling. ... The church is a collection of the elect.[4]

As I have said, too much comment and praise for Lloyd-Jones have by-passed his theology, or it is treated as quite secondary. Some might defend this neglect by saying they do not finding him writing or preaching about 'Calvinism', so it cannot be the key to understanding him. This is a major mistake. It is true the word 'Calvinism' is not common in Lloyd-Jones's books or recordings. He had no brief for parading a label, and he was not happy about those who did. But with regard to the fundamental truths which men have treated as though they came from Calvin, he not only believed them, they were at the very core of his life. His comfort in life and death rested in the sovereign grace of God. He wrote at the end of his life,

Finally nothing matters but the fact that we are in God's hands. We and our works are nothing. It is his choosing us before the foundation of the world that matters, and he will never leave us nor forsake us.[5]

For Lloyd-Jones, a preacher's relationship and knowledge of God is the great thing. Others may choose to interpret his life from a different standpoint, but if they do so they are not going to understand him. An understanding of the message has to come before there can be understanding of the messenger. The message, the word of God, is the important thing. It is to this that Luke, as an inspired historian, repeatedly traces the growth of the church in the Acts of the Apostles: 'the word of God increased; and the number of disciples multiplied';

'the word of God grew and multiplied'; 'So mightily grew the word of God and prevailed' (Acts 6:7; 12:24; 19:20).

LIFE-CHANGING EXPERIENCE

If it be asked how Lloyd-Jones came to the theology which he believed, the answer is not that it came from the religious tradition in which he was brought up. That may be surprising, for the denomination of his youth was the Presbyterian Church of Wales, also known as the Calvinistic Methodist Church. But, like other denominations of the last century, his denomination had departed from its doctrinal foundations. At the age of fourteen Lloyd-Jones became a communicant member without any examination of his beliefs. In fact he believed the opposite of what he would later preach. At that time he quoted the belief of Matthew Arnold in the autograph album of a school friend,

> For we are all, like swimmers in the sea,
> Pois'd on the top of a huge wave of Fate,
> Which hangs uncertain to which side to fall.
> And whether it will heave us up to land,
> Or whether it will roll us out to sea ...
> We know not.

This view of life did not fundamentally change until something very surprising happened to him at about the age of twenty-three. By that time he had completed a highly successful medical education at St Bartholomew's Hospital in London, one of the leading teaching hospitals in the world. His mentors were brilliant scientists and rationalists. The supernatural was ignored; evolutionary belief was the order of the day; and Lloyd-Jones came to mix with the men who were at the top of the medical world. A successful and lucrative career was virtually guaranteed for him. But then came a problem for which science had no answer. How do you deal with guilt, with pride, selfishness, greed, lust, envy? He saw these things in his colleagues and in himself. This awareness was his starting point: 'Repentance means that you realize you are a guilty, vile sinner in the presence of God. The moment a man understands the true nature of sin and character of sin he becomes troubled about his soul and seeks for a Saviour.'[6] In this way Lloyd-Jones became a Christian.

Now he and his ambitions were changed. So instead of going to the top of the medical profession, he went down the social scale and became the pastor of a mission hall in an industrial town in South Wales. 'I found myself', he says, 'living a kind of life I had never imagined for a moment. ... There is only one explanation—the sovereignty of God! The guiding hand of God! It is an astonishment to me.'[7] 'It is God who acts. It is God who intervenes. It is God who originates, who plans everything everywhere.'

This gave him a view of himself which would live with him. Thus, on one occasion after he had spoken in Edinburgh, the chairman paid him a glowing tribute and commented on the sacrifice he had made in leaving medicine for the Christian ministry. This was more than the preacher could hear in silence. He protested, 'I gave up nothing; I received everything, I count it the highest honour God can confer on any man, to call him to be a herald of the gospel.'[8]

The knowledge of God came to him personally, but not all at once. There were years of study and progress, and in the process he was led to authors, no longer popular among the churches, but men who had been teachers across the centuries. He was reading the Puritans early in his Christian life; he discovered Jonathan Edwards in 1929; and then B. B. Warfield in 1932. Warfield conveyed to him 'a profound impression of the glory and wonder of the great salvation we enjoy'.[9] That his doctrinal convictions only came to maturity gradually is illustrated by the fact that in 1935 he could still speak of Christ's death being on behalf of 'the whole of mankind'.[10]

But an increase in understanding brought him difficulty as well as help. In Wales he came to feel comparatively isolated; a newspaper described him as almost the 'last of the Calvinistic preachers'. When he left Wales and came to Westminster Chapel, London, in 1938, a sense of spiritual and theological loneliness intensified. Dr Campbell Morgan, his senior colleague at Westminster, had little interest in theology, and Arminian belief was pervasive in English evangelicalism. The ethos in important respects was alien to Lloyd-Jones. John Doggett, an editor and a contemporary, later wrote: 'In 1938 Dr Lloyd-Jones came to a city and to a country in which the Reformed faith of Calvin and the Puritans, of Whitefield and Spurgeon, was almost extinct.' One reason this was not entirely off-putting to the newcomer at Westminster Chapel was that he had indicated to Morgan his desire to remain in London only for a short period. He anticipated a return to Wales. He did not know in 1938 that God had purposed he would be in that pulpit for thirty years, and that during that time a major change would be introduced into English evangelicalism.

This was not a change which would have a ready welcome. At first none of the church officers at Westminster Chapel could sympathise with where he was coming from. One hearer was heard to protest after a Sunday morning service, 'I went to hear Dr Morgan, but it was that Calvinist.' It is not that Lloyd-Jones highlighted doctrinal differences. A first principle for him as a pastor was, 'We must take people as they are, not as we would like them to be.' He knew that people were not to be argued into truth. But the difference could not be hid, and it came out in his whole approach to the handling of Scripture. An early example of this came with the way he related Scripture to World War II which broke out in 1939. While many preachers used the occasion to offer optimism and comfort to worried families, Lloyd-Jones had something different to say. He preached that all things are under the control of God, and raised uncomfortable questions:

> What control have you really over your own life? You had not control over the beginning and you will have no control over

the end. … Had we a right to peace? Do we deserve peace? Were we justified in asking God to preserve peace and to grant peace? What if war has come because we are not fit for peace, because we do not deserve peace?[11]

CONTROVERSY OVER THE PREACHING OF THE GOSPEL

While English evangelicalism in the 1930s was Arminian, making conversion dependent on man's 'free will', in an important sense it was not theological at all. It was occupied with evangelistic witness, with how to gain a response, and had little interest in doctrine and theology. The message was about Jesus, about receiving forgiveness by his cross, and making a commitment to him. These, and belief in the authority of Scripture, were treated as the essentials. Other subjects were thought of as secondary and not matters for controversy.

Lloyd-Jones was not by nature a man who enjoyed controversy. He believed that all who are united to Christ are one. He knew that a person of weak understanding may be a true Christian, while another person of wholly correct belief may not know Christ savingly at all. The current situation therefore presented him with a question and a problem. Should he merge in with the existing evangelicalism, and not disturb the peace, or was he compelled to be different? He took the latter course because what he believed about God left him with no alternative.

He held that the prevalent idea of gospel preaching was wrong. It was wrong because it has lost sight of the truth that the message is 'the gospel of God'. It does not start with Jesus. It starts with God, with his holiness, with the demands of his law, and with his justice which requires that 'the wages of sin is death'. Only in the light of what God is, can the seriousness of man's sin and rebellion be seen.

Let me solemnly remind you of this: the gospel of Jesus Christ does not start even with the love of Jesus Christ. It starts with

It is no use going to people and saying, 'Come to Jesus', 'ome to Christ.' They say, 'We couldn't care less.' Why? Because they have never seen any need of him. That is why they do not come to Christ. The only people who truly come to Christ are those who have seen their own condition under the condemnation of the law of God and know that one day they will face God in eternal judgment.[12]

Much of customary evangelical preaching did not aim at conviction of sin in hearers, and an absence of conviction was recognised but misinterpreted. It was not traced to any defect in the message preached, but explained in terms of the current culture. The modern man was said to lack a sense of sin, and, instead of recognizing that this had always been true of mankind, it was supposed that some adjustment to the message would help to give it relevance at the present day.[13] If sin was not understood by hearers then a different approach to human need might be more effective. So increasingly the gospel was presented as designed for man's happiness, for man's satisfaction, with the offer of Jesus to be a friend, etc. Instead of bringing men to an end of themselves, this approach was an appeal to self-interest, and it left the impression that becoming a Christian was all in the hearer's own hands to determine.

In contrast, what Lloyd-Jones believed, was almost like a message from a different universe of thought. People were staggered to hear him say:

The popular teaching which says we have to preach the gospel to the natural man as he is, and that he, as he is, decides to believe on the Lord Jesus Christ; and that then, because he has believed, he is given new life, is regenerated,—this, I say, is a complete denial of what the apostle teaches.

Instead of making conversion more acceptable, he preached that man is in a position from which only God can deliver him. 'With man is it impossible but not with God.' 'You are without strength and totally incapable. ... We are altogether and entirely without spiritual ability.'[14] This is not to say that in conversion man is an insensible machine. If that were so there would be no place for preaching. But every individual has a conscience, and it is as conscience is awakened by the word of God that there comes a true knowledge of self: 'What things soever the law says, it says to them that are under the law: that every mouth may be stopped, and all the world may become guilty before God'. 'By the law is the knowledge of sin' (Rom. 3:19, 20).

Man's fallen condition is the biblical starting point for the presentation of gospel. While there is no one pattern of conversion, there is a common order or sequence in the way sinners are brought to Christ. According to Scripture, it is learning the gravity of their position before God and his wrath which makes the gospel relevant to the careless. To miss out the preaching of repentance because people have no sense of sin, and to speak to them only of 'accepting Christ', is to depart from the order of the New Testament.[15] The way Lloyd-Jones could conclude a sermon illustrates the difference. He could say:

> Have you ever faced the question of your attitude to God? Are you a rebel against God? Are you a hater of God? Do you feel you know better than God? If so, well I will tell you what you are suffering now is nothing to what you will have to suffer. That is the root cause of all ills and troubles, it is the cause of all suffering, all pain, all confusion. The only hope is to acknowledge it, to face it, to go to God in utter contrition and repentance.[16]

To think that such a presentation of the gospel would hinder a response misses the place of the supernatural in conversion. Under teaching which says that everyone is able to make 'a decision for Christ' there may be more 'results', that is to say, more professions of faith from people who have done what the preacher asked. But numbers are no proofs of spiritual realities. The New Testament warns of many who are 'believers' in Christ yet their *nature* has not been changed (e.g., Matt. 7:22; John 8:30-45; Acts 8:13, 18-23). While this may happen under orthodox preaching, it is far more likely to be the case when the message heard conveys the impression that receiving forgiveness is the individual's only problem. It is not. There must be a new life which can only be by a new birth.

This truth was thrown into the background in modern evangelicalism because of the teaching that converts are regenerated because they *believe*. So to call on people to believe became regarded as the same as calling upon them to be born of God. It was his denial of that teaching, quoted above, which put such a gulf between Lloyd-Jones's gospel preaching and so much that was contemporary. Certainly he called on all to believe in Christ for salvation, but where there is life-changing response it is because it has been given to believe. The natural, unregenerate man, 'receiveth not the things of the Spirit of God: for they are foolishness unto him' (1 Cor. 2:14). The person who receives Christ is no longer a 'natural man'. Faith is born of regeneration (John 1:12, 13).

A mistake here can have immense practical consequences. An older generation of evangelicals expected to see the evidence of a changed life in those who professed to have become Christians. It was believed that God-given faith is always accompanied with a new nature which will bring holiness, reverence for God, and love for Christ's command-ments. But the popular evangelicalism, recognizing a lack of spirituality in the churches, traced the problem to the wrong source. Because the meaning of regeneration was reduced, it was supposed people could be forgiven though not sanctified. So if professing Christians were too much like the world, the reason must be that they had not yet 'received the Holy Spirit'. They had only accepted Christ as Saviour, not 'as Lord'. What they needed was a 'second experience', a 'full surrender' (to which a charismatic variant would later be added). This became a staple part of evangelical teaching.

But the New Testament knows no separation between justification and sanctification. How the new teaching could ignore the scriptures which trace holy living to the new birth, or how it was supposed a person could be a Christian without the Holy Spirit, is a mystery. The greatest event for the Christian is what happens at the *beginning*. Certainly it is followed by progress but there will be nothing more radical and decisive than the change initiated by rebirth. 'If any man have not the Spirit of Christ, he is none of his' (Rom. 8:9); 'No one born of God makes a practice of sinning' (1 John 3:9).

When Lloyd-Jones addressed this fully in his sermons which were published as *Studies on the Sermon on the Mount* the repercussions were akin to sensational.[17] It led numbers to re-examine their whole theology.

In the course of time, Lloyd-Jones's understanding of evangelism brought on a seismic shift in the contemporary scene. Some evangelicals objected strongly and spread the opinion that the preacher at Westminster Chapel was not an evangelist at all, 'only a teacher'. They could not bring themselves to believe that anyone could be called an evangelist who did not call people to make public decisions in an evangelistic campaign. Others thought he must be a hyper-Calvinist, though they did not understand the term. A hyper-Calvinist believes that the preacher is not to call all to faith in Christ, or to present the invitations of the gospel to all, because Christ is only the Saviour of the elect. Such thinking certainly militates against evangelistic preaching and, by his practice and preaching, Lloyd-Jones opposed it. All men are to be called to repentance and faith; and the free offer of the gospel is an expression of the love of God for all, and all are responsible for their response, or lack of response. It is not the absence of love in God which shuts unbelievers out of the kingdom of God.[18]

All that are chosen will come to Christ, 'All that the Father giveth me shall come to me'; but it is with the second part of that verse that the sinner's consciousness of God's grace begins, 'him that cometh to me I will in no wise cast out' (John 6:37). The convert learns of his sin and his responsibility before he learns of his election. Romans chapters 1 to 3 come before Romans 9.

> It is not as persons convinced of our election nor as persons convinced that we are the special objects of God's love that we commit ourselves to him but as lost sinners. We entrust ourselves to him not because we believe we have been saved but as lost sinners in order that we may be saved.[19]

PUBLIC WORSHIP

Lloyd-Jones's theology brought him into inevitable disagreement over the direction in which evangelicalism was moving with regard to the public worship of God. A Christian newspaper, commenting on the worship at Westminster Chapel, was not intending to be commendatory when it said it had a form which would have been easily recognized by worshippers of 300 years earlier. There was prayer, praise, reading of Scripture, sacraments, preaching, and nothing more: no religious vestments, no pictures, no choir, no music director, and no orchestra. Now if someone had said a modern congregation should not imitate the vocabulary of the seventeenth century, Lloyd-Jones would have agreed. But that was not the issue. The issue, in his words, is that public worship is under God; it is not for us to decide what its content should contain. The form had stayed largely the same through time, not because of mere tradition, but because Christians sought to keep close to Scripture and to a biblical principle. In the words of John Owen, believers 'will receive nothing, practise nothing, own nothing in his worship, but what is of his appointment'.[20]

For Lloyd-Jones this also comes down to theology. 'As we think of God, so we will worship.'[21] Where there are high views of God, there will be high views of public worship. No one who understands the answer of the *Shorter Catechism* to the question, 'What is God?' is going to treat worship as something to be adjusted to his or her preference: 'God is a Spirit, infinite, eternal, unchangeable, in his being, wisdom, power, holiness, justice, goodness, and truth.' At the Reformation, from the recovery of the knowledge of God, came praise and reverence and a new understanding of what worship meant. So Calvin wrote, 'The worship of God is to be preferred to the safety of man and angels.' Again, 'Men allow themselves to devise all modes of worship, and change and rechange them at pleasure. Nor is this the fault of our age. Even from the beginning of the world, the world sported licentiously with God.'[22]

Take away sense and awareness of the glory and majesty of God, and a form of worship alien to Scripture will come in. It will no longer be fashionable to sing,

> Great God! how infinite art thou!
> What worthless worms are we,
> Let the whole race of creatures bow,
> And pay their praise to thee.

Lloyd-Jones believed that this change was directly connected with the way gospel preaching had become man-centred:

We conceive salvation not as something that primarily brings us to God, but as something that gives us something. And what is the result? A lack of sense of God in our services, a lack of reverence, a lack of awe, a lack of holiness, a lightness, a glibness, such as you will never find in the Scriptures.

Do you not see that if we started with the greatness of God, all our thinking would at once be revolutionised? ... It is because we have not taken the shoes from off our feet and realized that the God who made the world could blow upon us and make us vanish in a second that we speak as we do.[23]

DOCTRINE AND REVIVAL

This is another area where changed belief affects subject. A revival is a time which sees the ra ing of conversions and a marked advance in

Yet although numbers of converts enter into the difference with more normal times, the nature of conversion remains the same, whether in one or in many. An understanding of conversion therefore enters not only into an understanding of evangelism but of the meaning of revival. If individuals are thought to be converted because of their own decisions, it follows that multiple decisions will be thought of as a revival. This was the logic which led, in the United States, to evangelistic campaigns being called 'revival meetings' even before they had taken place. On this same understanding, revivals, it has been believed, are to be obtained by greater obedience on the part of Christians.

But the Calvinistic understanding of conversion leads to a quite different conclusion. An individual conversion takes place by the sovereign act of God—'No man can come to me, except the Father ... draw him' (John 6:44)—and, equally, revivals are special seasons which God has in his own power. In theological terms it is to be explained as a larger giving of the Holy Spirit. The Spirit lives in every believer, and there is his continuous work in the church as Christ as promised (John 14:16). But in the words of the Westminster divines, the work of the Spirit is 'not in all persons, nor at all times, in the same measure' (*Larger Catechism*, Q.182). Thus in the New Testament we read of times when 'great fear came upon all the church' (Acts 5:11); of churches being multiplied 'walking in the fear of the Lord, and in the comfort of the Holy Ghost' (Acts 9:31); of society being so affected in places such as Ephesus that books worth 'fifty thousand pieces of silver' were burned as people began clean lives (Acts 19:19). Scripture accounts for this in terms of times when the Holy Spirit was working in an extraordinary measure. They were not times planned or produced by men. Rather, as John Knox spoke of days during the Reformation, 'God gave his Holy Spirit to simple men in great abundance.'

History gives evidence that 'revivals' identified with evangelistic campaigns are not the same as what used to be called 'outpourings of the Spirit' or 'special seasons of mercy'. What is missing in the former is the widespread moral change in communities, changing the very course of history, as in New Testament times. The work of the Spirit is not uniform in all periods, and Lloyd-Jones believed there is only one explanation for times of extraordinary blessing, namely, the sovereignty of God in his administration of grace. For his own glory, God keeps times and seasons 'in his own power' (Acts 1:7). He intends to keep the church dependent on Christ, her head, from whom the 'supply' of the Spirit is given.

A mistake here produces wrong priorities. Lloyd-Jones feared that the evangelical churches were looking in the wrong direction for the larger influence which they coveted. They were too concerned with their own activities. He was shocked in 1959, when, on seeking to remind Christians of the great revival in America and parts of Britain a hundred years earlier, many seemed to think it had little relevance for the present day. There was too much interest in what *they* were doing. 'Do you think revival is near?' he was asked on one occasion. 'No, I do not', he replied, 'we are too healthy.' When dependence is on God, the priority is for prayer and the word of God (Acts 6:4). This was first with the apostles because they knew that the great thing was not what *they* might do, but what *God* would do. Wrong thinking on revival comes from wrong theology:

> Calvinism of necessity leads to an emphasis upon what God does to us: not what man does, but what God does to us; not our hold of him, but 'his strong grasp of us'. ... True Calvinism is bound to emphasize the element of revival, the 'givenness' of the activity of God, the visitations of God. It is only since the decline of Calvinism that revivals have become less and less frequent. The more powerful Calvinism is, the more likely you are to have a spiritual revival and re-awakening. It follows

of necessity from the doctrine. You cannot work up a revival. You know you are entirely dependent upon God. ... Nothing so promotes prayer as Calvinism. Calvinists who do not pray, I say, are not Calvinists. These things follow the one the other as night follows day. The true Calvinist is concerned about revival. Why? Because he is concerned about the glory of God. This is the first thing with him. Not so much that the world is as it is, but that the world is behaving like this, and that God is there. It is God's world, and they are under God. The glory of God! They are zealous for his name.[24]

On one occasion in a discussion of ministers which Lloyd-Jones was chairing, the question was raised why revivals are so periodic, and only found in certain places. One man rose to give what he believed was the solution. The explanation, he thought, was connected with race, 'Revivals had been found among the Celtic people of Wales and of North-West Scotland.' Lloyd-Jones was unimpressed and told the man that he was only right as far as the letter 'C'. He believed that in the English-speaking world, revivals have been most commonly found where the belief was Calvinistic.

Some have imagined he spoke of revival as the one panacea for the church's problems, and thus led people to hope for the future rather than to work in the present. That was not his position at all. He believed in the aid of the Holy Spirit as a present gift to be sought through prayer, and that such aid is given in the measure that is needed for the hour (Luke 11:13). And dependence on the Holy Spirit will rescue us from thinking that the church can only be successful if she takes care to adapt herself to the contemporary culture. 'How easy it is', he commented,

> to think in terms of human wisdom and strategy. The tragedy is that we do not believe in the power of the Holy Ghost as the apostle Paul did. Paul did not stop to ask, 'Will the Romans like this doctrine? I wonder whether, when they see that this is my message, they will stay away!' Paul knew that it all depended on the power of the Holy Ghost.[25]

THE IMPRINT OF FAITH ON LIFE

It was an insistent note in Lloyd-Jones's preaching that the test of how far truth has been received is its effect upon the life. Paul speaks of the correspondence between the form of teaching into which God puts the Christian and the stamp and the image of the doctrine on the life (Rom. 6:17). Humility is the sure consequence of believing that salvation comes from the grace of God alone: 'For who makes you different from anyone else? What do you have that you did not receive?' (1 Cor. 4:7). 'God has chosen the foolish things of the world … the weak things … things which are not … that no flesh should glory in his presence' (1 Cor. 1:27-29). 'Not of works, lest any man should boast' (Eph. 2:9). Near the end of his life, Lloyd-Jones read reviews of the biographies of two eminent Cambridge men, G. M. Trevelyan, historian and Master of Trinity College, and J. D. Bernal, a leading physicist. When a friend expressed a measure of surprise that these reviews had been arresting him, he replied with much feeling,

> They have turned out to be a great blessing to me. Here in Trevelyan is human nature at its best and it came to me with such force: Why did God ever choose to look upon me? Why *me* in contrast with these men and the despair in which they died?[26]

There were opponents of Lloyd-Jones who accused him of being the opposite of humble. They interpreted the authority with which he spoke as pride; he was, one critic asserted, 'a pope'. Professor F. F. Bruce once heard Dean Matthews of St Paul's describe an address the preacher had given as 'extra-ordinarily bad'. What Matthews did not understand, said Bruce, was that Lloyd-Jones's assurance 'was based on his confidence in the God whose message he was commissioned to proclaim'. And Bruce added: 'He was a thoroughly humble man. Those who charged him with arrogance were wildly mistaken.'[27]

John Murray once commented, 'Much evangelical preach-ing suffers from the absence in the preacher himself of the note of contrition and humility.'[28] This comes from a lack of experience of God. In the words of Lloyd-Jones, 'The greatest trouble is our lack of spirituality and of a true knowledge of God.' To have such knowledge 'is to have a deeper view of sin … sight of your own ugliness and vileness.'[29]

SIX RULES FOR PREACHERS

Of one thing Lloyd-Jones was sure, for better days there had to be a change in preaching. On this subject he said much. His earliest published critique of contemporary evangelical preaching was the Inter-Varsity booklet, *The Presentation of the Gospel*, and his fullest is his, *Romans, Exposition of Chapter 1*. His longest treatment on preaching is in his *Preaching and Preachers*.[30] In addition there is an address on 'Preaching' in *Knowing the Times*, and an item not to be missed, 'Raising the Standard of our Preaching', in my *Lloyd-Jones: Messenger of Grace*.[31] The following is the briefest summary:

1. Be clear about the purpose of preaching. It not merely to communicate information, nor even to pass on knowledge of the word of God. A sermon will do both these things, but they are not enough. The preacher is speaking not only about God, but for God, as in his presence, 'as of God, in the sight of God speak we in Christ' (2 Cor. 2:17). If the business of pulpit prayer is to lead men and women into the presence of God, no less is it the business of preaching.

In 1968 Lloyd-Jones, in convalescence after surgery, was not preaching for about four months and heard many sermons. His comments on that experience were given to the Westminster Fraternal of ministers, and at their heart were these words:

> It is a great thing to be a listener. You want something for your soul, you want help. I don't want a great sermon. I want to feel the presence of God—that I am worshipping him, and considering something great and glorious. If I do get that I do not care how poor the sermon is.[32]

He would have agreed entirely with an older writer who said, 'We need men of God who bring the atmosphere of heaven with them into the pulpit and speak from the borders of another world.'

2. Be sure the whole act of worship is in unity with the message to be delivered. The idea that, provided the pastor of the congregation preaches, the reminder of the service can be arranged and led by others was entirely foreign to him. Every part of the worship of God is of equal importance, every item sung, and its tune, came under his care. If the sermon needs to begin with an interesting story to gain attention, there has been something seriously wrong with what has gone before.

3. The preacher must know himself. There are different gifts, different abilities, and different levels of maturity. The first need is to be natural, not to take someone else as a model. The ministry of Lloyd-Jones gave rise to a whole generation of men who thought that the only way to preach was to proceed, week by week, through a book of Scripture. They missed the fact that he had been preaching for a quarter of a century before he began to adopt that procedure and, even then, it was a gradual development. What he could not do in the 1920s or '30s he had grown into by the 1950s. The name 'expository preaching' does not rightly belong to only one form of preaching. Preaching must be according to the state and needs of the people. They also must be known. He warned, 'I wasn't always a long preacher; we must bring the people up to it.'[33]

4. The effectiveness of the message is closely related to the form in which it has been planned. For clarity it needs a main thrust, supported by clear divisions. An emotional, sentimental, devotional talk may make a pleasant impression but it is not preaching. An address on disconnected subjects is not a sermon. Nor is an exposition, so-called, which meanders through a number of texts without a unifying, compelling burden:

> A running commentary is not a sermon. The whole notion of a message—'the burden of the Lord'—needs to be

recaptured. There ought to be an impact; whereas just to give an 'exposition', in which no message comes through, is to make preaching intellectual only.[34]

Although the way a sermon is put together is not the most important thing, if it is not clear, logical, and rational, it will rarely be compelling.[35] Because Lloyd-Jones spoke little on the practical side of what is involved in the preparation of a sermon, it has sometimes been thought that he gave minimum attention to it. That was far from true. Once he knew his text he might give much time to arriving at a convincing plan of arrangement, and he is on record as saying that his best sermons were commonly those on which he had worked the hardest. The preacher is responsible to speak in the simplest, clearest manner possible and those who neglect this will surely limit their usefulness.

5. *Gospel preaching is the pre-eminent calling of every preacher and pastor.* All preaching does not fall under that heading. There is teaching which is primarily for the people of God, and evangelical truth is, of course, bound up with it. But there are texts and passages of Scripture especially relevant to those who are not Christians, and gospel preaching is preaching deliberately directed to the unconverted. As all Scripture is inspired of God, it is sometimes argued that it is all equally applicable to every hearer, and there is no need for sermons specifically for the non-Christian. Lloyd-Jones regarded that opinion as a serious mistake. He was once asked by a would-be critic, 'When did you last have an evangelistic campaign?' He was not joking when he replied, 'I have one every Sunday night.'[36]

Sermons born out of a concern for unbelievers, and to lead them to Christ, formed *half*, if not more, of his entire ministry.[37] When he first preached at Westminster Chapel as a visitor in 1935, both his sermons were evangelistic.[38] Later this would be the pattern every Sunday night, and it was commonly the same as he preached around Britain, mid-week, through forty years. When he was asked to speak at Melton Mowbray on the eve of a General Election, he took for his text Acts 24:25: 'And as he reasoned of righteousness, temperance, and judgment to come, Felix trembled'. At a service convened during annual meetings of the British Medical Association at Cardiff, he introduced his subject by saying it was a particular danger for doctors that they could treat dying patients and forget that they too would one day be in the same condition. He therefore chose as his subject the teaching of Christ on a 'successful man' who seemed to have provided for everything, 'But God said unto him, Thou fool, this night thy soul shall be required of thee: then whose shall those things be, which thou hast provided?'(Luke 12:20). Some of his medical hearers had tears in their eyes when he closed with the words, 'I beseech you not to allow the profession to make you forget yourself, that you are a man and not merely a doctor.'[39]

He not only believed that such preaching is a chief part of the ministry, it is a burden which drains the preacher more than any theme. For the first ten years of his ministry it was to the evangelistic sermon that he gave most attention in preparation and it remained his primary concern.

6. It is the work of the Holy Spirit which makes preaching powerful. It was in 'the power of the Spirit' that Christ began his ministry (Luke 4:14), and it was so with the disciples, not simply at Pentecost (Acts 2:4), but the pattern was repeated many times, 'They were filled with the Holy Ghost and spoke the word of God with boldness' (Acts 4:31). Church history witnesses that such preaching was not restricted to the apostolic age, but also that there are eras when such preaching almost disappears and the power is gone. It was to this that Lloyd-Jones was referring in his statement, 'The greatest need in the church today is to restore authority to the pulpit.'[40] He knew that there is a world of difference between listening to sermons and hearing God speak through the preacher. Effective preaching is hearing Jesus himself (Eph. 4:21). This is the amazing conjunction in true preaching, 'I labour', says Paul, 'striving according to his working, which worketh in me mightily.'[41]

Gospel preaching cannot be sustained without this element. The wonder of the person and work of Christ is dimmed. Concern and compassion for the souls of men and women are lost. Preaching sinks into a routine. It is heard with no thrill or expectancy and the listeners go home as they came, instead of not being the same again.

When Lloyd-Jones made such observations in his last address on preaching to theological students at Westminster Seminary, it was in order to plead with them, individually, to recognise that the giving of the Holy Spirit is the ongoing work of Christ.

> Nothing but a return of this power of the Spirit in our preaching is going to avail us anything. Seek him! Seek him! What can we do without him? Seek him! Seek him always. But go beyond seeking him; expect him.[42]

The one who raises up preachers has an inexhaustible supply of the Spirit to give, and his promise stands for all generations: 'If anyone thirsts, let him come to me and drink ... and out of his heart will flow rivers of living water' (John 7:37, 38).

NOTE: WAS LLOYD-JONES AN AMYRALDIAN?

A review of J. E. Hazlett Lynch, *Lamb of God, Saviour of the World: the Soteriology of David Martyn Lloyd-Jones* (Bloomington, IN: Westbow, 2015; ISBN: 978 1 49088 190 4).

Our interest in this book lies in the author's wish to present the 'soteriology'—i.e., the doctrine of salvation—of Dr Lloyd-

Jones. The word is not actually appropriate, for the theme of the book is not the *nature* of the atonement but its *extent*. It concentrates on the question, For whom did Christ die? Since the Reformation there have been two predominant and different understandings of that question among evangelical Christians: (1) that Christ's death met the guilt of all mankind, and (2) that he suffered for those whom the Father had given him and whom he will certainly bring to glory. There is, however, a third understanding, which appeared early in the seventeenth century, traceable to several evangelicals of that period, but commonly called Amyraldianism (after Moise Amyraut or Amyraldus).[43] It faded after Richard Baxter, but had continuance among evangelicals in the Church of England, and saw a resurgence in Wales in the teaching of Edward Williams (1750–1815).

Christians of Amyraldian persuasion recognize that scriptural teaching on the gospel contains both universal and particular elements but these they arrange in a way which differs from both Arminian and Calvinistic understandings. There is agreement with the Arminian in saying that all mankind has been potentially reconciled to God through the death of Christ, and with the Calvinist in holding that the faith which brings personal experience of salvation is not within the capability of fallen man but is the consequence of divine election. So there is a 'hypothetical redemption' which is universal, from which all may benefit on the exercise of faith, but which, on account of sin, none do benefit except an elect number. This view thus seeks to bring together the biblical strengths of what is in both Arminian and Calvinistic teaching. There is a *potential* salvation for all (which is said to warrant the universal preaching of the gospel) and a *definite* salvation for the elect.

Dr Lynch puts before us the main features of this doctrinal construction: 'Redemption can be achieved for all yet the sinner remains unpardoned' (p. 169); 'The moment he [the sinner] puts his trust in the Saviour, his sin and guilt are cancelled. But if he refuses, his sin and guilt have been atoned for but because he had not applied the remedy to his own case, his guilt remains on him'(p. 168); 'The success of the gospel is the fact that the message will be effective in the elect' (p. 116); 'Christ's death purchased and made available to the whole world a great salvation, while simultaneously guaranteeing the eternal salvation of God's elect people' (p. 121).

This thinking is supported by the argument that if there is no universal redemption, no general atonement, the imperative of the evangel is lost. The gospel cannot be good news for all 'if Christ did not die for all'. To preach a universal offer, while not believing there is a universal atonement, is said to be 'contradictory if not hypocritical' (pp. 157, 170). A lack of evangelistic passion in the current reformed scene is traced to this source.

What Dr Lynch presents in such words is not original and the subject can be followed up elsewhere. We are concerned here with what is original in his book, namely, his wish to prove that 'the Doctor's soteriology was clearly Amyraldian' (p. vii). We are told that those who teach a limited atonement 'invalidate the Amyraldian position held by DML-J' (p. 167). Again, 'This study has shown beyond reasonable doubt that Rev. Dr David Martyn Lloyd-Jones's soteriology is soundly Amyraldian' (p. 247).

On the contrary, except for apparent belief in a universal atonement in his early ministry, we believe that Dr Lloyd-Jones's teaching is unmistakably contrary to the main tenets of Amyraldian belief.[44]

THE LLOYD-JONES POSITION

In the decree of God, Amyraldianism puts election after the atonement. It teaches that an atonement is made equally for all but, because sin hinders its acceptance, divine election has to come in to make it effective for some. Lynch rejects an eternal determination of the saved by God, arguing that if faith is predetermined by a 'decision taken by God in eternity, and, therefore, unchangeable', then those who are non-elect cannot be responsible for their destiny 'their eternal lostness is not their fault, but God's' (p. 159). Election must come in after redemption, for it would be unjust if God did not give the same possibility to all.[45]

This view of Scripture is denied by ML-J in innumerable places. In preaching on the Eternal Decrees of God, he said, '*God had an unchangeable plan with reference to his creatures.* The Bible is constantly using a phrase like this—"before the foundation of the world" (see Eph. 1:4) … God has a definite plan and purpose about creation, about men and women, about salvation, about the whole of life in this world.'[46] This planned salvation is not for all, but for particular individuals: 'Does he say, "As thou hast given him power over all flesh, that he should give eternal life to all flesh"? No—"that he should give eternal life to *as many as thou hast given him*" [John 17:2] … God, from before the foundation of the world, had chosen these people. He gives a particular people to his Son, and he says, I give them to you for you to save them for me.'[47]

In another sermon he shows, from a whole series of passages, that it is an error to think that Christ died to make us God's people: 'He did not; we were the people of God first, and it was God who gave us to him. If that comes as a surprise to us, it is because we read our Bibles with prejudiced eyes instead of looking at what it really says. "Thine they were, and thou gavest them me"' (John 17:6).[48]

In preaching on Romans 5, on the whole doctrine of Christ's headship over his people, he sees the same truth as vital to the exegesis: 'God made a covenant with his own Son. Having appointed him as the Head and Representative of his people, he makes a covenant with him, and the covenant is that if he bears their sins he will deliver them and they shall be his people.'[49] Both Adam and Christ are representative heads:

'those who are connected with Adam fell with Adam, and those who are connected with Christ are saved with Christ'. He explains:

> This word 'all', as it is often used in Scripture, is limited by conditions which Scripture itself makes clear; this is very true of the words we are looking at here—the 'all' and the 'many'. The limit here is perfectly clear in [Romans 5] verse 17: 'For if by one man's offence death reigned by one'—and Paul has just been saying that it reigned over all, and he has kept on repeating his statement—'much more they which receive abundance of grace and of the gift of righteousness shall reign in life by one, Jesus Christ.' He does not say that 'all' have received abundance of grace and the gift of righteousness. What he says is that they, and they alone who receive that grace, are the people who are going to 'reign in life by one, Jesus Christ'. There we notice, a limit is introduced. All died in Adam, but not all are going to reign in life ... This is not a limit introduced by me; it is a limit that the apostle himself has deliberately introduced.[50]

In other volumes the same truth is stated more directly as it arises in the text. Thus on the words of Ephesians 5:25, 'Christ also loved the church, and gave himself for it', he quotes the words of Christ in John 17:2, and comments, 'here we are reminded that Christ died for the church. We must never lose sight of this; he died for nobody else ... his purpose in dying was to redeem the church'.[51]

Further, ML-J was in opposition to Amyraldianism on the very meaning of the atonement. Dr Lynch virtually by-passes treating the nature of the atonement. But its nature is vitally related to its extent as some of the quotations given above have already indicated. Does the New Testament represent atonement, reconciliation, propitiation, and redemption as only *potentially* able to remove the guilt of sin? Did Christ obtain only a possible forgiveness, or was he dying as the surety and substitute for all he came to save? Did Calvary *secure* the whole salvation of those for whom he suffered, or was it only a possibility? Lloyd-Jones's gospel preaching depended on the definite, accomplished redemption of all for whom Christ died. The gospel he preached, and freely offered, was not about a potential salvation. Along with such evangelists as George Whitefield and C. H. Spurgeon, he preached that the sins of the very worst who trust in Christ have been covered; the ransom has been paid (Matt. 20:28); the curse of the law has been borne by the Son of God (Gal. 3:13). Faith is instrumental in salvation but it is not *because* of faith that we are saved. Amyraldianism, in its anxiety to make the atonement universal, does not, and cannot, present the work of Christ in this way. For if it did, it would have to explain how so many are finally lost whose debt Christ supposedly paid, and whose condemnation he endured. Under Amyraldianism the real meaning of substitution is evaporated.[52] As Warfield has written, 'The nature of the atonement is altered by them, and Christianity is wounded at its very heart ... the real hinge of their system turns on their altered doctrine of the atonement.'[53] This is exactly what ML-J believed was the most serious error of Amyraldianism, as I shall document further below. We have to choose, in Warfield's words, 'between an atonement of high value, or an atonement of wide extension'. Or better, as Dr Nicole states it:

> The choice here is not between limited and unlimited atonement, but between an effective atonement limited in breadth to the redeemed, and a universal atonement limited in depth to the point of ineffectuality.[54]

CONTRARY EVIDENCE PROPOSED

It is not disrespectful to Dr Lynch to say that his treatment of the subject is hindered by his lack of experience under the ministry of Lloyd-Jones. This appears in the two main lines of 'proof' which he offers for his claim that the gospel message at Westminster Chapel was according to Amyraldian thinking.

One line is a lengthy string of quotations taken from Lloyd-Jones's published books. But the quotations given are not relevant to the issue. For instance, Lynch says that ML-J 'warned sinners not to turn their backs on the salvation Christ purchased for them' (p. 142). We are then given six quotations to support the accuracy of Lynch's statement. But none of them do so. The only one that is pertinent reads: 'If you believe this message that you are a vile, damned sinner, that Christ the Son of God has borne your sin and your punishment and has died for you and risen again, if you believe that, then God pronounces you righteous'. Now those who attended the Lloyd-Jones ministry understood that there was a variation in his sermons, and their application, depending on the particular people whom he was seeking to help. His words often are best understood according to the time and place where they were spoken. The passages I have quoted from him above, from several volumes, come either from Sunday morning sermons (addressed chiefly to believers), or from Friday night addresses to the same constituency. To *that* congregation he might readily say, 'Christ died for those the Father gave him to redeem'; while to a Sunday evening congregation, when he was primarily concerned to speak to the non-Christian and the enquirer, he would say, 'Christ died for all who repent and trust in him.' Both statements are accurate, but both are not equally suitable for every occasion. The quotation given by Lynch belongs clearly to a Sunday night sermon. Picture a large and hushed congregation when the drop of a pin could be heard. Some are sitting on the edge of their seats, some are rejoicing, some are offended, but others are under real conviction and concern—each feeling he is the 'vile and damned sinner' the preacher is addressing. This is no hypothetical description. There were times when the preacher, conscious of the presence of God as he spoke, knew that there were such hearers before him. It was to them that he would speak such words as those quoted. The idea that they express belief in a universal atonement is an entire misunderstanding. I am not saying that he only addressed the gospel to such convicted hearers. He did not. But he preached *for conviction of sin* and knew when there was special need to speak to those aware that they were lost. His whole approach to evangelistic preaching had no resemblance to the message which says, 'Won't you accept what Christ purchased for you?'

Dr Lynch also seems to misunderstand Lloyd-Jones's readiness to emphasize the gospel for 'the world', as though he must be speaking of a universal redemption. Texts, such as 2 Corinthians 5:19 and 1 John 2:2, are quoted by the author in that connection. But those very texts, in ML-J's mind, contradicted any hypothetical redemption. The 'reconciliation' of which Paul spoke was brought about by *substitution*—'he hath made him to be sin for us' (2 Cor. 5:21). And the blessing for 'the whole world', of which the apostle John speaks, is nothing less than 'propitiation'—the momentous change from guilt to favour which Christ obtained for sinners when he died in their place. To say that the 'world' in such texts is not speaking of the sins of every individual of mankind is not 'forcing Scripture': the very meaning of the gospel depends on it.

I must touch briefly on another line of alleged evidence that Lynch seeks to use. These are statements attributed to Lloyd-Jones which have been passed on to him by others. One of these relates to a reference to limited atonement in a conversation when Lloyd-Jones is reported to have said, 'I never preached it, you know ... only once on Romans 5:15 and I was in great difficulty when I did so' (p. 113). The omitted words have not been given. Taken in the light of his whole thought and ministry, the statement only makes sense if we understand that Lloyd-Jones did *not* 'preach on limited atonement', nor did he ever preach on 'the Five Points of Calvinism'. That is to say, he never gave sermons with these *labels*. He did not want people simply to embrace controversial terms. He wanted convictions grounded in a clear understanding

SEVEN LEADERS: PREACHERS AND PASTORS

of Scripture itself. Under his ministry Christians learned the meaning of definite redemption without ever hearing him use the words 'limited atonement'. He often made this point in advising ministers. He was against any hurrying of people into an acceptance of 'Calvinism'.[55] That could well have been the context from which this quotation comes. Equally his words 'in great difficulty' do not have the meaning that Dr Lynch seems to give them. In his sermon on 'the Eternal Decrees of God', ML-J uses the very same language: 'I want to admit very frankly that I am again calling your attention to an extremely difficult subject. I do not apologize for that because, as I shall show you, this is not a question of choice. The business of someone expounding the Bible is to expound the whole Bible.' His 'difficulty' had nothing to do with any uncertainty about the teaching; it lay rather in the profoundly awesome and overwhelming nature of the subject. Nothing demands greater care, reverence, and humility in the preacher. Anyone who finds it 'easy' to preach on divine sovereignty should not be in a pulpit. Dr Lloyd-Jones often confessed that there were truths involved beyond his understanding. Speaking on the sovereign choice of God in salvation, from Romans 9:18, he said: 'We are not told what determined this in God, we are obviously not meant to know; it is too big for us.'[56]

Another alleged evidence comes from someone who over-heard a conversation during which the *Westminster Confession of Faith* was mentioned. The occasion was ML-J's visit to 'a newly founded reformed church at Gateshead' when he was asked if he advised that the *Westminster Confession of Faith* be adopted as the doctrinal basis. 'No, no', he is quoted as replying, 'that's much too Calvinistic.' By which, we are told, he meant, 'it was too theologically extreme in its orientation' (p. 115n). No such interpretation is required. In a newly formed independent church, and at a time when Calvinistic belief was little understood, to require the adherence of the membership to such a full and detailed confession was not to be recommended. Even in traditional, orthodox Presbyterian churches, members are not required to accept the *Westminster Confession*. The terms for church membership should be no more than the terms of repentance and faith required in the New Testament. A doctrinal standard which ministers may be asked to uphold is a different matter. The ministry of the Welsh Calvinistic Methodist Connexion—the denomination to which ML-J belonged—was built on a doctrinal standard the same in essence as in the *Westminster Confession*.

QUESTIONS OF HISTORY

Martyn Lloyd-Jones and J. I. Packer led the influential annual Puritan Conference at Westminster Chapel from 1950 to 1969. In the formative early years, from 1952 to 1960, the conference secretary was David Fountain, who has made this observation:

> Those in attendance were generally, but not always, sympathetic to the Puritans, but one incident stands out as indicating how few fully grasped the doctrines of grace. It was during Dr Packer's paper on Richard Baxter in 1952 that dwelt at some length on the fact that Baxter did not hold to the doctrine of Particular Redemption, but followed the view of a French Seminary at Saumur, believing that it 'hindered evangelism' and dishonoured God. Baxter differed from the vast majority of Puritans in this, as in other things. This provoked some discussion in which the Chairman [ML-J] pointed out that if you really believe in Universal Atonement you are confronted with the question, 'Will sin be punished for people whose sin has been atoned for? This cannot be.' I remember that Dr Lloyd-Jones was the only one at the Conference in 1952 prepared to defend the doctrine of Particular Redemption (the proper out-working of substitutionary atonement). ... Dr Lloyd-Jones, many years later, reminded me of this occasion when he stood alone on the subject of Particular Redemption.[57]

The next year at the Tyndale Summer School at Cambridge in 1953, the subject was 'The Plan of Salvation', and Professor

John Murray gave an address on definite (as opposed to universal) redemption. Lloyd-Jones would later say that he was the only person in the room who rose to support what Murray had taught, and his speaking drew the protest of an Anglican clergyman, 'I am not going to be ruled by your logic.'[58]

Addresses such as the one by John Murray had given had probably never been heard before at an Inter-Varsity conference.[59] Jim Packer was present on that occasion but remained silent on the point in dispute. That he was thinking hard on the subject is certain, for in 1953 he was engaged in finalising his thesis on 'The Redemption & Restoration of Man in the Thought of Richard Baxter', which he would present the following year for the degree of D.Phil. at Oxford. In this now published thesis, the thinking of Baxter on universal redemption is carefully and fully stated, as he had given it more briefly at the Puritan Conference of 1952. But there was one great difference. He was no longer speaking as an advocate for that teaching. He would continue to be an admirer of many features of Baxter's life and ministry, but he had reached the conclusion that the pastor of Kidderminster was no sure guide on the theology of redemption. The crisis point had been Baxter's understanding of the nature of the atonement.

Lloyd-Jones has recorded how much this change in the thinking of his friend meant to him: 'I will never forget one morning when the Puritan Conference was due to start. Packer came rushing up to me and said, "I am now a complete Calvinist, Doctor!" He had finished with Baxter and turned to Owen. At first I alone was contending for limited atonement.'[60]

Another piece of evidence from history has to do with Dr Lloyd-Jones's part in the origins of the Banner of Truth Trust. When the magazine of that name began in 1955 he was one of its first supporters. The Trust itself came into being at Westminster Chapel in 1957, its two founders being members of that congregation and one of them his assistant. In 1957 the proposed doctrinal schedule for the Trust was first submitted to him and had his approval. It included:

> The Covenant of Redemption in which Christ undertook from eternity to perfectly deliver all those whom the Father gave him (the elect) from the pollution, guilt and power of sin by sustaining the office of a prophet, priest, and king.

> The substitutionary death of Jesus Christ as a propitiatory sacrifice which infallibly secures all the benefits of salvation for those whom he represented in his death and resurrection.

Dr Lynch is standing the truth on its head in the way he explains a supportive reference to particular redemption in a Lloyd-Jones sermon about the time the Trust first published John Owen's *The Death of Death in the Death of Christ* in 1959. The book contained a compelling and 'awakening' Introductory Essay by Dr Packer.[61] 'Dr Lloyd-Jones', Lynch writes, 'did not want to cause a theological or commercial stir at a time when the Trust was in its infancy. So it appears that he provided that particular limited atonement emphasis at that time, despite this emphasis being well out of sync with his view of the atonement as demonstrated in his published sermons' (p. 114). For anyone who was present at that time, and knew the relationship between the minister of Westminster Chapel and his two junior friends who founded the Trust, it would be impossible to take this suggestion seriously. And the idea that Dr Lloyd-Jones would temporarily tailor his beliefs for such a purpose is something he would have called a prostitution of preaching.

It is regrettable that Lynch should draw inferences which more information would show to be unfounded. He makes the same mistake when he hints that ML-J may have parted company with the Banner of Truth Trust in the mid-1960s for doctrinal reasons (p. 129). This is based on the fact that ML-J only attended the Leicester Ministers' Conference (organized by the Banner) twice. But it was *after* that date that Lloyd-

Jones made Banner his main UK publisher, as he wrote in one of his books given to me in 1973, 'To my very dear friend, Iain Murray, and now my publisher.' It was to the same publishers that he entrusted the preparation of an authorized biography. Much else could be said of his link with the Banner of Truth Trust, including the input of his advice on authors to be reprinted, among them George Smeaton, whose work *The Apostles' Doctrine of the Atonement* carries a short but comprehensive critique of Amyraldianism.[62]

With respect to the Banner of Truth Trust, Lynch makes an observation which needs comment:

> The Banner of Truth Trust publishes most of DML-J's major writings. It either regards Amyraldianism as being within the Reformed Faith and church (as evidenced by the number of Amyraldian authors whose works it has published). Or it suffers from theological schizophrenia and does not know it. It is a staunch 'five point' Calvinist publishing house. Therefore only those authors who subscribe to the human mnemonic TULIP have their books published by it (p. 128).

This is not true. A great deal of most helpful material has been written about, or by, Christians who have not taught the 'five points'. The Banner's range of books goes from Wesley to Amy Carmichael. In selecting authors we seek to remember Richard Baxter's words: 'It is a grand and pernicious error to think that the same men's judgments must be followed in every case. And it is of grand importance to know how to value and vary our guides, as the cases vary.'[63] To segregate Christian authors—evangelical and Bible-believing—and to put them in opposing camps with labels, too often contravenes the command, 'As much as lieth in you, live peaceably with all men' (Rom. 12:18). It is one thing for publishers to publish books containing statements over which Christians differ, but another to publish titles which have a mission to undermine the faith which they conscientiously confess.

Christians may fall into errors with the best of motives. It was a worthy motive of Amyraut, and others who have followed, to want to meet an objection to the gospel which they saw as an obstacle to its success. It concerned the need to uphold the justice of God. How, it was said, could that attribute be safeguarded unless God is seen to provide an atonement for all? Dr Lynch follows this view in saying, 'The limited atonement camp has cast a dark cloud over the goodness of God to all mankind' (p. 142). But does the alternative really remove the objection of injustice? To say, according to Amyraldian thinking, that election is planned to be operative after redemption, only amounts to saying that God has provided an atonement from which none can benefit except the elect. In this apologetic, the part of sovereignty has only been moved to another point. But, as Nicole observes, 'A universal redemption on condition of faith is not a blessing which issues in any concrete advantage to the non-elect.' The truth is that God only requires us to *believe* his sovereignty in salvation, not to silence objections to it. The response to which the truth calls is worship and humility (see Matt. 11:25-27). Scripture shows us the problem is not in divine justice, it is in man's sinful pride which only wants a salvation which he can explain, and to which he believes he is entitled. Most objections to Christianity arise from an absence of conviction of sin.

Dr Lynch is right to be critical of preachers lacking in evangelistic passion. We are all deficient there. More fervent, persuasive, appealing, preaching of Christ is indeed needed. As the dying Legh Richmond once told fellow preachers, 'We are none of us more than half awake.' But the case that Amyraldian belief leads to a better hold on Scripture, and to a better hold of Christ, is mistaken. Dr Packer's testimony, in this regard, is that of many. He came to see that the view 'which at first seems to magnify God's love by proclaiming its universality, actually discredits it. Orthodox Calvinism was consistent in teaching that God's love is powerful and effect-ive; that whom he loves he saves through the work of his Son and Spirit.[64] The Amyraldian view of the atonement *secures* nothing. It does not speak of a ransom paid which has pur-chased a sure deliverance. It cannot say with the *Confession of Faith of the Calvinistic Methodists* that for those redeemed by Christ 'all things—that is, grace and glory—are obtained. … Thus the redemption ensures their calling, justification, sanctification, perseverance, adoption, and glorification.'[65] The force of one of the greatest promises to believers is taken away: 'He that spared not his own Son, but delivered him up for us all, how shall he not with him also freely give us all things?' (Rom. 8:32). The business of the church is not to proclaim the extent of the atonement to the world. It is to preach the Christ who saves, who keeps, who brings his own to glory. Only on receiving this Saviour may we say, 'He loved me and gave himself for me.'

'Speaking for myself,' Dr Lloyd-Jones concludes, 'I know of nothing that gives me greater consolation than this particular doctrine. I do not hesitate to say that nothing gives me greater comfort than to know that behind me, little creature as I am passing through this world of time, there is this doctrine of the eternal decrees of God himself.'[66] 'The astounding thing is that this eternal, absolute Being is interested in me, even me, as an individual and as a person, and that I was in his mind when he conceived this amazing plan that includes the incarn-ation and the cross, and the resurrection and the ascension, and the reign of his Son at his side that is going on now. What a staggering, yes, but what a glorious thought!'[67]

W. J. Grier:
Against Frittering Life Away

'May our lives not be frittered away—in the days ahead—on a multitude of petty things! May we rather be "much in the main things". May we concentrate on the goal—on the glory of God and the bliss of heaven!'

W. J. Grier, Meditation 'On Toward the Goal'.

ULSTER was a largely Scots/Presbyterian plantation settled in the north of Ireland in the early seventeenth century. In the following centuries her churches supplied many eminent pastors and missionaries, often little known beyond Ireland or the mission fields to which they gave their lives. William James Grier might have remained among that number had it not been for the calling God gave him when the Reformed faith was at a low ebb in the early twentieth century.

To be known as 'William' at home, and later 'Jim' to his friends, the third son of John and Elizabeth Grier was born in County Donegal on 18 November 1902. Had the parents not made special sacrifices for his education he might have remained a farmer as did the first son, George, or been an emigrant to North America as John, the middle brother. Instead, at the age of thirteen, Jim left the small family farm at Little Ards, near Ramelton, to attend Foyle College, Londonderry, for four years of further schooling. He stayed with an aunt in that city during term time until, at seventeen, he proceeded to Queen's University, Belfast (1920–1923). At the latter date, with the BA degree in classics behind him, he became a candidate for the ministry of the Presbyterian Church.

In Northern Ireland a young man's route to a Presbyterian pulpit followed a long established pattern. After an Arts degree there would be three years of theological training at the denomination's Assembly's College in Belfast or Magee College in Londonderry. For Jim Grier, however, this course did not fall out as expected, which needs to be explained. Christian teaching and orthodox belief had been familiar to him from childhood. He had belonged with his family to the Presbyterian Church at Ramelton, with occasional visits to a

Reformed Presbyterian congregation at Milford. This background seems to have given him some early discernment, for at Londonderry he had by-passed the local Presbyterian church for another where there was a Bible class with an earnest evangelical teacher. Of course, with the *Westminster Confession* as its creed, the Presbyterian denomination was reputedly evangelical but, in some quarters at least, the experience of rebirth was more assumed than preached.

Once in Belfast, Jim Grier was to find the nature of evangelical preaching to be a matter of dispute. A disturbance had arisen around the ministry of W. P. Nicholson (1876–1959). Born an Ulster Presbyterian, Nicholson's life was far from the usual. From the age of sixteen to twenty-one he was a seaman far from home in South America, after which he worked on the Cape to Cairo railway. A turning point came the night after his return to Ulster when he identified with Salvation Army people on a street in Bangor, his hometown. After some Bible training in Scotland, Nicholson joined with American evangelists and was ordained as an evangelist by the Carlisle Presbytery of the Presbyterian Church in the USA in April 1914.

In 1920, Nicholson returned to his native Ireland for a 'brief tour', burdened for a spiritual awakening. It was not unusual for God to choose unlikely means, and for many years to come Nicholson's unexpected preaching was to be remembered as a time when there was remarkable movement of the Holy Spirit. This was evident in the provincial towns where he preached in 1921—Portadown, Lurgan, and Newtownards—where hundreds professed saving faith in Christ. In other places, and especially in Belfast in 1922, the numbers grew to thousands. It is said that '12,000 people passed through his enquiry rooms in two years'. As the quotation suggests, Nicholson adopted some of the evangelistic methods which American 'missioners' had made popular but there is no need to base the evidence of a revival simply on the high numbers of converts and of inquirers reported, for it is evident that there were changes in public life which no methods can produce. At Newtownards, it was reported, 'Business people have had debts, long since written off as irrecoverable, paid in full. Money wrongfully used has been returned. At the last petty sessions only one man was brought for trial.' At Londonderry, Nicholson was said to have 'been a liberating force to vast numbers who have too much associated religion with outward dignity and decorum instead of peace and joy'. In East Belfast, 'the Belfast shipyard found it necessary to allocate a special store to accommodate stolen tools and materials that were being returned'. A 'State of Religion' report of the General Assembly of the Presbyterian Church recorded that over 100 congregations had seen a revival of spiritual life, with prayer meetings, communicant classes, and volunteers for Christian service multiplied across the Protestant denomination.

This tide of new life came to Belfast during Grier's second and third years at Queen's University. At this time he was attending Ravenhill Presbyterian Church, East Belfast, where the minister, John Ross, was a supporter of W. P. Nicholson's work. At a Nicholson mission in this church, so great was the crush of shipyard workers seeking to enter the building that a stone pillar upholding the gates was moved off its foundation. Charlie Ross, son of the Ravenhill minister, was a friend and fellow student with Grier, and in long walks together over the Castlereagh Hills he spoke to him of his need of a saving knowledge of Christ. When Grier first heard Nicholson is not recorded, but he certainly did so at Rosemary Street Presbyterian Church, Belfast, on October 22, 1922, a date he was known to refer to as the time of his conversion. When Jim shortly after met Charlie Ross on University Avenue, it was to tell him, 'I am the Lord's.' The two young men became founding members of a students' prayer meeting at Queen's. Grier would later recall how one's ankles might be kicked if a companion thought you slow to pray as they knelt on the floor!

Nicholson preached for repentance in a manner that had been uncommon for years. 'Nothing is so alarming', he believed, 'as the absence of alarm in the churches. Nothing so dreadfully terrific, to my mind, as that sinners have no terror.'[1] He spoke plainly of hell, and of Christ as the only Saviour, in whom, 'the moment a man believes in Christ, he is clothed in the spotless righteousness of the Redeemer in the sight of God!'

I have said above that in 1923 Grier became a candidate for the ministry in his denomination. That had not been his intention at the time of his conversion the previous year, but in his last year at Queen's the conviction had grown that he was being called to preach the gospel. 'I put it from me', he tells us, until a crisis point one Saturday afternoon, on a 'lovely summer's day', when he was visiting his home in Donegal. A local friend arrived to surprise him with the news that he was needed to speak at the Mission Hall in Milford the following night. To that point Jim had done no more than give his testimony, and lead a study group once at Queen's on Romans 8. The friend, however, 'just would not take "No" as an answer'. What made the request so critical for Jim was not so much the prospect of speaking, as whether he could address an audience in the name of Christ while inwardly battling a call on his own life. In much perplexity, he recalled,

> I took a book and went out away over the fields. The book was a book by Bishop Ryle with the title, *Knots Untied*.[2] And the knot was untied for me that afternoon. I remember saying to the Lord I didn't know my own mind, whether I was willing to go on for the Lord, or not willing. But one thing I did know, I was willing to be made willing for whatever his will was. I never had another moment's struggle. And I went the next evening to Milford, four miles away, and the best part of the sermon was the text. It was John 3:3. He was speaking to that very respectable man Nicodemus. The Lord said to him:

'Verily I say unto thee, Except a man be born again, he cannot see the kingdom of God.' I often thanked God that I had a battle for months over this matter, because I could always feel sure that I had been called [83].[3]

With his final year at Queen's ending that same summer of 1923, Grier's local presbytery in Donegal accepted him as a student for the ministry, and theological training was the next step. The normal way ahead was obvious, but Nicholson's preaching had raised serious questions for him. He had reason to doubt how far instruction given at the Assembly's College— the theological seminary of his denomination—could co-exist with evangelical zeal. It also troubled him that, *before* his conversion, a professor at this college had directed him towards a career in the Church. Surely, he wondered, it could not be common for the unconverted to be so encouraged. This, and kindred subjects, must have been discussed with Charlie Ross and his father at the manse of the Ravenhill Presbyterian Church. The path taken into the ministry of the denomination by Allen Ross, the elder brother of the family, was brought to Jim's attention. For theological training Allen had been allowed to take the year 1920–21 at Princeton Theological Seminary, New Jersey. This was light for Jim who 'had heard of Princeton's reputation for orthodoxy'. On request to his presbytery, he was allowed to plan for two years at Princeton, with one final year back in Belfast at the Assembly's College.

All was settled before the end of the summer in which he had picked up Ryle's book. Complications over travel arrangements were overcome, and, after a farewell to his family, he departed by train from Londonderry in memorable circumstances. It was near the end of the period in which fighting had broken out in a rising of republicans in 1916 against British rule in Ireland. A treaty in 1921 had recognized the Irish Free State in the south, leaving just six of Ulster's nine counties part of the United Kingdom according to the wish of the majority in the north. This concession to Ulster's continuance as part of

Britain was rejected by the Irish Republican Army (IRA) who demanded a republic for the whole of Ireland. Two hundred and sixty-four people were killed in the six counties in civil war in 1922 and it was the tail end of this fighting which Grier experienced as he was leaving Londonderry railway station, where gunfire caused him to lie on the floor of the train.

PRINCETON THEOLOGICAL SEMINARY

Jim Grier's two years at Princeton were to prove the most formative period of his life. He arrived in the quiet country town in New Jersey a week before classes were to begin. If he felt loneliness that is not what he recalled:

> That week I attended the midweek service in the Second Presbyterian Church. The speaker was Professor Oswald T. Allis and his text was, 'Give diligence to present thyself approved unto God, a workman that needeth not to be ashamed, handling aright the word of truth' (2 Tim. 2:15). I imagine I was the only theological student in the meeting, and that address seemed especially for me, an unforgettable message of God for my soul. So Dr Allis was the first of the 'men of Princeton' whom I saw and heard. It was a foretaste of things to come [88].

The year 1924, Grier's second year at Princeton, was to be memorable for several reasons. During November 3-7, he heard the eighty-two-year-old former president of the Seminary, Francis L. Patton, give five lectures on 'The New Christianity'. His subject had become one gaining wide attention in North America. The popular New York preacher, Harry Emerson Fosdick, along with others, had just signed the Auburn Affirmation which denied the virgin birth and other truths. 'Not dogma but life' was the call of many who wanted to reconstruct the New Testament. Patton spoke on the change in religious thought and practice in the last fifty years, convinced that 'This different Christianity appears as a disease and an epidemic.' Referring to historic Christianity, he told the students, 'it is a system so co-ordinated, whose doctrines are so concatenated, which has been so logically constructed, that if discovered by an excavating palaeontologist he would be forced to remark: "Gentlemen, this belongs to the order of vertebrates."'

That same year, J. Gresham Machen had caused uproar in the Presbyterian Church by his book *Christianity and Liberalism* which argued that the teaching of liberals was not Christianity at all. Machen, assistant professor of New Testament at Princeton, had been a pupil and friend of B. B. Warfield (d. 1921), and the former professor of systematic theology had taught him that 'a broadly based evangelicalism was not enough—it was the full-orbed Reformed faith which alone was consistent biblical Christianity and consistent evangelicalism'.[4] Not all the Seminary's faculty were of this 'Old-School' persuasion. Charles R. Erdman, professor of practical theology, as Machen would later write, 'does not indeed reject the doctrinal system of our Church, but is perfectly willing to make common cause with those who reject it, and is perfectly willing on many occasions to keep it in the background' [89].

The broader policy of such men was to win in 1929 when the constitution of the Seminary was revised. In Grier's years there was still a group of teachers, additional to Machen, committed to see the doctrinal standard of the Seminary kept as it had always been. These were the men to whom Grier gravitated. At their head was Caspar Wistar Hodge Jr (grandson of Charles Hodge). It was in an optional course of lectures by 'Caspar Wistar' on 'Imputation' that Jim first met John Murray, a new student in 1924. Murray remembered the young Irishman pressing to the front for more information once the class was dismissed.

Others among his favourite mentors were Robert Dick Wilson and Oswald T. Allis in the Old Testament department, and William P. Armstrong as well as Machen in the New.

Wilson, recognizing Grier's gift for languages, wanted him to study four cognate languages, which would better qualify him to be a teacher. But the Ulster student had no ambition with respect to the classroom and only took two. He was set on the gospel ministry. In that regard he was helped by the long-established ethos of the seminary, in which the priority had ever been given to the training of preachers. As an enthusiastic sharer in that vision, he readily took a place among students who were to serve vacant congregations in the continuing Presbyterian Church in Canada in the summers of 1924 and 1925. In the former year he spent several weeks in the prairie province of Saskatchewan, and in the latter, fifteen weeks (May to August) at River Denys Station, Cape Breton Island, Nova Scotia. In both places his brother John was able to visit him.

It was not only by some of its contemporary professors that Grier was imbued with all that was best of Princeton Seminary. He learned and absorbed its history from the days of its first professor, Archibald Alexander, in 1812. The work of Alexander, and of his three sons, 'J. W.', 'A. A.', and 'J. A.', was as familiar to him as if he had personally known them all. The biography of Archibald Alexander was one of his favourite volumes, well-marked, and deservedly said to leave 'a precious memory, embalmed in many hearts'.[5] The seminary of the Alexanders and the Hodges was a nursery of missionaries, as well as a theological school, and Alexander treasured a white-bone walking stick, given him by a chief of the Sandwich Islands, with the charge, 'You must leave this to your successor in office, that it may be handed down as a kind of symbol of orthodoxy.'[6] Archibald Alexander, by life as well as word, was the means of doing untold good. When a friend visited him for the last time before his death in 1853, he said, 'I felt that I had been breathing an atmosphere redolent with the very fragrance of heaven.'

At Princeton Grier saw and felt biblical doctrine, delivered with scholarship and in love and devotion to Christ. Both from the older and the contemporary examples, he learned what Warfield expressed in the words, 'It is *the vision of God and his majesty* which lies at the foundation of the entirety of Calvinistic thinking.' Such was the theme of the last lecture Grier heard from Caspar Wistar Hodge in 1925. Its subject was 'the glories of the Reformed faith', and many years later Grier could give us the chief points:

> It is consistent evangelicalism. It gives all the glory to divine grace, and so bestows the crown where it belongs. Salvation is by grace alone. And so Dr Hodge sent us forth in that closing lecture to cast men on the mercy of God. We are to hold aloft Christ as Saviour and look for results to God. We are to preach and pray but God alone can regenerate.[7]

In the application of the Bible to the contemporary situation no one among the seminary's teachers impressed Grier more than J. Gresham Machen. One of the last sermons he heard from Machen in 1925 was on 'The Separateness of the Church'. 'Gradually', the preacher told his students,

> the church is being permeated by the spirit of the world; it is becoming what the Auburn Affirmationists call an 'inclusive' church; it is become salt that has lost its savour and is henceforth good for nothing but to be cast out and trodden under foot of men.

Then came the charge to the young men:

> What are you going to do, my brothers, in this great time of crisis? What a time it is to be sure! What a time of glorious opportunity! Will you stand with the world, will you shrink from controversy, will you witness for Christ only where witnessing costs nothing, will you pass through these stirring days without coming to any real decision? Or will you learn the lesson of Christian history; will you penetrate, by your study and your meditation, beneath the surface; will you recognise in that which prides itself on being modern, an enemy that is as old as the hills; will you hope and pray, not for a mere continuance for what is now, but for a recovery of the

gospel that can make all things new? God grant that some of you may do that![8]

His Princeton days over, and a summer of preaching in Cape Breton Island coming to a close, Grier wrote to Machen of how 'he had enjoyed the ministry of the word very much'. So had the groups he had served who wanted him to settle with them. But, after picking up his belongings from Princeton, he was headed for home. Behind him were friendships which would last a lifetime, including that of Machen. In reply to Grier, Machen wrote to him on September 3, 1925, 'All summer I have been desiring to write you, but did not know your address. … I shall miss you ever so much next year and wish that it were possible for you to stay with us. But wherever you are I shall have a deep personal interest in you, and shall always be appreciative of news about you and about your work' [92].

PRESBYTERIANS IN TURMOIL

The dark days of civil war were passing when Grier entered the third-year class at the Assembly's College in October 1925. Trouble of a different kind was now at hand. An early sign of the storm brewing was an appeal that had been made by students at the college that the confessional standard they were required to accept be modified by the Church. In particular, they wanted removed the identification of the 'word of God' with the Bible. In characteristic fashion, the hesitating General Assembly of 1925 appointed a 'Formula Committee' to decide whether any change was necessary or desirable. Simultaneously, and in contrast with the attitude of these college students, W. P. Nicholson had returned to Belfast for another mission, and supported the formation of a Bible School at which Friday evening classes began on September 11, 1925. How far it was hoped that the Bible School might stop the drift in the Presbyterian Church is not stated, but no one who heard Nicholson could question what he thought of an unbelieving teacher of theology:

> That sucker can get into a college, and may rob your boy or mine—who, we are proud to think, might be a minister—rob him of his faith, the dirty, immoral rascal; taking Presbyterian money to wreck Presbyterian faith; taking Baptist money to wreck Baptist faith; taking Methodist money to wreck Methodist faith. If such people had decency, they would quit their jobs. ... The only thing that keeps me quiet is the knowledge that there is a judgment.[9]

Nicholson did not exactly practise keeping 'quiet' and there were those in Belfast in 1924 who scarcely welcomed his return. One of his supporters in the Bible School was John Ross of the Ravenhill Church, and another was the Rev. James Hunter who had recently retired after thirty-five years of service at Knock Church, in the eastern suburbs of Belfast. Hunter was known for his resolute commitment to Scripture. With a special concern for foreign missions, he had visited Manchuria in the early 1900s and been one of the first to raise questions over the orthodoxy of some men who were being accepted by the Foreign Missions Board of the Irish Presbyterian Church. Perhaps to avoid showing partiality, the Assembly of 1925 had made Hunter a member of the Formula Committee mentioned above.

As he did not return to Belfast until the autumn of 1925, Grier cannot have followed closely the developments in his denomination. He was soon thrown in at the deep end. It was quickly apparent to him that the twenty-three college students appealing for a relaxation of the doctrinal standards were but the spokesmen for their more cautious mentors. In a number of the theology classes which he now attended at the college, the contrast was immense between what he listened to and what he had heard at Princeton. In his later report of the experience he wrote:

> When he was only a few weeks at the college, Professor J. E. Davey stated that Paul did not claim anywhere that

Christ pre-existed as God before he came into this world. The writer challenged this, quoting Philippians 2:6-7. At the beginning of the following lecture, Prof. Davey admitted that the objector was right and Paul did so claim, but added, 'My faith is not in Paul.'[10]

In due course he would hear James Haire, professor of systematic theology, giving six reasons for not believing in the inerrancy of Scripture. Coming into contact with the Rev. James Hunter, Grier passed on to him his notes of what was being taught in the college. While the older man was startled, he was not altogether surprised. As a member of the Formula Committee, Hunter was hearing its convener, Francis J. Paul, Principal of the Assembly's College, say that 'experience' came before Scripture, and that 'infallible' should not be applied to Scripture because 'there is no external infallibility'. When Hunter, at one meeting, quoted the words of Christ, 'The Scripture cannot be broken', an ex-moderator replied with a wave of his hand, 'He only said that in controversy.'

The information from Grier clearly played a main part in Hunter's determination to fight this 'modernism' in public. In Grier's words, he resolved to 'press the battle to the issue'. Accordingly he formed 'The Presbyterian Bible Standards League' which launched three pamphlets from his pen in April and May 1926. Entitled *SOS to Irish Presbyterians*, the first was 'FAITH OR INFIDELITY, which is it to be?' and had the subtitle 'THE ASSEMBLY'S COLLEGE, A SEED BED OF RATIONALISM' [112]. In response, on May 24, seven students were called to appear before the College Committee to give evidence on what was taught in the college. With one exception, the interviews were brief, the exception being Jim Grier who was closely cross-questioned for fifty minutes. He was clearly recognized as the supplier of information to Mr Hunter. Hunter had alleged that 'Prof. Haire strives to have his students believe that the Bible is not infallible, and that the Lord Jesus Christ was not infallible.' He was contradicted by

Haire who affirmed that 'he did not impress this teaching on his students, but took pains to controvert it'. When the committee reported that Haire's response had been 'fully borne out by the evidence of the students' they interviewed, Hunter asked whether the seven students had been examined on the truth of his allegation. 'Not directly', the convener replied. But it has been put *directly* to at least one of the seven. In his notes of the meeting of May 24, 1926, written on the same day, Grier noted, 'I was asked if it were correct to say that Prof. Haire did *strive* to have his students believe that the Bible was not infallible, and that the Lord Jesus Christ was not infallible, I replied, Yes.'[11]

So truth was a casualty at the outset as the controversy took an ugly turn. Censure of its esteemed professors was the last thing which the denomination's leaders intended to allow, especially in a form which could carry information to church members. The Belfast Presbytery now censured Hunter for his conduct and for what he had published. Against this Hunter appealed to the General Assembly, meeting in June 1926. The outcome was the dismissal of his appeal, and the censure of the Presbytery upheld by 499 to 115. The public excitement had now reached a pitch which was not going to be allayed by such a decision. 'Many believers within the Church had long felt that something was wrong—now the seat of the trouble had been found and its hidden source exposed.'[12]

Not prepared to be muzzled, James Hunter took the formal course required by the Church in such cases, and tabled charges of heresy against Professor J. E. Davey before the Belfast Presbytery. The heresy trial, which took fourteen sessions between February 1 and March 29, 1927, was a foregone conclusion, despite Davey's acknowledgement of the substantive accuracy of the statements quoted as evidence against him. There were, he said, 'discrepancies' in the Scriptures, indeed, 'without hesitation I should say there are literally hundreds of discrepancies or direct contradictions in Old and New

.s.' 'We are not as Christians committed to an intel-
fallibility of either Christ or the Bible.'

: course of this trial the presbytery resolved by a large
majority to inhibit 'all who are under its jurisdiction from
every kind of public reference to the case until the appeals
have been heard by the Assembly'. When an ex-moderator
proposed that there should not even be reference made in
prayer, 'he looked exceedingly irate when Mr Hunter laughed
outright at this suggestion'.

There was to be no brotherly discussion in the courts of the
Church that summer. When an appeal was taken by Hunter
from the presbytery to the General Assembly, the Rev. Charles
Hunter (brother of James) sought in vain to make his voice
heard before the final vote: 'He was howled down and could
not even be heard at the press table beneath the platform where
he stood.' It would have made no difference. In Grier's words:
'The lack was not evidence, but rather of theological discernment and of backbone—in a word, of loyalty to Christ and
his holy word.'[13] The General Assembly approved Davey by
a vote of 707 to 82, and he was subsequently made Principal
of the College. The guilty party was not the professor but the
few who had brought the case against him, as they were duly
admonished.

By June 1926, when Grier had finished his compulsory
third year at the Assembly's College, he was in a very tense
situation. It was clear, that same month, during Hunter's
rejected appeal to the General Assembly, the allegations of
heresy rested, in part, on the evidence of at least one college
student. There had been cries in the Assembly on June 8 of
'Name, Name?' Hunter was about to give the name when
others wanting to shield Grier from the rage of the other
side, shouted, 'Don't, Don't.' The next night, however, Jim
identified himself at a large public meeting in the YMCA Hall,
asserting that 'every reference Mr Hunter has made in his
leaflets to the teaching in Assembly's College is true'.

Machen was following events in Ulster from afar, and on June 11, 1926, Grier wrote to him: 'It was no light thing for me to take that stand. I felt that it was one of the most tremendous decisions in my life. The Lord indeed stood by me, and strengthened me, as I am persuaded he will continue to do' [116]. In another letter to Machen he added that he was 'being looked on in some quarters as responsible for the whole rumpus'.

It is well that at this point Grier was under the jurisdicion of his home Letterkenny Presbytery who licensed him to preach on 21 April 1926. But his way ahead was far from clear. There appeared to be three options. One was to accept a call which had come from the congregation he had served in Cape Breton. Another was to give himself to the work of the Bible School which Nicholson had started with others, and where he was already teaching New Testament Greek, and a third was to pursue his original purpose of settlement in a congregation under the Presbyterian Church of Ireland. The decision on the first of these possibilities was more easily settled. Events since his homecoming had deepened his commitment to the cause of the gospel in Ulster, but between the second and third a decision was far more problematical. Nicholson had publicly denounced the college professors for their unbelief, and a continued association with his work would carry a price with respect to any future service in the Presbyterian Church. For the time being he took an assistant-ship in Richview Presbyterian Church, Belfast, in April 1926, being in charge during the temporary absence of its minister [108]. It was here that fourteen-year-old Joseph McCracken met Mr Grier for the first time, as he recalled:

> One night at the Bible School it was announced that an all-night prayer meeting was to be held in Richview Presbyterian Church. I sent word to my folks at home that I was going to that meeting. It was here that I first personally met Jim Grier. He was in charge of Richview Presbyterian Church while

the minister was on prolonged leave. I was so impressed by the earnestness and sincerity of this young minister that the next day I walked the four or five miles through the City to hear him preach. I found the Church packed, with seats in the aisles. Mr Grier preached with great power and I was not surprised to hear of conversions taking place [252].

By the end of the summer of 1926 Grier's career took another turn following the months in which Hunter had formed the Presbyterian Bible Standards League and later launched the 'Ulster Pamphlets'. The public support given to this development warranted the appointment of a full-time deputation secretary, involving a call 'to speak on behalf of conservative groups "up-and-down" the country' [118]. For Hunter, Grier was the obvious man for this need and, ending his assistantship at Richview in September 1926, Jim began to work full time with the League.

By October 1926, however, there was a change in the role Grier was expected to play. It was influenced, no doubt, by the effect of the literature the League was producing. He wrote to Machen that he would be 'organizing and taking charge of a large, new Bookstall of the PBS League. ... The main part of my duties will be the sale of *defensive* and *offensive* literature.' As a base for the work, the League acquired the use of 15 College Square East, Belfast, as a shop and office. October 1, Grier wrote to Machen, 'Am now engaged in superintending new book room. It is thought essential to our work. It is certainly a change for me ... the Lord has been prospering and we look to him for further blessing. We begin on our knees each morning.'

This change of emphasis did not stop the convening of public meetings. 'We could fill the largest hall in Belfast', Grier told Machen. The League 'has been most enthusiastically supported and the people are joining in large numbers.' When the Belfast Presbytery inhibited all further public discussion relating to the controversy in March 1927, pending Hunter's appeal to the Assembly in June, Hunter ignored the order. Public meetings continued, culminating in those at which Machen came to speak—four times in Belfast and once in Londonderry—at the beginning of June, on the eve of the 1927 General Assembly. A Sunday evening meeting in the Ulster Hall saw 1,600 or 1,700 people present. The Princeton professor reported: 'The interest is intense. The meetings at which I have spoken are of course connected with the ecclesiastical situation, though naturally I have not referred to the personal details in my addresses' [160-61].

It has been asked whether Hunter's disobedience to the Presbytery's inhibition did not play a major part in the failure of his appeal. Both the 'Ulster Pamplets' (seven out of nine from his pen) and the public meetings had continued despite the injunction of the Presbytery. This behaviour was referred by the Presbytery to the June Assembly of 1927 which appointed a Commission to correct him and any others who took the same course. Short of Hunter's public repentance there was only one course of action for the Commission to take, the termination of his status as a minister. It is probable that Hunter saw that outcome as inevitable before he determined to ignore the inhibition. As Grier would later record, 'There was to be no more liberty for upholders of orthodoxy.' Without waiting for the deliberation of the Commission, in July 1927 Hunter gave notice to the Belfast Presbytery that he had discontinued his membership in the Irish Presbyterian Church and demitted his position as a minister of the denomination. He wrote to Grier on July 27, 'Surely it is not the will of the Lord that people should remain banded together who have so little in common as the Modernists have with those of the old faith' [183]. The next month his young friend, still only 24 years old, took the same decision; Christians did not belong in a 'broad, inclusive church'. In New Jersey Machen passed on news of the Belfast situation, and reported:

Heroic work has been done by Mr Grier our Seminary graduate. He has thrown away all his ecclesiastical prospects for
the sake of the cause. His work is now in the conduct of the
Bookshop of the Bible Standards League. Most of the pulpits,
of course, are closed against him [161].

THE IRISH EVANGELICAL CHURCH

The question now concerned the way ahead, namely, how
converts of the Nicholson missions, the Bible School, and the
supporters of the Bible League, could organise themselves to
form churches uncompromised by the prevalent defection.
With that need in view, Hunter called for six meetings at a
café in Fountain Street between September 1927 and February
1928. At the first of these there were only twenty men and
women; the figure would increase yet, as far as numbers were
concerned, the low turnout was startling. What had happened
to the crowd who met in the Ulster Hall? Four other ministers
had signed most of the heresy charges, but were not committed
to secession. Many were too long accustomed to the ethos of
'No one is afraid of heresy; all are afraid of "schism".' Certainly
there were exceptions, especially among elders. Some church
sessions were aroused, as at the Ravenhill Church where there
was a vote for closer loyalty to the denomination's confessional
standards. But while such votes achieved nothing, a call for
separation had few hearers. In the words of a later observer,
'the great public interest in the controversy evaporated' [379].
Twelve months later it was probably Grier who wrote in the
Alliance News magazine of the Christian Workers' Union:

> Many are sitting today on the top rail of the fence, like sleeping
> fowls, and from their theological roost they insist on peace.
> And from the other side—from the modernist camp—the cry
> is re-echoed: 'Let us have peace.' Yes, the Modernist does love
> peace—peace to propagate his own views—for 'there shall be
> false teachers among you, who *privily* shall bring in destructive
> heresies' (2 Pet. 2:1).

A special cause for disappointment was the lack of support from the many evangelical lay people active in the public meetings, the Bible School, and the Bible League. Evangelism had their backing but, lacking in theological instruction, and in measure confused by Professor Davey's representation of himself as an evangelical, they failed to see the gospel itself was being abandoned. Davey, at his trial, assured the General Assembly that he had received 'the second blessing' at the Keswick Convention, yet at the opening session of the college in the autumn of 1928 he could assert that anti-Christian writers such as H. G. Wells and Bernard Shaw were 'certainly converted' and 'Christians'.[14] Yet the seceders were represented as those departing from the tradition of Christianity, as though their ideas on separation were novelties. Their opponents had no ears to hear what Paul wrote in 2 Timothy 2:21, or Bishop Ellicott's words on those verses which Grier quoted: 'There must be no communion on the part of God's servants with impugners of fundamentals. It was imperatively necessary … to break off from all church fellowship, from all friendship' with such.[15] In Hunter's words, many saw no 'need for separation from those who cast discredit upon God and his word'.

The result was that on October 15, 1927 the small company gathered at the café in Fountain Street decided to proceed with the formation of a new church organisation. By the end of the following month, the name was settled as the 'Irish Evangelical Church'. Eight Articles of Faith were signed by a company of twenty-seven, and a council of eleven men was appointed, with Grier as the Interim Clerk. He, and Mr Hunter, were the only ones who had been preachers in the Presbyterian Church. No congregation had joined them, and the Bible Standards League had decided to continue its existence to work within the Church.

Yet the mood of the few was far from one of disheartenment. Interest and numbers slowly increased, through smaller public 'conferences', and the work of the bookshop. A new monthly, the *Irish Evangelical*, was published. Prayer meetings were marked by earnest prayer, individuals were converted, and Grier wrote to Machen of there being 'much more contentment—feeling that we are doing a positive work—than in our previous situation where we were fighting a hopeless battle as far as numerical strength was concerned'. By the end of 1927 three congregations were meeting, sometimes in temporary locations. By 1932 the number would rise to ten. Not all were in Belfast itself. One new congregation came about through the enquiry from troubled members of the Presbyterian Church at Crumlin, Co Antrim, who invited Grier to meet with them. He was happy to do so, and set off on his bicycle, believing that Crumlin was at the end of Crumlin Road, close to the city's boundary. Instead he was to discover it lay across hills eighteen miles away. By the time he arrived, drenched with perspiration, a delay was necessary before he addressed the waiting company!

PERSONAL TRIALS

With James Hunter now in his mid-sixties much of the burden of the new work fell upon Grier. As well as the management of the bookshop, he now had the care of two congregations, one at Botanic Avenue, the other at Lisburn Road (until 1942), with a Bible class and prayer meetings occupying three evenings every week, and open-air meetings in the summer months. A monthly report on his congregational work in May 1933, recorded fourteen services at both charges and visitation of 160 families, where there were 37 sick. In addition he had the main responsibility for the preparation of the *Irish Evangelical* every month. He lived in lodgings and had no means of transport other than his bicycle. It was a small measure of respite when the church council decided in January 1929 that his presence at the bookshop should be limited to mornings only.

Ernest Brown speaks of his 'nigh impossible schedule' at this date, and notes concerns expressed for his health. At the time of the heresy trial he developed a facial twitch which was to remain for several years. Helen McCracken, later a missionary in South Africa, remembered how this could affect his preaching when he was overtired, but added, 'his heart was so in his message, his anxiety for sinners so great' [252]. His mother, who remembered how her brother had died from excessive study, was dismayed to see the tiredness of her son when she visited Belfast to attend a missionary rally in 1926. An unplanned meeting which she had with an ex-missionary, Catherine Gillespie, was to have a long-term consequence. On listening to Elizabeth Grier's anxiety, Catherine Gillespie promised to invite Jim to their home at Knockdene Park South. From every point of view it was an address as attractive as the name may suggest and, with few breaks, Jim was to be there Saturday afternoons from mid-1926. His hostess was a sister of James Hunter, who had married a medical missionary, Dr John Gillespie. With her husband, Catherine Gillespie had returned from Manchuria, and he was at this time a medical officer of health. There were two young people in the home at Knock, Catherine, aged thirteen, and her brother James, aged twenty, whom Catherine was to remember wrestling with Jim Grier on the lawn.

The Gillespie family were closely involved in the witness of the Irish Evangelical Church from the outset. Dr Gillespie was a member of the council and a main supporter of the editor of the magazine. His son, James, became the closest companion for Jim Grier. While he was still twenty-one, and before he graduated in medicine, James published an effective refutation of the disbelief in Scripture.[16] He was expected to become one of the denomination's major leaders for the future. In 1931 he and Grier went together to Palestine, a break which the latter much needed.

The early years of the 1930s remained particularly difficult for Jim as a bachelor. Ernest Brown speaks of 'a time of intense loneliness for him and a feeling of isolation would sometimes threaten'. Criticism of the infant denomination was common. One day he overheard two ministers standing talking outside the bookshop. Women who happened to come into the shop at the time asked him, 'Did you hear what those two ministers outside were saying?' He replied, 'I was meant to hear.' They were saying that he and the shop had no future.

The difficulties he faced were many, and one of the chief was finding supplies for their pulpits, especially after he became responsible for co-ordinating pulpit supplies in 1932. With the increase of congregations the lack of suitable preachers was serious and the more so when a controversy occurred within the denomination in 1933. Three years earlier, Dr Lewis Sperry Chafer of Dallas Theological Seminary had been a welcome visitor and one of his students settled to serve with them. Chafer, a Presbyterian, was strong in commitment to Scripture and it would appear that the dispensational teaching, promoted at Dallas, was not at first regarded as introducing any serious discord in the preaching. Was there not room enough for difference provided preachers believed in the second coming of Christ? But a few years were to prove that while Christian fellowship does not depend on a uniform belief in unfulfilled prophecy, the dispensational system introduced interpretations into the handling of Scripture which made for real inconsistency in the message of the infant denomination's pulpits. For Grier this underlined the inadequacy of the Eight Articles of 1927 as the only standard to which the ministers had to subscribe.[17] Matters came to a head in 1933 when the council adopted an additional subscription which affirmed the Catechisms of the Westminster divines 'to be founded on, and agreeable to, the word of God'. Five Council members refused to sign, and two ministers were to be lost to the denomination. Shortly before, in February 1933, a Canadian minister also resigned after a few months' service.

In addition to such losses, there was abiding sorrow over a number who had been friends in the 1920s and whose zeal for upholding Scripture had grown cold. Some of these men remained in the Presbyterian Bible Standards League but that organisation also settled down into an acceptance of the *status quo* and was to pass out of existence in the 1940s. One special grief, which came to Grier on February 25, 1934, was more sudden. He arrived to take a Sunday evening service that night in such distress that it appeared doubtful whether he could proceed. He did so 'with great difficulty and had to cut it short' [278]. The explanation was news just received that James Gillespie, in London for a three-month medical course, had been killed in a road accident after leaving church that morning. He was only twenty-seven and no one had meant more to Jim Grier in his hopes for the Church. When he went to Knockdene Park South to console Catherine Gillespie—her father being in hospital at the time—it was he who needed the consolation. 'Don't cry, Mr Grier', Catherine told him, seeing him in tears, 'The Lord gave, the Lord hath taken away.'

As Ernest Brown has written, the 1920s and '30s were Grier's training and development years. Several things came to mark his life and the life of the Irish Evangelical Church.

The first was the place of prayer. What was prominent in his own life was seen also in the people. An Australian visitor to the Irish Evangelical Church, coming as a stranger to Belfast in 1934, wrote of the two things which impressed him:

> One is the spiritual fervour of the members with whom one comes in contact. They are zealous for the glory of God in the salvation of souls. The other is the great volume of earnest and definite prayer rising from the church to the throne above. Such zeal and prayer must have results [255].

Even before the new Church began, a group of women, kneeling on the tiled floor at the back of the bookshop, were meeting monthly for prayer. Ernest Brown comments, 'It is impossible to estimate the Church's indebtedness to this group of praying women' [268].

The opposition the Church faced worked for good. Luther's saying that trials make a minister of the gospel was proved true again in Grier's life. Loneliness, criticism, and difficulties entered into making him the man he was. Ambition for position and popularity was early mortified. Machen already saw evidence of benefit from what his former pupil was suffering when he wrote to him on August 24, 1926: 'Some men fall under opposition; others only become clearer in their insight and braver in their service. It is cause for the greatest rejoicing that you belong in the latter category' [177]. His protégé, Ernest Brown, would later write:

> The battles of the 1920s had taught him to strengthen himself in the Lord, and he developed courage, alertness and a commanding presence. He was indefatigable, he worked quickly and achieved objectives. The addition of a ready mind and powerful memory-recall made him formidable in debate.

Another consequence of these years was the maturing of his conviction that the doctrines of the reformed faith need to be spelt out definitely and in distinction from the 'fundamentalist' type of evangelicalism then prevalent in Ulster. As already seen, he owed a debt to evangelicals of the latter school and maintained friendships with many of them, including W. P. Nicholson. But he recognized the weakness which was in the Protestant churches on account of the lost doctrinal standards of their earlier history. Evangelistic activity was not enough. Sound teaching and good literature were no less important. It was his leadership which led the denomination in 1933 to advance beyond their eight Articles to the Westminster catechisms. He felt so strongly on that account that he said he would have left the Irish Evangelical Church and 'started all over again' if the controversy over doctrine had not been settled [275]. He speaks on this issue in the following words:

> In the days of the Heresy Trial it was the vital and common fundamentals of the faith which were at stake, and it was to the defence of these that we betook ourselves. As time went

on, however, we saw that it was not a minimum of Christia[n]ity to which we should pledge ourselves but the most full-orbed and complete expression that we possess. This is what we felt we had in the Westminster standards. Henry B. Smith declared, 'One thing is certain—that Infidel Science will rout everything except thoroughgoing orthodoxy. ... The fight will be between a stiff thoroughgoing orthodoxy and a stiff thoroughgoing infidelity.'[18]

THE DECADES WHICH FOLLOWED

The 1940s brought great sorrows to Ulster. Unlike the neutral Irish Free State, which retained a German delegation in Dublin throughout World War II, Northern Ireland was prominent in the part she took in resisting Hitler's aggression. Between 35,000-40,000 of her people joined the Armed Forces. Her shipyards and factories became a major supplier of aircraft and ships. Inevitably Ulster drew the attention of the enemy and, once France fell in 1940, she was within range of the Luftwaffe. Yet Belfast was poorly prepared for aerial attack, and some 900 of her people were killed in one air raid on April 15, 1941. In the crisis years of the war, when the German U-Boat fleet was at its deadliest, trans-Atlantic supplies to the ports of Liverpool and Glasgow continued because, in Churchill's words, 'loyal Ulster gave us the full use of the Northern Irish ports and waters. ... But for the loyalty of Northern Ireland, we should have been confronted with slavery and death.'

In addition to the occasional Days of National Prayer called for by the king, the Irish Evangelical Church had its own times of prayer meetings for the nation. On one such occasion March 25, 1942, a main service was held at Botanic Avenue Church, conducted by James Hunter. His long ministry was almost over. A few months later, when in the midst of writing an article on 'Exulting in hope of the glory of God' (Rom. 5:2), his work was done. The last sentences of the unfinished article were these:

Justification by faith means that the undeserving sinner through simple faith in the Saviour is forgiven and accounted righteous by God, and he is there and then introduced into the standing ground of grace. Grace or the free favour of God is the streaming sunshine of heaven that is always enveloping the believer whether he sees it or not.[19]

James Hunter died on September 20, 1942 in his 80th year. Had he lived a year longer it would have been his joy to see Jim Grier married to his niece, Catherine Gillespie, on October 12, 1943. A graduate in classics of Queen's University, by ways unrecorded she had ceased to address the minister of the Botanic Avenue Church and long-time friend as 'Mr Grier'. In her acceptance of his proposal he was given an ideally suited wife. Since Catherine was twenty-one, she had helped with the *Irish Evangelical*, taking the place of her brother in writing the children's page. As they became blessed with a family, in the persons of James, John, and Hunter, the old home and garden at 28 Knockdene Park South came into new life.[20]

By the 1940s Grier was prepared to lead the denomination. Despite losses in the 1930s, the position of the Irish Evangelical Church had been strengthened. One means through which this had come about was the care he had given to teaching and enthusing young people who were now themselves ready for positions of leadership. Joseph McCracken was one of the first of this group. We noted him earlier, attending an all-night prayer meeting. Grier took him, when he left school at the age of fourteen, to help at the Evangelical Book Shop, where he would begin to study 'the rudiments of reformed theology' as well as the book trade. Another was Charles E. Hunter. In 1932 both McCracken and Charles Hunter were candidates for the ministry and about to go to Dallas for their theological training. But the controversy over dispensational teaching led them instead, under Grier's oversight, to the College of the Free Church of Scotland in Edinburgh. This marked the beginning of a long-term cooperation between the two denominations. In John Macleod, the Principal (1927–42), the Free Church had an outstanding teacher.[21] In 1935 McCracken was to write, 'If I went to Edinburgh a professed Calvinist, I have returned a convinced Calvinist. ... The College staff are uncompromising in their opposition to modernism' [253]. Two other future ministers of the denomination, W. J. McDowell and C. H. Garland, would also go to study in Edinburgh in the 1930s, the former after six years' valuable work in selling Bibles and books across Ireland. Ernest Brown records: 'Such was the shortage of preaching and pastoral resource that the Council placed these men in congregational charges from the beginning of their training!'

By the 1940s this group of men, all friends and sharing a close relationship with their leader, were making a real difference in the denomination. And Grier's influence did not stop with ministers and office bearers. From his Young People's Bible Class, three young women, Nan Dunlop, Annie Wilkinson, and Florence Donaldson, were to go out as foreign missionaries without further training. They went to the work of the Free Church of Scotland in India and Peru, the two denominations having joined forces in Foreign Mission. With the same mission, Harold Lindsay went to Peru in 1937 and Joseph and Helen McCracken to South Africa in 1944. Another member of that Bible class, Ella Ball, would serve in the work of the Evangelical Book Shop 1942–1975.

The 1950s brought clear evidence of the fruitfulness of the literature ministry to which the Church had been committed from the outset. A deficit in the funds of the Evangelical Book Shop had not stopped its continuance. The denomination met the need until faith was rewarded. This was a time when very little Calvinistic or Puritan literature was published or promoted anywhere in Britain. In the 1930s new books in that tradition, shipped from the United States, had their distribution point at the Evangelical Book Shop and when that source of supply had ended, during the years of the World War II, it is indicative of the optimism of the owners that good stocks had been built up beforehand. By the 1950s the *Irish Evangelical* was known in the British Isles by an increasing number of those who loved 'the old paths'. In its columns reformed books were reviewed, or advertised month by month, and the shop at 15 College Square East, Belfast, had become the best known place to obtain them. It was a reflection of the esteem in which Grier was held that on the thirtieth anniversary-number of the magazine in 1958 there were greetings from readers in Australia, New Zealand, the Netherlands, USA, Canada, Scotland, South Africa, and Sweden. The success was not in the number of copies sold (never high) but in the help the magazine gave to those who, in turn, were the leaders of others. Dr Lloyd-Jones was one of them. He wrote from London in 1958:

> I look forward to its coming month by month with great pleasure. It always seems to me to have the ideal blend as regards matter—theology, devotional element, first-class book reviews, pungent comment on current affairs, biographical material, and choice extracts from the writings of the masters. The industry and the versatility of the Editor astound me more and more.[22]

That same year, 1958, saw a major advance in the publication of evangelical literature in Britain. An interdenominational Trust had been formed by two members of Westminster Chapel 'to make available in our times some of the best expository and evangelical works of former centuries'. This was an ambitious plan, not attempted without prayer, and one which could not have proceeded without the input of the three men named in the Trust's first advertising material: W. J. Grier, Martyn Lloyd-Jones, and Professor John Murray. The name, Banner of Truth Trust, indicated the continuation of a work begun with a small magazine of that name in 1955. It was the preparation of that magazine that first put the present writer in touch with 'Mr Grier' (as he was always known to me), and he had invited me to preach in Belfast in 1956. As he was away at that time with his family on holiday, I spent a good deal of my visit with William and Sadie McDowell and in conversation over books. I believe it was in the welcoming home of the McDowells that I had my first lesson on the authors of old Princeton Seminary. William McDowell had never been there, but he glowed with the same enthusiasm that I would later see in his mentor. Two Princeton authors (Charles Hodge and T. V. Moore) were among the eleven titles reprinted by the Trust in the first five months of 1958.

To the surprise of many, this publishing venture went forward at a rapid pace and with large sales. The young and inexperienced staff of the Banner of Truth Trust felt that they were only seeing the fruit of the labours and prayers of others which had gone before when a hunger for reformed and Puritan theology had been little seen. The Evangelical Book Shop had played a significant part in that preparation, as had the ministry of Dr Lloyd-Jones, the Puritan Conference (begun with Jim Packer at Westminster Chapel in 1950), and the Evangelical Library, London. There was an informal co-operation between all these agencies, with the friendship of Lloyd-Jones and Grier (which developed after the war) being a significant factor. The minister of Westminster Chapel was an admirer of Grier's book, *The Momentous Event*,[23] and the Ulsterman became a much-appreciated visitor to his pulpit. Ernest Brown's description of his preaching accords with the memories of many who heard him in London:

> Grier was an earnest, serious, expository preacher and teacher. He always knew his subject, delivering substantial sections of his sermons without reference to his notes and engaging powerfully with the congregation. His facility in quoting Scripture from memory was remarkable. His passion for souls was vigorously evident in the pulpit and it characterised the whole of his life [326].

The 1960s was perhaps the busiest decade of his life. He had ceased to be daily in the book shop but otherwise nearly all the local activities of early years continued. He never missed church prayer meetings, and was still to be found speaking at open-air meetings. He did not miss the Boys' Camp, an annual open-air occasion under canvas which had begun with one Bell tent in 1939, noting it in 1959 as 'the best ever camp'.

His engagements in England and Scotland had increased by this date. He was a member of the council of the Lord's Day Observance Society, and of the British Evangelical Council formed in 1953. The latter was intended as a link between churches outside the ecumenical movement, and its leaders were G. N. M. Collins for the Free Church of Scotland, E. J. Poole-Connor for the Fellowship of Independent Evangelical Churches (FIEC), and Grier for the Irish Evangelical Church. The three men were strong friends. Only after 1967 did the BEC gain wider public attention with the addition of Dr Lloyd-Jones to its membership. For a time it was to have a rapid increase of support but difficulty arose over a call for unity 'at the church level', making the BEC seem to be promoting more than a linking organisation. A statement of faith for any such 'church' body would have had to avoid being specifically Calvinistic, and while this was acceptable to the FIEC, it did not have the support of its Scots and Irish leaders.[24]

A parallel issue had already arisen in connection with the Leicester Ministers' Conference. This conference had arisen out of a discussion which I had with the Rev. J. Marcellus Kik, the thought being of providing a conference with the specific intention of helping preachers and students for the ministry. Kik, who lived in New Jersey and was a trustee of Westminster Theological Seminary, promised to discuss the matter with Professor John Murray at Philadelphia. Mr Grier became involved, for anything supported by his friend John Murray had appeal to him. In 1958 he had urged me, 'If you see John Murray, it would be well to ask his views as to future publications', and in a further letter, 'Glad you met John. He is a very fine fellow and a very able theologian—so loyal to the Reformed heritage. He usually wields a powerful pen and is clear and incisive in his style.'[25]

So Murray and Grier were founding members and speakers at the first Leicester Conference which met for four days in July 1962 in the Midlands of England. Lloyd-Jones also participated in the conferences of 1964 and 1965, but at the latter date there was a measure of disagreement over whether a closer union of churches would require a definite Calvinistic confession. Lloyd-Jones believed that for pastoral reasons—the recovery of reformed theology being so recent in England—the time was not ripe for such a development. Murray and Grier on the other hand were against a movement to unity on the church level which had only a broader evangelical consensus.[26]

It needs to be added that while Grier wanted 'devotion to the Reformed Faith, as over against a bare evangelicalism', there was a yet greater priority which he brought to the Leicester Conference. His emphasis was on prayer and knowing the presence of God. In an address on that subject entitled 'The Church at Prayer', he took Acts 1:12-14 as his text, where 'we see the little congregation gathered under the protecting hand of the sovereign, all-controlling God whose purposes can know no defeat'. 'Prayer had priority in those days. The professing church today has often got her priorities all wrong … unless we look up to God in heaven, we can never work effectually on the earth below.'[27] Both by word and example Grier's presence at Leicester was to be a continuing witness in successive conferences. From 1967 he and John Murray were to be the regular chairmen.

After the 1920s the IRA was mainly dormant until the late 1960s when a 'civil rights' movement, led by Irish nationalists, led to violence in Ulster after they had defied the government. It was a new attempt to overthrow the constitutional government of the province, the main justification being the allegation that the government discriminated against the Roman Catholic section of the population. Grier never belonged to a political party. In Donegal he had been reared where the majority were Roman Catholic and, in later years, where there was discrimination he spoke against it. But he believed that the charge was greatly exaggerated for political purposes, and that there were no grievances to justify 'the riots, the wrecking of shops and factories, the wanton destruction of property to the amount of millions of pounds'.[28] It would have been well if the real cause of the 'troubles' had been understood by leaders on both sides. He set it out for American readers in an article, '"Troubles" in Northern Ireland', from which I have just quoted. He continued:

> Why is it that these troubles have been permitted by our sovereign God? Why have our foes been let loose to assail us on every side? It is a judgment of God. Centuries ago a Protestant church in this island refused to give the Irish people the Bible in their own language, the Gaelic. The church was more intent on anglicizing the people than making them Christians. And in this 20th century, our Protestant churches have been weakening in loyalty to the word of God. In our large churches we have been bowing to the altar of ecumenism which has abandoned the gospel of the redeeming blood of Christ.
>
> We have not given the gospel to our fellow-countrymen, Roman Catholic and Protestant. This has brought judgment upon us. May God in his mercy pour out his Spirit and revive his work among us. Then Roman Catholics and Protestants shall bow at the foot of the cross, reconciled through Christ's blood. This is the real cure.

CORRESPONDENCE ON BOOKS AND AUTHORS

Grier maintained an extensive correspondence, and among the most important part were the letters of counsel and comment on the publication programme of the Banner of Truth Trust. These letters which he wrote to me, beginning before the first Banner publications of 1958, ran to hundreds, and no one played a fuller or more important part in decisions on books thereafter published than he did. A number of the Trust's reprints had their origin in his suggestion. They included George Smeaton, *The Doctrine of the Holy Spirit*, Archibald Alexander, *Thoughts on Religious Experience* (both titles with Foreword or Introduction by Grier), David Brown, *The Four Gospels*, and D. C. MacNicol, *Robert Bruce*. His opinion also entered into decisions on many other titles.

A stranger today, taking up his letters to me, could be forgiven for believing the writer must have been an academic, living in the world of books. He can have had few equals in the range of his knowledge of Christian books. Rarely would he be asked for an opinion on a title formerly published, whether expository, exegetical, or biographical, on which he was not ready to give a definite opinion.[29] Nor were his comments merely general. Errors with respect to Hebrew or Greek would not escape his notice, the truth being that, among his other gifts, he was a linguist. He read the Book of Psalms through in the original language once a year, and before breakfast at the annual Boys' camps could be seen reading his Greek New Testament outside his tent. He was the only person I have met who had read all the volumes of Emile Doumergue's biography of Calvin in French.[30]

It was as a pastor that our friend assessed books. His was not the interest of a *litterateur*, rather he wanted books that would be of lasting worth for readers. If a volume had admirable qualities, yet was dull or heavy, he would not favour it. As much as possible he wanted simplicity to be the guide if the book was being considered for general readers. And he wanted the writing of history to be alive, as the two volumes of J. Merle d'Aubigné's on *The Reformation in England* which he counted 'thrilling' reading.

I constantly found his ability to discriminate impressive. He would not approve or question a title proposed for reprinting, simply on the reputation of its author, but point out that a man's judgment may change at a different stage of life; A. W. Pink's early works, for instance, being less dependable than his later ones. The reverse, he judged, to be the case with the writings of Klaas Runia.[31] Much as he admired the Princeton divines, even they were not exempt from occasional criticism. The Old Testament commentaries of J. A. Alexander he rated above his New Testament work. Cornelius Van Til (a friend from student days at Princeton) he faulted for lack of lucidity in style but, referring to his value, he went on to write, 'I believe he is right in saying that even Hodge and Warfield (and sometimes Bavinck) did not carry out the true Calvinistic principle. For example, Hodge sometimes uses the universal practice of humanity as an argument for a biblical doctrine. I thoroughly agree with Van Til on such a point.'

That all should be tested by Scripture was paramount. He did not believe that because some evangelicals have supported the teaching of a universal redemption, or a hypothetical atonement, that the error should be regarded as insignificant. For the same reason he believed it was wrong to say that Roman Catholics were orthodox on the work of Christ. 'Any view of the work of Christ must teach IMPETRATION—that it actually procures the benefits it was intended to procure' (19/3/63).[32] What Christ did in making an atonement, and in *applying* the benefits of that atonement, are both sure and definite. Thus, while he valued the sermons of J. C. Ryle, he regretted his notes on the extent of redemption which appear in his *Expository Thoughts on the Gospel of John*. A commentary which opposed particular redemption he would not commend, ast, without a word of warning.

On the subject of unfulfilled prophecy he urged caution against dogmatism on the grounds that the interpretation of certain passages of Scripture is uncertain. In commentating on differences among authors on Romans 11 holding to an a-millennial understanding of the second coming, he wrote:

> There is an amount of latitude. Hendriksen and Berkhof do not understand that there is to be a conversion of Israel on a widespread scale—Dr Lloyd-Jones and Dr Basil Atkinson would follow this line.[33] I raised a question on that point in their presence at Cambridge (Tyndale House) in 1953. J. G. Vos and John Murray believe that there will be such a conversion and I feel they are right. The late Ned Stonehouse (to whom I was attached) felt also that Romans 11 was big with promise. John Murray and I have prepared a Report on Eschatology for the Reformed Ecumenical Synod (meeting in Grand Rapids in August [1963]) and the Report presents this interpretation. Of course, alongside the promises of a wide extension of the church, there are Scriptures which warn of apostasy and unbelief and antichrist (Luke 18:8; 2 Thess. 2:1-12). The reign of truth will be extended but the forces of unbelief will muster strength also, and the universal sway of the kingdom of God will not come from missionary effort alone; it will require the direct divine interposition at the close (3/12/62).[34]

In 1960 Grier sought to begin preparing a guide to Christian literature. It was a major undertaking for which he could only give limited time, but the valuable result was eventually published by Banner of Truth in 1968 under the title, *The Best Books*. The scope was limited to books in print at that date, with the comment, 'Many fine works are still difficult to obtain, but what a wealth lies within our reach.' Few such guides have been as careful to be reliable as this book. Popular 'Christian' books, unfaithful to Scripture, such as William Barclay's commentaries on the New Testament, found no space.[35]

It is not easy for a commentator to be as critical, where necessary, on contemporary authors as on those departed.

Grier did not avoid this difficulty, as instanced to me when he mentioned a deficiency in *The Banner of Truth* magazine for which I was responsible:

> I have heard from a very few sources of desire on the part of some younger men for more Bible exposition with the setting forth of Bible doctrine and life founded on doctrine. It would perhaps be good to have an article of moderate length, say 3 or 4 pages, on such lines, if possible, in each issue (24/1/75).

The observation, too kindly delivered, was warranted.

THE LAST YEARS OF WORK

While Jim Grier reached the age of seventy in November 1972, he knew no retirement age for ministers of the gospel. He admired the words of Charles Simeon, 'I am so near the goal that I cannot help running with all my might.' His health had appeared to falter for some months in the late 1960s, but the old vigour was renewed. After the 50th anniversary of the denomination in 1977 he wrote to me: 'We have much to thank God for. But we must look up and forward. Time is short. I have been rather tired at times in the past few months, but I would like to labour on while God gives me strength' (26/10/77). He was to continue in public ministry for a further two years, and as magazine editor for three. In 1979 he preached in Cheltenham at the annual BEC Conference, with heaven as his subject, and also, for the last time, at Leicester, on 'Praying always with all prayer and supplication in the Spirit' (Eph. 6:18). Since 1974, when John Murray could no longer attend, he continued to be the chairman at the conference. He had long communicated to us his love of old Princeton and in that connection would quote the words with which A. A. Hodge concluded a series of lectures, 'We shall not meet here anymore. Let us pledge one another, as we part, to reassemble in heaven.'[36]

The 1970s brought to him both special trials and special blessings. Foremost among the trials was the political trouble now bringing loss and death to large numbers in Northern Ireland. The IRA activity in 1968–69 had only been a beginning. Much worse in the way of armed conflict was to follow with 3,000 British soldiers involved in seeking to preserve peace. In 1972 nearly 500 people were killed, just over half being civilians. The IRA were now split between the 'Official' and the 'Provisional'. In that same year the Provisionals were said to have killed some 100 members of the security forces and wounded 500 others.[37]

Belfast was at the centre of suffering with twenty-two bombs set off in the city centre on July 21, 1974. These were planted almost indiscriminately to disrupt commercial life. On November 19, 1974 the Evangelical Book Shop was burned severely by a firebomb and made unusable for a time. Being in the city centre the shop was virtually in a 'bomb alley'. Repaired, it was broken into, and then bombed a second time in 1976. This damage and its cost did not distress Grier so much as the human suffering of so many in a country he loved. His pastoral visitation was more needed than ever and gave, as he wrote in a letter of March 24, 1978 'some precious opportunities of personal work'. At that date he mentioned 'calling almost every week' on grandparents where a grandchild, husband and wife had been killed by a bomb. The church building where he had formerly served at Lisburn Road would later be destroyed by a bomb in 1986.

It was characteristic that he wrote in the midst of these events: 'We need to pray and seek the Lord's face. While there are problems, there are also great blessings—both at Shop and in Church.' First among the blessings at the shop was the arrival of his son John in 1974 to take over the management of the work. John's decision to end his career in London for this purpose could not have been more timely. He was to remain at that post for thirty-eight years to June 2012. The Christian commitment of the Griers' two other sons, James and Hunter, meant much to their parents.

The blessing in the Church came in connection with a seeming set-back. In 1970 the church at Botanic Avenue, where he had served since 1930, was required to move as the site was required for demolition on account of planning for a ring road. This led the church to a new building and a new location at Stranmillis, where the congregation grew and experienced a quickening of spiritual life. In 1975 he wrote in a personal letter of this blessing and of the sense of the presence of God being given to them.

In the closing years of his ministry he was to see growing numbers in more than one field. He rejoiced in the increase of men at the Leicester Conference, and in the way books, once little known and unobtainable, were being sold in Britain and the United States.

In June 1979 his long pastoral ministry came to an end as failing memory led him to lay down his charge at Stranmillis. The next year he wrote, 'I can still take an occasional service when called upon, though I feel my weakness more than ever.' It was a time of change in the Evangelical Presbyterian Church and in that same letter he wrote of close friends from the denomination's early years: 'Mrs W. J. McDowell is in hospital and is very seriously ill. Willie [McDowell] retired from the ministry just recently, and C. H. Garland has retired too.' In this situation it was a joy to him how God had raised up a band of able young men in the 1970s to ensure the continued work of the denomination.

His mental powers now deteriorated considerably, as though his mind was worn out. In the very last letter I had from him, November 17, 1981, his handwriting was as firm as ever it had been but his mind wandered to things which remained clearest to him:

> I was born near Ramelton in Co. Donegal and not long ago, in last summer, my wife and I spent a few weeks in that county. I studied at Princeton for a few years (not very far from Philadelphia) .... The Lord bless you and use you for his

glory and the salvation of souls. Yours most cordially in our Lord Jesus.

On December 3, 1981 Catherine Grier wrote to me, 'He thinks he won't be here for long and has great desire to depart and be with Christ.' In July 1983 he still lingered, unable now to communicate, and inactive save for one thing, in Catherine's words: 'He can still pray, and I believe *that* world is still real to him.' The next month, on August 6, he entered 'the land of pure delight, where saints immortal reign'.[38]

The life of Jim Grier exemplifies what can be seen by those who rely on God's word and promises when success all seems to point to the need for compromise. It took faith to say 'unity in error is unity in ruin' in a day when most saw the separation which Scripture requires to be far from ruinous. It was not easy to hold firm in a 'day of small things', when many claimed that successful churches could be built by an easier route. The fall off of support, as already noted, had been marked in the 1920s and 1930s. The seceders were said to represent ideas which 'belong to the mentality and outlook of bygone ages'.[39] Critics regarded with incredulity, if not amusement, Grier's words, 'We have a solemn charge to guard the precious deposit of Bible truth committed to our trust. We must hand it on undiluted and undiminished to succeeding generations, if the Lord tarry.'

For a time there was small success in the work which he led. The first literature ministry was only a trestle table on a Belfast street stall. Even in 1962 the monthly print run of the *Evangelical Presbyterian* was not more than 1,200 copies. But the scene would change. The God lives who can take the things that are not to 'put to nought the things that are'. There is truth for all Christians in the ancient promise, 'Gad, a troop shall overcome him: but he shall overcome at the last' (Gen. 49:19). History is to be judged, not by first successes or defeats, but by what happens 'at the last'. As John Bunyan said, 'at the last' means for ever, for nothing can come after the last.[40]

In the quarter century I knew Mr Grier he was to me a man of zeal. The first time I set eyes on him it was without knowing who he was. I was walking behind him to a Sovereign Grace Union conference at Grove Chapel, London, in the autumn of 1955. The road to it was uphill and I was surprised to see I was being outpaced by the older man ahead. Later, when I first visited the Grier home at Knockdene Park South, it was to find him cutting his lawns at a speed closer to running than walking. This was zeal which belonged to him as a natural gift. But his zeal as a Christian came from another source. Without it, mere natural zeal could have taken him in quite a different direction. He would have been well able to make a name as an author, and to attain to higher academic distinction. But he saw the work to which God had appointed him as higher work. The pastorate and the recovery of the reformed faith were his calling and in that context he would point others to the ambition of William Cunningham who declared before his death in 1861,

> the only credit due to him either in the pulpit or in the [professor's] chair was this and no more, that he had resuscitated Reformation doctrine, like Hodge, and caused the churches to look at its noble features.[41]

His life was fed by the prayerful devotion to Christ which led him to write:

> 'O for more zeal for the Lord and his good cause in the days ahead! May each one of us be able to say:

> > Loved of my God, for him again
> > With love intense I burn;
> > Chosen of him ere time began
> > I choose him in return.'

NOTE: THE RECOVERY OF
THE OLD PRINCETON SEMINARY AUTHORS

Among the earliest titles reprinted by the Banner of Truth Trust were *Lectures on Revival*, W. B. Sprague, 1958, 2007; *Princeton Sermons*, Charles Hodge, 1958, 1960, 1979, 2011; *The Way of Life*, Charles Hodge; *Thoughts on Religious Experience*, Archibald Alexander, 1967; *The Log College*, Archibald Alexander, 1968; *Counterfeit Miracles*, B. B. Warfield, 1972; *Faith and Life*, Warfield, 1974, 1990; *Outlines of Theology*, A. A. Hodge, 1972; *Thoughts on Preaching*, J. W. Alexander, 1975; *Biblical Theology*, Geerhardus Vos, 1975; *The New Testament, An Introduction*, J. Gresham Machen, 1976; *Evangelical Theology*, A. A. Hodge, 1976; *Studies in Theology*, B. B. Warfield, 1988; *Biblical Doctrines*, B. B. Warfield, 1988; *The Saviour of the World*, B. B. Warfield, 1991; *Grace and Glory*, Vos, 1992; *Princeton Versus the New Divinity, Articles from the Princeton Review*, 2001; *Life of Charles Hodge*, A. A. Alexander, 2010; *Pastor Teachers of Old Princeton, Memorial Addresses of Faculty*, ed. J. M. Garretson, 2012; *Princeton and the Work of the Ministry*, 2 vols., ed. J. M. Garretson, 2012.

In addition to the above, a number of valuable volumes by contemporary authors have been made available by various publishers.

For the history of Princeton Seminary, the best introduction is, *Princeton Seminary (1812–1929), the Leaders' Lives and Works*, Gary Steward (Phillipsburg, NJ: P&R, 2014). No less readable but much fuller are the two volumes by David B. Calhoun, *Princeton Seminary, Faith and Learning, 1812–1868*, and *Princeton Seminary, The Majestic Testimony, 1869–1929* (Edinburgh: Banner of Truth Trust, 1994 and 1996).

A number of outstanding books of biographical character have appeared, rightly led by a reprint of J. W. Alexander's

Life of Archibald Alexander (Harrisonburg, VA: Sprinkle Publications, 1991). None of the trilogy by James M. Garretson should be missed: *Princeton and Preaching, Archibald Alexander and the Christian Ministry* (Edinburgh: Banner of Truth Trust, 2005); *An Able and Faithful Ministry, Samuel Miller and the Pastoral Office* (Grand Rapids: RHB, 2014); and *Thoughts on Preaching and Pastoral Ministry, Lessons from the Life and Writings of J. W. Alexander* (Grand Rapids: RHB, 2015).

The work of the Evangelical Book Shop, 15 College Square East, Belfast, BT1 6DD, continues today. Copies of *'By Honour and Dishonour': The Story of the Evangelical Presbyterian Church* by Ernest C. Brown are available, as are a number of audio recordings of messages and addresses by Rev. W. J. Grier.

7

John MacArthur:
Preaching and Scripture

'The dominant strategy of Satan since the creation of the world has been to undermine trust in God's Word. It started in the Garden of Eden when he asked Eve, "Has God said?" In that devious, highly consequential question he was casting doubt on God's Word, and he hasn't stopped doing so since.

From that point forward, Satan's objective has been to lead as many people as possible to eternal destruction. And what has been the focal point of his attack on people's souls? Fomenting unbelief in and rejection of God's Word. Undermining people's confidence in the objective truth of Scripture, thereby taking away their only hope of salvation. "Has God said?" has become the battle cry of the entire world system in which we live.'

John MacArthur,
January, 2015.

I N February 1968, Martyn Lloyd-Jones ended his thirty years at Westminster Chapel, London. In the same month a year later, John MacArthur became pastor at a chapel in Sun Valley, California. No observable connexion existed between the two events; no more than there seemed to be any connexion between the death of Matthew Henry and the birth of George Whitefield in 1714. It is only with hindsight that we see more of the purposes of heaven. If Christ were ever short of true witnesses the very stones would cry out.

MacArthur was called to Grace Community Church as a twenty-nine-year-old Californian, and in that same charge he remains to this day. Born of godly parents—preachers on his father's side through many generations—and happily married in 1963, there is much which could be said about him. But to do so would not leave time to speak of what is of first importance. The *message* is more important than the messenger. What such men as Matthew Henry and George Whitefield *believed* is now of far more enduring significance than how they lived, and so it will always be, 'For all flesh is as grass ... But the word of the Lord endures forever' (1 Pet. 1:24, 25).

There is also the possibility that a concentration on Dr MacArthur's life might be more of a discouragement than a spur to contemporary preachers. It is not given to us to speak to thousands on the Lord's Day, or to yet larger numbers by radio and recordings across the world on weekdays. To hear of such ministry we can admire and be thankful, but it may have little apparent connection with our own circumstances. To speak and think of his message, however, should discourage no faithful pastor. Here we are on sure ground, and ground which our subject would be the first to endorse. John MacArthur wants no disciples. He insists: 'It's not the man;

it's the truth of God and the power of God in the man. The power is in the word—the truth that we preach—not in us. It is God's revelation for every generation.'

Yet a few biographical details are necessary to provide context for what follows.[1] I will limit myself to a few which were of a life-changing nature.

BIOGRAPHY

Brought up in a Christian home, and under his father's ministry, John did not know a time when he was not savingly related to Jesus Christ, but it was a car crash in his second year at Bob Jones University, South Carolina, in 1959, which God used to call him to the gospel ministry. Thrown out of the car in which he was a passenger at seventy miles an hour, the third-degree friction burns he suffered necessitated three months in hospital. Life was suddenly serious for him in a way it had not been before. His own thoughts of what his future might be were laid aside, together with a resistance to becoming a preacher.

That calling to the gospel ministry led to a firm purpose. He finished his Bachelor's degree in California, then proceeded to Talbot Theological Seminary, also in his home state. It is what happened after Talbot that I mention as another life-changing decision. Whether by the advice of others or his own choice, in 1964 he sought to prepare for entrance to Claremont School of Theology to study for a doctoral degree in theology. This involved two terms in the study of the German language, and familiarity with about 200 titles required by the reading list given to him. It became apparent to him that the list contained little other than liberal theology and humanistic philosophy. Further, a course had to be taken on 'Jesus and the Cinema', which involved watching a number of contemporary films and deciding whether or not they were supportive of the 'Jesus ethic'. For a young man of twenty-five, eager to find entrance for the gospel in wider circles, there must have been a temptation to go through the training for the prestigious degree which Claremont offered. But he made the right decision. His divine Saviour reduced to an 'ethic' was too much for him. Taking his college papers back to his adviser, he told him, 'I have spent all my life learning the truth, and I cannot see any value in spending the next couple of years learning error.' The academic door closed, and a far greater one was to open.

Life-changing in the fullest sense of the word was MacArthur's marriage to Patricia Sue Smith in August 1963. It had the foundation of every happy Christian marriage, first, commitment to Jesus Christ, and then to each other. Only then will priorities be in the right order. Without Patricia his whole life and ministry could not have been what they became. In his own words: 'The degree to which I have enjoyed success as a father, as a husband, and as a minister of the gospel, is a result of the investments she made in me each day.' On their fortieth wedding anniversary in 2003 he would write:

Through Patricia, God has filled our home with love, grace, and kindness. He has provided for me a godly partner and a daily source of joy, support, and accountability.

If whom we marry is the next most important thing to being a Christian, it is doubly so for every pastor. John Watson, advising students for the ministry on this point, warned that of all men, they 'ought to be most careful in the choice of a wife, for she may be either a help or hindrance not merely to his comfort but to his work'. A good wife, he continued,

advises her husband on every important matter, and often restrains him from hasty speech ... receives him weary, discouraged, irritable, and sends him out again strong, hopeful, sweet-tempered. The woman is in the shadow and the man stands in the open, and it is not until the woman dies and the man is left alone that the people or he himself knows what she has been.[2]

At the nineteenth-century date that Watson spoke these words, it was hardly necessary for him to add, 'One does not mean that a minister had better marry a woman who can preach and conduct meetings, in order that he may divide his duties with her.' By the time that John MacArthur began his ministry, Feminism was beginning to present a new idea of true womanhood, which he was called to oppose. But he was to do so, not by making woman the same as man, but by giving her the high place which the word of God gives to her:

> Eve was created ... a token of the marvellous grace of God to man. She was in no way an inferior character made merely to serve him, but she was his spiritual counterpart, his intellectual co-equal, and in every sense his perfect mate and companion.[3]

Thomas Charles, leader the evangelical awakening in North Wales at the beginning of the nineteenth century, once said, 'People are seeking this or that quality in their wives. I say, "Give me a praying wife."' For him, and for John MacArthur, that desire was fulfilled.

MacArthur's first ten years at Grace Community Church were comparatively quiet formative years, then, in 1979, events occurred which brought new dimensions to the ministry. The change began with a sudden outbreak of opposition. On February 3, the *Los Angeles Times* attacked his preaching under the heading 'Woman's Place is at Home'. More hostile media followed two months later when a young man who belonged to the church shot himself after a broken relationship with his girlfriend.

Closer still was a blow from close associates. While his elders were supportive, some of his pastoral staff, unknown to him, were not. To his shock it came into the open at a staff meeting in the early summer of 1979, when the leader of a mutiny told him, 'If you think we are your friends you have another think coming.' Significantly, all this happened while he was preaching a series on the Sermon on the Mount, spoken of as the most used series in the first eleven years of his ministry.

John himself saw those sermons as 'a major turning point in the life of our church'.[4]

It so happened that the summer of this same year 1979 had been planned as his first extended family break. For three months, with Patricia and their four children (Matt, Marcy, Mark, and Melinda), they toured the United States in a van. John would later speak of the time as 'the most interesting and memorable vacation we've had'. But it also had spiritual significance and 'ended up being important in shaping my ministry at Grace Community Church and at Grace to You'. Before this date, numbers at the church had risen steadily, and an organization within the congregation (later to be called 'Grace to You') took care of the circulation of tape recordings and the contacts with a few radio outlets. John recalled: 'While the ministry was growing, it was still small. Yet I had no idea how far-reaching and in demand it had already become. The trip my family took helped show me.'

What was planned primarily as a sight-seeing tour had led to many encounters with Christians and churches which were new to him. These unplanned meetings brought home to him that the pulpit of Grace Community was exercising an influence far wider than he had realised. The words of one young pastor stayed with him, 'John, don't do anything different and don't let anything change, because so many of us are depending on this kind of teaching.' Instead of being swayed off course by opposition, the summer of 1979 saw him confirmed in his belief in the power of the word of God. It was the same lesson he found at home on their return in September when, as Phil Johnson reports, his preaching of three months earlier 'was still ringing in the hearts of people in the church'.[5]

In the providence of God, this year 1979 also saw MacArthur make his first visit to Britain. The outreach of Grace to You was becoming international.

FAITH IN THE WORD OF GOD

I turn now to the subject on which there is perhaps most to be learned from his ministry. On occasion there have been enquiries made at Grace Community Church for information on how the numbers attending were made to grow, and what kind of programme produced the success. The assumption being that there must surely be a formula of some kind which others could adopt. Such enquirers meet with a disappointment. What MacArthur told them was not the answer they expected: 'I must ascribe our church's spiritual and numerical growth to the will of our sovereign God. There are no marketing techniques or modern methods that can explain it.'[6] He believes that God put him into the ministry at a time and in a place when there were numbers of the disillusioned and the confused whose hearts were to be opened to Christ. Such times and seasons are directed from heaven. There was no template to secure the same result elsewhere.

He was conscious that there were 'faithful saints in churches all across the country who sense that no matter how hard they work, no matter how faithful they are, their church still struggles, falters, veers off course and loses ground'. Obedience, not success, is the great thing. What counts supremely is the truth that is preached and in due course, one way or another, men will reap if they do not faint.

Of course, John MacArthur's thinking and belief has matured with the years, but its foundation has not changed in the slightest. From his youth the 'Fundamentalist' conviction, despised by so much of the professing church, possessed him: Holy Scripture is divine revelation, inerrant and infallible, delivered to us not in the words which man's wisdom teaches, but in the words the Holy Spirit teaches, God so directing the writers that '*all* Scripture is given by inspiration of God'. This a Christian believes, not because of the testimony of others, but because the same Holy Spirit bears compelling witness in his heart. The mark of the non-Christian is disbelief in 'the record that God gave of his Son'. 'He that believes on the Son of God has the witness in himself' (1 John 5:10).

The foremost characteristic of MacArthur's ministry has been the way God has enabled him to hold to the authority, sufficiency, and the finality of Scripture. I write 'enabled' deliberately, for making Scripture supreme is so inconsistent with this fallen world that continued obedience to its truth requires the Holy Spirit's work: 'That good thing which was committed unto thee keep by the Holy Spirit which dwells in us' (2 Tim. 1:13, 14).

It was his view of Scripture that led MacArthur into his first pastoral charge. Other forms of Christian service were possibilities for him, but his overriding desire was to be settled where the study of the word of God would be his chief occupation. He believed then, as he does now, that 'Scripture is an inexhaustible treasure that demands a lifetime just to begin to understand its riches. No one ever outgrows it or exhausts its immeasurable depth.' His deacons, on inviting him to Sun Valley, were surprised to hear him say he would need thirty hours a week alone. They came to understand what he meant, and the congregation felt the result. Phil Johnson, who joined Grace Community Church in 1983, found himself among a people with 'a fervent passion to understand and obey the word of God'. Scripture has now sustained John in the same congregation for almost half a century and supplied the sermons which go round the world in radio broadcasts and on the internet. No subject means more to him than the sufficiency of the word of God.

The lesson is the same at all periods of history. In 1816–17 a revival began among theological students in Geneva on account of the visit of Robert Haldane from Scotland. He invited these young men to the guest house where he stayed, and put Bibles, opened at the Epistle to the Romans, on the table at which they all sat. As this went on for several days, the contrast between what Paul wrote and what his hearers were being taught by their theological professors became very clear. It was Haldane's method, in response to questions or objections, simply to put his finger on the text. At a later date, when these guest-house meetings in Geneva, and the remarkable result, were being discussed, one of the men who was present was asked, 'How did Mr Haldane do it?' 'Oh, it was not Mr Haldane', was the answer, 'it was his finger'.

Such was the example MacArthur sought to follow as he, in turn, gathered young men around him—a grouping which led to formation of The Master's Seminary in 1986.

One of the best ways to understand MacArthur's ministry is to consider his convictions on what happens when the authority of Scripture is undermined, displaced, or not taken seriously by those who profess to believe it.

WITHOUT SCRIPTURE THE KNOWLEDGE OF GOD IS LOST

Although God is our Creator, sin has so corrupted us that the natural mind is 'at enmity to God' (Rom. 8:7). 'And because I tell you the truth, ye believe me not', Jesus said to the Jews (John 8:45). 'There is none who understands ... that seeks after God' (Rom. 3:11) 'The things of God knoweth no man' (1 Cor. 2:11). Deliverance from this darkness can only come by the action of God in making himself known, and this is what he has done in Scripture. Here is revelation. The infinite, eternal and unchangeable, speaks to us fallen mortals. Until we know him we are all idolaters, with no fear of God before our eyes. We have no concern for his glory, no care about being under his condemnation. No reverence for him.

This opens a question fundamental to the whole understanding of evangelism. The opponents of MacArthur's book *The Gospel According to Jesus* were correct in seeing that he was proposing teaching which was very disruptive of the popular evangelistic practice. He was saying that the presentation of the gospel must begin with God. The starting point is not what Jesus can do for you. The message must start with bad news, namely that God is holy and that in the light of that holiness the sinner stands condemned and worthy of hell. The first thing men need to hear is how contrary they are to God and that 'repentance towards God' is demanded of them. 'Trust in Jesus' is not the starting point.

> Evangelism must take the sinner and measure him against the perfect law of God so that he can see his deficiency. ... It is meaningless to expound on grace to someone who does not know the divine demand for righteousness.[7]

But to this the reply is given that surely our business is to make it easier, not harder, for people to believe. That statement reveals the depth of the disagreement. It treats salvation as something that is in man's hands, and ignores what is the real obstacle to conversion:

> There's only one reason why people who know the truth of the gospel are not willing to repent and believe. It is because they will not see themselves as the poor, prisoners, blind and oppressed. It has nothing to do with the style of music your church offers, the drama and skits you stage, or the quality of your laser light show. It has everything to do with the spiritual deadness and blindness of pride. God offers nothing to people who are content with their own condition, except judgment.[8]

> The Western church has subtly changed the thrust of the gospel. Instead of exhorting sinners to repent, evangelicalism in our society asks the unsaved to 'accept Christ'. ... This modified gospel depicts conversion as a 'decision for Christ' rather than a life-transforming change of heart involving genuine faith, repentance, surrender, and re-birth unto newness of life.[9]

It is no wonder if such words produce serious controversy. It means that many who believe themselves to be custodians of the gospel, have missed the way the Bible presents salvation as the work of God.

> Salvation always results because God first pursues sinners, not because sinners first seek God. ... No one seeks God unless God has first sought that person (cf. Rom. 3:11). Salvation is first of all a work of God and in no sense the result of human enterprise or individual longing. A blind man has no capacity to restore his own sight. Spiritual sight depends on God's initiative and God's power, offered in divine and sovereign grace.[10]

The parallel here with the preaching of Martyn Lloyd-Jones is marked. The two men never met, but it is not surprising that the truth they shared had the same effect on their ministries. As Steven J. Lawson has written, 'These are both no-nonsense men, marked by sobriety, gravity, and dignity.'[11]

WITHOUT SCRIPTURE A SENSE OF SIN IS LOST

The essence of sin is dependence on self, and esteem for self rather than God. Man worships and serves the creature more than the Creator who is blessed forever. He loves darkness rather than light. The condemnation pronounced on King Belshazzer belongs to the whole human race: 'You have praised the gods of silver and gold, bronze and iron, wood and stone, which do not see or hear or know; and the God who holds your breath in His hand and owns all your ways, you have not glorified' (Dan. 5:23).

Only the truth of Scripture reveals the true seriousness of sin. Jeremiah said of his contemporaries that they were so accustomed to sin, they could no longer blush; man is so habituated to the realm of sin that he is said to drink it 'like water'.

The great intention of Satan is to keep men in ignorance of the real nature of sin. Accordingly he orchestrates society and culture to hide the truth from them. He makes swearing popular because it demeans the character and the works of God. In a multitude of ways, we are conditioned to think nothing of sin, as if it is a matter of small consequence. One contemporary form of that conditioning has been to remove from public hearing some of the key words of Scripture. Such terms as 'sin', 'repentance', 'judgment', and 'hell', are gone. At the same time other words of Scripture are constantly misused. Trivial items or events are described as 'awesome'. The very name of God is turned into an exclamation useful for any sudden surprise. Our language has been so deliberately deconstructed that the traditional title for a married woman has come close to disappearing, while homosexuals are credited with being 'gay'.

MacArthur sees this programme for taking away the seriousness of sin as worthy of being called frightening.

> Remove the reality of sin, and you take away the possibility of repentance. Abolish the doctrine of human depravity and you void the divine plan of salvation. Erase the notion of personal guilt and you eliminate the need for a Saviour.[12]

WHERE THE BIBLE IS NOT UPHELD THE CHURCH TURNS TO OTHER MEANS TO PROMOTE HER INFLUENCE

Scripture teaches that there is a definite opposition between the wisdom of men and the wisdom of God, one is from beneath the other is from above. When this antithesis is passed over, the inevitable result is that the difference between the church and the world is toned down. This, in turn, justifies the introduction of changes in the church's work which are calculated to be more effective and acceptable in current society. So pastors 'stylize church meetings to look, sound, feel, and smell like the world, in order to remove the sinner's resistance and lure him into the kingdom down an easy and familiar path'.[13]

MacArthur has often spoken on this subject, and he does so with care. He does not hold that there is never change or adjustments in the way the church organi and her worship. There are areas of her life where alterations may be beneficial; Scripture does not lay down such things as the hours or length of public worship, nor the type of building in which Christians should meet. There can be no objection to changes on things not governed by Scripture, provided they are not contrary to Scripture. But what makes this subject so controversial today is that the call for change too often comes from a giving way to pressure from the world:

> The church in our age has abandoned the confrontive stance. Instead of overturning worldly wisdom with revealed truth, many Christians today are obsessed with finding areas of agreement. The goal has become *integration* rather than *confrontation*. As the church absorbs the values of secular culture, it is losing its ability to differentiate between good and evil.[14]

What has changed is not a question of details but of a whole mindset. The biblical mindset is for the church to put first the approval and honour of God. This has been displaced in many churches by the so-called need to 'contextualise' the gospel, to make it 'relevant' to our self-centred culture. 'Relevance' and 'accessibility' have become an obsession. It is not to be denied that the motive is sometimes good, namely, to speak to the people in meaningful language, but something is seriously wrong when relevance comes to be an excuse for toning down or suppressing biblical truth.[15]

An example will show that this danger is not imaginary. The New Testament makes clear that the church is holy, and that where the lives of her members contradict that character, action needs to be taken to preserve her purity. In the 1970s, preaching from 1 Corinthians 5, MacArthur had to address the scriptural teaching on this subject, but, not long after, when a situation arose in the membership requiring action, he discovered that church discipline was a long-neglected subject. When he discussed it with two other pastors, he describes their response: 'It won't work. The church will be wrecked. You can't have everyone looking out for other people's sins.'

MacArthur replied: 'The Bible says we are supposed to be accountable to one another. Let's just do it and see what God does.'[16]

The aim of discipline is, of course, the restoration of the offender. Love requires discipline, but in cases of serious sin, where there is no repentance, the matter needs to be addressed publicly, according to the scriptural direction, 'Them that sin rebuke before all, that others also may fear' (1 Tim. 5:20). But the above incident is an example of how no action is advised on a plain biblical duty because it is judged to be inexpedient in terms of the possible outcome. Supposed 'usefulness' is thus elevated and the pragmatism of the age rather than Scripture is given superiority. But Scripture has given clear warning against our being wiser than God. There was radical church discipline in the infant church at Jerusalem. Ananias and Sapphira, generous supporters of the work, were struck dead for telling a lie. The result was 'great fear came upon all the church, and upon as many as heard these things' (Acts 5:11). Did this become a hindrance to the spread of the gospel? Not at all! On the contrary, Luke tells us, 'believers were added to the Lord, multitudes of men and women' (Acts 5:1-14). It is as the church is most God-centred that there is the greatest impact on the world. So we read in the same history, when the churches were 'walking in the fear of the Lord', they also knew the 'comfort of the Holy Spirit' and 'were multiplied' (Acts 9:31).

Those who think that wider usefulness necessitates keeping as close as possible to the culture have cause from MacArthur's ministry to think again. His preaching is heard daily from India and the Philippines to Scotland and South Africa. Large numbers of the earth's population, in entirely different cultures, hear the very same message that was recorded in southern California. Since recordings of his sermons became available freely on the web in 2008 more than 100 million have been downloaded. Can preaching so lacking in 'contextualization' be effective? The evidence is that it can. How could it be otherwise? The word of God towers above all the details of time and cultural difference. It confronts mankind across the world and across the ages. It calls, this preacher would say, not for salesmen but for prophets, and dismisses the allegation that treats 'preaching the word and boldly confronting sin as archaic, ineffectual means of winning the world'. To the plea for cultural relevance he responds:

> Church history is strewn with examples of those who thought they could mould the message for their own time—but ended by corrupting the truth. … If church history teaches us anything, it is that different times do not require different messages. Those who preach anything other than the unadulterated gospel forfeit the power of God in their ministries. Nothing is wrong with the message. … If they don't hear the truth, cool music won't help. If they don't see the light, power-point won't help. If they don't like the message, drama and video won't help. They're blind and dead. Our task is to go on preaching not ourselves, we carry a supernatural message of everlasting life.[17]

When asked. 'How do you translate into other languages and cultures?' he replied: 'That has never been an issue. Because if you teach the Bible it transcends every border, every language, every culture. It is as relevant today, and will be tomorrow, as in all the years since God put it down.'[18]

WHERE SCRIPTURE IS NOT HONOURED DOCTRINE IS DISCOUNTED

The contemporary evangelical situation demonstrates that it is possible for there to be regular preaching, with quotation from Scripture, and devotional application, and yet the sermons may have little or no doctrinal content. It may be pleasant preaching, it may be replete with stories and illustrations, and require little or no mental effort on the part of hearers, but it is a long way from a proclamation of 'the whole counsel of

God'. Doctrine has to do with the distilling of biblical truth into principles which can be definitely stated and seen as part of a coherent whole. A piecemeal understanding of truth is not enough, we need to know how one doctrine relates to another; how does law relate to grace; how does divine justice relate to the atonement; how does regeneration relate to faith, and so on. Without this, the capacity for discernment in a Christian will be greatly weakened. In MacArthur's words:

> Doctrine is not the exclusive domain of seminar professors. All true Christians must be concerned with understanding sound doctrine. It is the discipline of discerning and digesting what God is saying to us in his word so that we can live lives which glorify him. Doctrine forms the belief system that controls behaviour. What could be more practical—or more important?[19]

Doctrine gives stability and permanence. On the question whether sermons should come in a series on a consecutive passage of Scripture, or in distinct and individual texts from week to week, there is room for differences of opinion. But on the question whether sermons should have doctrinal content there should be no debate at all.

Yet it has been the experience of all faithful preachers that doctrine is commonly not regarded as desirable. This has certainly been MacArthur's experience. He has sent books to evangelical publishers and received the comment 'too doctrinal'. Doctrine, supposedly, is divisive. John goes as far as saying that for 'much of the visible church nowadays ... the idea of actually *fighting* for doctrinal truth is the furthest thing from most churchgoers'.[20] He is surely right in saying that this attitude has filtered down from what he calls 'the elite echelons of the evangelical academic world'. He is referring to those whose first concern is not to transmit the spiritual heritage of the past, but rather to interact with contemporary thought and scholarship in a way to make evangelical belief more popular and respectable.

The question of whether the latest trend is dangerous or not is not a welcome question in most evangelical circles anymore. Whatever happens to be popular at the moment is what drives the whole evangelical agenda.[21]

What lies behind this development is a loose view of Scripture as the only rule for faith and conduct. In practice, Scripture is no longer treated as sufficient and final. It is as though God has not revealed certainties worth dying for. After MacArthur published his book, *The Gospel According to Jesus*, he tells us that what disappointed him was not the negative comment it received, it was the nature of that comment:

> The overwhelming majority of criticisms have nothing what-ever to do with biblical matters. Some reviewers have complained that the lordship issue is too divisive, the message too hard, or my position too dogmatic. Others have argued semantics or taken exception to my terminology ... none of them deals with the *biblical* particulars.[22]

In referring to how he came to publish that controversial book, MacArthur has commented on how the material came out of the Gospel of Matthew. When he took up that Gospel for Sunday preaching in 1978 he had supposed it would not be 'doctrinally taxing', rather a break 'from the more didactic and doctrinal style of the Pauline Epistles'. He was mistaken: 'Matthew brought my doctrinal convictions into sharp focus and amplified several truths in my heart and mind that continue to be the backbone of everything I preach.'[23]

SCRIPTURE AND UNITY

On occasion, MacArthur has been prominent in controversies which have divided evangelicals. Those taking an opposing view have had their own reasons, sometimes claiming that they were acting in the interest of preserving unity. Too often, however, there has been a failure to recognise that Scripture does not allow Christian leaders to teach only a minimal statement of faith. MacArthur has had to differ with evangelical voices raised for unity who have argued for 'mere Christianity' and insisted only on the so-called 'Apostles' Creed'. That creed has been regarded as enough for a united stand for super-naturalism against anti-Christian forces; but, as MacArthur has pointed out, this supposed minimal basis says nothing on such essential truths as the sole authority of Scripture, and on how a sinner is justified by Christ alone—works playing no part in the obedience which justifies before God. A unity which ignores such crucial issues constitutes an indifference to the rule of Scripture.[24]

Despite necessary controversy, and sometimes because of it, John MacArthur's ministry has played a leading part in the formation of a much stronger unity among Christians. The past forty years have seen a major re-alignment of preachers and churches in the United States. Before that date evangel-icals identified with Fundamentalism had little connexion with evangelicals adhering to the Protestant and reformed confes-sions of an earlier generation. That latter tradition had faltered and weakened in a general theological decline. But then a new interest in Scripture, with the same understanding as marked the Reformation and Puritan periods, began to appear in dif-ferent parts of the United States, and has transcended the former party and denominational groupings.

This brought men of different backgrounds to stand to-gether in a new way. I had seen something of the change before 1997, but it was in that year that I experienced how strong this influence was in Dr MacArthur's congregation. The occasion was a Shepherds' Conference, a gathering of a few thousand pastors, among whom such authors as Jonathan Edwards and Martyn Lloyd-Jones were being read with enthusiasm. The tide had turned, even if not all present were clear why. In a Question and Answer session one man asked why the minister of Grace Community Church was being identified with 'the reformed'. Others saw in what was happening a fulfilment of what Spurgeon had said before his death in 1892: 'I am quite willing to be eaten of dogs for the next fifty years; but the more distant future will vindicate me.'[25] The truths preached by a former generation had re-appeared, and forgotten authors were being studied again. Thus MacArthur, in answering the claim that 'mere Christianity' is enough, gave effective quotes from Herman Witsius and Francis Turretin,[26] and, when asked to list the books that had the greatest impact on his life, he named Thomas Watson's *The Beatitudes* and *A Body of Divinity*, and Stephen Charnock's *Existence and Attributes of God*.[27]

Out of this doctrinal re-awakening across the United States came strong convictions, strong enough to cause a break in some former ties, but big enough to forge a wider, spiritual, and gospel unity. In his own deepening commitment to the evangelicalism of a former generation, John MacArthur had lost some of his earlier connexions. He had also made a stand against such popular things as mass evangelism, and the charismatic movement, conscious in doing so that he might lose rather than gain support. He kept to the principle 'Do what is right, regardless of the consequences'.[28] Yet instead of being isolated, his ministry became a unifying influence and a focal point for many of a younger generation, and that not only in the English-speaking world. When Robert Provost was in the Soviet Union in 1989 he asked an evangelical leader, Yakov Dukhonchenko, if he had he heard of John MacArthur. 'Do you mean the brother who wrote the book *The Charismatics*?' was the reply. When Dr Provost said, 'Yes', Dukhonchenko pounded his big fist on his desk while exclaiming, 'I believe like that brother!'[29]

Iain D. Campbell, a British reviewer of my biography of Dr MacArthur, thought it 'quite remarkable' that I should have written it, 'Separated by continents, ecclesiastical affiliations, and even points of doctrine, the subject is a strange one for the author.'[30] The comment is understandable. My subject and I come from different traditions, he a Baptist and I a

Presbyterian. My writing his biography, however, involved no hiding of differences; rather it was an example of how unity and esteem, under the rule of Scripture, is a reality even where there is not unanimity in understanding all that Scripture teaches. Those who wait for the fuller light, and the perfect brotherhood in heaven, can in the meantime do all they can to support one another. As Archibald Alexander once said at the end of his long life:

> Real Christians agree much more perfectly in experimental religion, than they do in speculative points; a more intimate acquaintance among Christians of different denominations would have a happy tendency to unite them more closely in the bonds of brotherly love.[31]

One factor in John MacArthur's ministry is too important to be left out in this chapter. It is that he could never have done what he was given to do had he not also been given the support of a wide circle of fellow Christians. The work grew as the circle grew, with the love and devotion to Christ of his own congregation at its centre. To say he had a 'team' of helpers would be an understatement. Rather, *Moody Monthly* in 1973 called Grace Community Church 'The Church with Nine Hundred Ministers.' What was meant, as I came to appreciate on subsequent visits, was that a common spirit is to be seen in the church—a love which unites, enlarges, and energises the whole. Truth came first, but not as an end in itself, it is in order to conformity to Christ. As Paul writes, that we 'speaking the truth in love, may grow up into him in all things, which is the head, even Christ' (Eph. 4:15). Essential as sound doctrine is, love is the final test which shows how well Christ has been received: 'By this all people will know that you are my disciples, if you have love one for another' (John 13:35). And humility goes with love. The more we know Christ, the more we feel our present lack. Every church and every preacher is presently in an unfinished state. But 'when he appears, we shall be like him', and made perfect in love: 'They shall not find faith there, for that is gone into vision, nor hope there, for that is gone into fruition; but they shall find love there, yea, there they shall find nothing but love. "There abideth faith, hope, and love, these three; but the greatest of these is love" (1 Cor. 13:13).'[32]

NOTE: THE INERRANT WORD

The Inerrant Word: Biblical, Historical, Theological and Pastoral Perspectives (Wheaton; Crossway, 2016), ed. John MacArthur.

In this important book, published after the preceding chapter was written, there is the fullest coverage of Scripture as the word of God. It consists of addresses given at the Shepherds' Conference, Los Angeles, California, in 2015, with two chapters, a Foreword, and an Afterword, by Dr MacArthur. We know of none more qualified than he to speak of the dangers facing contemporary Christianity, as a few quotations illustrate:

> In order to gain acceptance in a postmodern society, the church became soft on sin and error. Capitulation was masked as tolerance; compromise redefined as love; and doubt extolled as humility. So-called evangelicals started to champion the message that 'we all worship one God'. And those willing to stand for truth were dismissed as divisive and uncouth.
>
> Some books can change a person's thinking, but only the Bible can change the sinner's nature. It is the only book that can totally transform someone from the inside out. When

God's word is proclaimed and defended, it goes forth with Spirit-generated power.

The church has always managed to grow amid the fiercest worldly antagonism. It's a pattern that was established in the first generation of church history. Acts 12:1-2 records how James, the first apostolic martyr, was killed by direct order of Herod. That immediately launched a violent systematic, worldwide persecution. But don't miss how Luke summarises the impact of this persecution on the church. He ends that same chapter with this report: 'The word of God increased and multiplied' (Acts 12:24). By the second century, Tertullian was saying that the blood of the martyrs was the seed of the church. The pattern continues even now. Just in the past half-century, the church has grown behind the Communist Iron Curtain amid horrible persecution—while in free Western Europe, a fascination with theological novelties and a corresponding move away from Scripture has left churches moribund.

Survey all church history and you will discover an unsettling fact: the most pernicious and spiritually devastating assaults on the church have always come from within—via subtle attempts to undermine the authority of Scripture. Artful deceit is more dangerous and more destructive than open rebellion. Wolves don sheep's clothing. Satan and his demonic minions disguise themselves as angels of light. They always insist that the church must adapt her strategy and methodology or she will lose the next generation. That very claim is a subtle attack on the authority of Scripture.

Endnotes

CHAPTER 1

[1] The two titles are now republished in one volume, Edward Morgan, *John Elias, Life, Letters and Essays* (Edinburgh: Banner of Truth, 2004).

[2] In later years, after Elias had learned English, it would be said of him by Dr Jenkyn 'that he had collected more of the Puritan theology into his mind than any man of his age'.

[3] John Morgan Jones and William Morgan, *The Calvinistic Methodist Fathers of Wales*, translated by John Aaron, vol. 2, p. 754. The two volumes under this title were originally published in 1890 and 1897 as *Y Tadau Methodistaidd*. Hereafter cited as *Fathers of Wales*.

[4] I have written on Charles in *Heroes* (Edinburgh: Banner of Truth Trust, 2009), pp. 317-42. *Thomas Charles's Spiritual Counsels, Selected from his Letters and Papers* (1836; Edinburgh: Banner of Truth Trust, 1993) is a valuable book.

[5] D. E. Jenkins, *Life of Thomas Charles of Bala*, (Denbigh: Jenkins, 1910), vol. 2, pp. 89-91. This three-volume biography is regrettably rare. This was the first awakening in North Wales. Speaking of the country as a whole, Charles says in the same letter: 'Within these fifty years there have been five or six very great awakenings: a land of darkness and the shadow of death hath seen great light.'

[6] *Ibid.*, pp. 97-98.

[7] Morgan, *Elias*, p. 17.

[8] Owen Jones, *Some of the Great Preachers of Wales* (London; Passmore & Alabaster, 1885), p. 272. Writing more than forty years after the death of Elias, some of the anecdotes given by this author need to be treated with care. Yet, as Spurgeon said in reviewing this

title, 'Mr Jones's remarks upon the unction of the old Welsh preachers, and that mighty prayerfulness which was their main strength, deserve to be written in letters of gold.' *Sword and the Trowel* (1886), p. 83.

[9] Most of such statements by Elias are drawn from a short piece of autobiography written in the last year of his life when he was 66, and recorded in his *Life* by Edward Morgan.

[10] *Fathers of Wales*, vol. 2, p. 653.

[11] *Ibid.*, p. 658. One of the 'Rules of Discipline' later set down for Society members was, 'They must avoid all those modes and fashions of dress which tend to foster pride, wantonness, or extravagance, and "adorn themselves in modest apparel, with shamefacedness and sobriety, as becometh those professing godliness". 1 Tim. 2:10; 1 Pet. 3:2.' *History, Constitution, Rules of Discipline and Confession of Faith of the Calvinistic Methodists, or the Presbyterians of Wales* (1823; repr. ed., Carnarvon: General Assembly, 1900), p. 25. Below I will cite as *Confession of Faith*.

[12] Morgan, *Elias*, p. 101.

[13] *Ibid.*, p. 267. 'The observance or profanation of this holy day is like a weather glass, shewing signs of the rise or fall of a nation. This is also applicable to particular persons' (p. 384).

[14] *Fathers of Wales*, vol. 2, pp. 653-4. This was wise advice Elias himself would offer with respect to a young preacher who was to visit Liverpool: 'Don't praise him, especially before his face, for he is but young. On the other hand, don't look cross or stern on him, despising his youth, that he may not be discouraged, but pray for him.' Morgan, *Elias*, p. 245.

[15] Morgan, *Elias*, pp, 75-76. The authors of *Fathers of Wales* (vol. 2, p. 660) comment, 'the Methodist Connexion should thank heaven for the wives of preachers for without them the preachers, however great their talent, could not have accomplished the work they did'.

[16] Morgan, *Elias*, pp. 294-95.

[17] *Ibid.*, pp. 297, 289.

[18] *Ibid.*, p.123.

[19] *Ibid.*, p. 89.

[20] R. Tudur Jones, *John Elias, Prince Amongst Preachers,* Annual Lecture (Bridgend: Evangelical Library of Wales, 1975), p. 11, whose account of this event I have followed.

[21] An outline of another Elias sermon on the same text is given in the second edition of Morgan's *Elias* (Leicester: Spencer, 1863), pp. 115-19.

[22] *The Great Sermons of the Great Preachers, Ancient and Modern* (London: Ward and Lock, n.d.), p. 328. In contrast to the practice of Elias, I recently heard a lecturer on preaching advise that starting a sermon with a text was likely to be boring!

[23] *Fathers of Wales*, vol. 2, p. 722.

[24] Tudur Jones, *Prince Among Preachers*, p. 9.

[25] *Ibid.*, p. 6.

[26] I have evidence for this beside me as I write. A copy of the *Works of Andrew Gray* (repr. ed. Falkirk, 1789), carries the pencil inscription, 'John Elias's Book Bought it at London Jan. 23, 1806 for 2/6'. Among other London purchases were *The Christian Minister*, by Charles Bulkley (London, 1758), and *Sketches and Hints of Church History*, by John Erskine (Edinburgh, 1797).

[27] Jenkins, *Life of Charles*, vol. 3, p. 36.

[28] *Ibid.*, p. 402.

[29] *Ibid.*, p. 271. He reports how a speech of the Rev. Rowland Hill contributed to this break with the Church of England. Hill said: 'He loved the ministers who preach the gospel within its pale; but that, inasmuch as the generality of its ministers deny the doctrine to which they have once pledged themselves, pious people have been obliged to leave it, and that the children of God cannot live on chaff.'

[30] *Ibid.*, p. 570.

[31] See Elias's 'Thoughts on the Bible', and 'On the Use of Reason', in Morgan, *Life*, pp. 339-49.

[32] Martyn Lloyd-Jones was no more handicapped than was Elias. Yet a recent writer thought it necessary to tell us that Lloyd-Jones 'had undertaken no formal study of theology, but neither had he any formal qualifications or academic standing as a biblical scholar'. T. A. Noble, *Tyndale House and Fellowship: the First Fifty Years* (Leicester: IVP, 2006), p. 70.

[33] *The Experimental Knowledge of Christ, and Additional Sermons of John Elias*, tr. Owen Milton (Grand Rapids; RHB, 2006), p. 40.

[34] Quoted in the *Banner of Truth* (April, 1959), p. 8.

[35] Morgan, *Elias*, p.142.

[36] *Confession of the Faith*, p. 23.

[37] Morgan, *Elias*, p. 300.

[38] *Fathers of Wales*, vol. 2, pp. 742-43.

[39] D. M. Lloyd-Jones, *Revival* (Basingstoke: Marshall Pickering, 1986), p. 152.

[40] Emyr Roberts, *Revival in Wales, Addresses in the Bala Ministers' Conference*, ed. John Aaron and John Emyr, pp. 153-54.

[41] Morgan, *Elias*, p. 249.

[42] *Ibid.*, p. 259.

[43] Morgan, *Elias*, pp. 228, 234. Elias grieved that, 'For every one of Christ's listeners, I have ten. ... Men take great delight in listening to us, without ever listening to him.' *Experimental Knowledge of Christ*, p. 38.

[44] *Ibid.*, p. 70.

[45] I write 'source', but the first publisher in Wales is said to have been his pupil, John Roberts of Llanbryn-Mair.

[46] Further information on this will be found in W. B. Sprague, *Lectures on Revivals*, (1832, repr. Edinburgh: Banner of Truth Trust, 2007); *Princeton V. the New Divinity, Articles from the Princeton Review, between 1830 and 1842* (Edinburgh: Banner of Truth Trust, 2001); and my *Revival & Revivalism: the Making and Marring of American Evangelicalism* (Edinburgh: Banner of Truth Trust, 1994).

[47] Owen Thomas, *Cofiant John Jones, Talsarn* (Wrexham, Hughes, 1874).

[48] *The Atonement Controversy in Welsh Theological Literature and Debate, 1707–1841*, Owen Thomas, tr. John Aaron (Edinburgh: Banner of Truth, 2000). The translation of this work, and the same translator's work in making available the two volumes of *Fathers in Wales*, has constituted a major opening into Welsh church history for English readers. The personal bias of Owen Thomas can be seen in his condemnation of the Introduction by Elias to John Hurrion's

book, *Particular Redemption*. This title, with Elias's Introduction, is scheduled for republication by the Trust in 2017.

[49] *Atonement Controversy*, p. xxvi.

[50] W. T. Williams, *Edward Williams, His Life, Thought and Influence* (Cardiff: University of Wales), p. xl. No evidence is provided that there was much hyper-Calvinism in North Wales. We are told only that a book by the English hyper-Calvinist, Willliam Huntington, was printed in Welsh, and that one unnamed minister once told his congregation, 'If I knew who here today was predestinated to eternal life I would not say one word to the rest.' *Fathers of Wales*, vol. 2, p. 605. Yet Owen Thomas claimed, 'the land was to a significant degree leavened with very high Calvinistic ideas' [terminology used inter-changeably with 'hyper-Calvinism', there being no exact word for the latter in Welsh]. *Atonement Controversy*, p. 161.

[51] Edward Morgan, *Life and Times of Howel Harris* (Holywell: Morris, 1852), p.139.

[52] *Atonement Controversy*, p. 291.

[53] 'Let a man go to the grammar school of faith and repentance, before he goes to the university of election and predestination.' *George Whitefield's Journals* (London: Banner of Truth Trust, 1960), p. 491.

[54] The hymn, 'And was it for my sin', translated by Noel Gibbard, is #199 in *Christian Hymns* (Bridgend: Evangelical Movement of Wales, 1977). I am indebted to John Aaron for the story behind its composition.

[55] Morgan, *Elias*, p.317.

[56] Letter of August 17, 1819, quoted in Tudur Jones, *Prince Amongst Preachers*, p. 27. This was the standard teaching among Puritans. Richard Sibbes, in answer to the same question put to Elias, replied: 'The gospel runs, whoever believes in Christ shall have the fruits of the death of Christ, shall have everlasting life. Thus whosoever believes and casts himself upon Christ, doth the act, shall have the fruit. Away with idle questions … "Did he die for me?" Go to the act; if thou hast grace to cast thyself upon Christ, to assent when he offers and invites thee, it is well.' 'Salvation Applied', *Works*, vol. 5, pp. 390-91. John Owen has the same answer, 'Many disputes

there are whether Christ died for all individuals of mankind or no. If we say, "No, but only for the elect, who are some of all sorts", some then tell us we cannot then invite all men promiscuously to believe. But why so?' *Works*, vol. 6, p. 523.

[57] Williams, *Edward Williams*, pp. 125-26.

[58] *Ibid.*, p. 105.

[59] Preface to Welsh 1820 edition of the sermons of John Hurrion, *The Scripture Doctrine of Particular Redemption, Stated and Vindicated*, translated by John Aaron in *Banner of Truth*, issue 638. Owen Thomas was very critical of Elias for this Preface, *Atonement Controversy*, p. 88. The distinctions drawn by Williams were praised by his admirers as able 'to clear away those mists and offensive vapours which had arisen from the deep valley of partial or particular redemption'. 'Memoir of Edward Williams' in John Morrison, *Fathers and Founders of the London Missionary Society*, vol. 2 (London: Fisher, n.d.), p. 371. But the distinctions were not new. Similar terminology had been used in the seventeenth century by Richard Baxter who supported the idea of a hypothetical redemption. See the critique by J. I. Packer in *Redemption & Restoration of Man in the Thought of Richard Baxter* (Vancouver: Regent College, 2003), pp. 223-36. The sermons of Hurrion were delivered as part of the Lime Street Lectures and can be found at https://archive.org/details/defenceofsomeimp184phil. They are also scheduled for republication by the Trust in 2017

[60] *Atonement Controversy*, p. 294. As had been done in the seventeenth century, the attempt was made to get round this by arguing that in the redemptive work of Christ, there is no equivalence between the *price* (his own divine person) and the *debt* sinners owe. But the price was being paid by a divine person because divine justice demanded propitiation of such greatness. Equivalence was therefore a legitimate term and was so used by orthodox theologians, including Thomas Charles. It would appear that prolonged debate on this point by opponents of particular redemption was a diversion from the plain scriptural sense of ransom. Charles was right to comment at an early stage in the controversy: 'We judged it also unnecessary to assert of debate, whether Christ's death is, or is not, a sufficient atonement for the whole world, nor whether he would have had to

suffer more if every man was saved. No one shall be lost through a lack of sufficiency in the atonement, but for all that will be lost it will be because they would not come to Christ to be saved, and these shall have no excuse for their neglect of him. It is best to leave our speculations aside and confine ourselves within the appropriate limits of scriptural statements.' *Atonement Controversy*, p. 292. This counsel was not heeded by subsequent promoters of the controversy.

[61] *Confession of the Faith*, p. 74.

[62] The party of younger men, wanting revision, advanced the view which would later be popularized, that the 'narrow' statement on redemption was contrary to the beliefs of the founders of the denomination. Howel Harris wrote: 'I think we all agree with the good old orthodox Reformers and Puritans; I hold their works in great esteem—We do not think the Baxterian Scheme [of a universal atonement] orthodox.' Morgan, *Life and Times of Howel Harris*.

[63] John Owen, *Works of John Owen*, ed. William H. Goold (1850–53; repr. London: Banner of Truth Trust, 1965–68) *Works*, vol. 10, p. 433.

[64] So the rebirth, by which alone the individual is able to 'receive the things of the Spirit of God' (1 Cor. 2:14), is supposed to follow, not precede, faith in Christ, contrary to John 6:44; Acts 16:14; etc.

[65] For references and fuller discussion see, Murray, *Revival & Revivalism*, pp. 261-62.

[66] *Confession of Faith*, p. 75. Christ 'purchased, not only reconciliation, but an everlasting inheritance in the kingdom of heaven, for all those whom the Father hath given unto him' (*Westminster Confession of Faith*).

[67] Morgan, *Elias*, pp. 363-64. See also p. 240.

[68] *Atonement Controversy*, p. 324.

[69] Morgan, *Elias*, p. 268.

[70] *Fathers of Wales*, vol. 2, p. 745.

[71] *Fathers of Wales*, vol. 2, p. 745.

[72] John Owen believed the same influence was at work in those teaching a general redemption in his day: 'It is a thing of the saddest consideration possible, that wise and learned men should once

suppose, by tempering the truths of God ... to remove the scandal and offence ... to force the mysteries of the gospel to a condescension and suitableness unto the unpurged relics of the wisdom of nature.' *Works of John Owen*, vol. 10, p. 432.

73 *Thomas Charles's Spiritual Counsels*, p. 388.

74 T. Rees, *History of Protestant Nonconformity in Wales* (London: Snow, 1861), p. 464.

75 *Atonement Controversy*, p. 363. The words which immediately continue to point to a different situation then existing at the level of church membership: 'Furthermore, and in one sense even more valuable, the people nearly everywhere not only tolerate this but demand it.' The change had to be the result of a fear Elias had expressed in his later years, 'There are but few ministers that fully show that salvation springs entirely out of the sovereign grace of God.'

76 *Confession of Faith*, p. 130.

77 *Atonement Controversy*, translator's Introduction, p. xviii.

78 Quoted in Roberts, *Revival in Wales*, p. 169.

79 Owen, *Edward Williams*, pp. 149-50.

80 *An All-round Ministry* (1900; repr. London: Banner of Truth Trust, 1960), p. 285.

81 Morgan, *Elias*, p. 259.

82 Jenkins, *Life of Charles*, vol. 2, p. 98.

83 It is noteworthy that the great need which Elias emphasised near the end of his life is the same as would be emphasised by J. C. Ryle. He complained of sermons lacking 'life, and light, and fire, and love', and asked, 'Can nothing be done to restore health to our Zion? I answer, Nothing, in my opinion, but outpouring of the Holy Spirit. More schools and universities will not set us right. They touch heads but not hearts. Spiritual is the disease, and spiritual must be the remedy. In plain words we need among us more of the "real presence" of the Holy Ghost. For this let us all pray and besiege the throne of grace continually.' *Charges and Addresses* (Edinburgh: Banner of Truth Trust, 1978), pp. 352, 368.

84 William Williams, tr. William Howells.

CHAPTER 2

[1] W. Robertson Nicoll, *Princes of the Church* (Hodder & Stoughton, 1921), p. 55. He added; 'Let those who think we have praised this book too highly read it: they will not think so then.'

[2] K. R. Ross, under Bonar A. A., in *Dictionary of Scottish Church History and Theology* (Edinburgh: T & T Clark, 1993).

[3] John Macleod, *Scottish Theology: In Relation to Church History Since the Reformation* (Edinburgh: Banner of Truth Trust, 1974), p. 277.

[4] Fergus Ferguson, *Life of Andrew A. Bonar* (Glasgow; Rae, 1893), p. 202. The same book tells us that when Andrew Bonar was 'dux' at Edinburgh High School, those placed second and third were men who would be, respectively, Archbishop of Canterbury, and Lord President of the Court of Session.

[5] I have written on Horatius Bonar in Iain H. Murray, *A Scottish Christian Heritage* (Edinburgh: Banner of Truth Trust, 2006).

[6] Thorngreen, Sacher, and Kinrossie.

[7] Cotton Mather, *The Great Works of Christ in America* [*Magnalia Christi Americana*],(repr. Edinburgh: Banner of Truth Trust, 1979), vol. 1, p. 562. Bonar's variation of that statement was, 'God can do anything by or for a man in Christ.'

[8] 'The Holy Spirit Convicting', in Andrew Bonar, *Sheaves After Harvest: A Group of Addresses* (London: Pickering and Inglis, n.d.), p. 77.

[9] *Narrative of a Mission of Inquiry to the Jews from the Church of Scotland in 1839* (Edinburgh: Whyte, 1842); repr. *Mission of Discovery*, A. Bonar and R. M. M'Cheyne, ed. Allan Harman (Fearn, Ross-shire: Christian Focus, 1996).

[10] Andrew A. Bonar; *Diary and Letters*, ed. Marjory Bonar (London: Hodder & Stoughton, 1894), p. 85 [p. 58]. My quotations from the *Diary* are from this edition. It was reprinted by Banner of Truth Trust, 1960 and 1984, where the pagination differs by four pages, i.e. p. 85 of the original is p. 81 in the reprint. In 2013 the Trust issued a retypeset edition, and page references to that edition are supplied in square brackets.

[11] *Reminiscences of Andrew Bonar*, Marjory Bonar (London: Hodder & Stoughton, 1895), p. 14 [p. 305]. This book, most of which was reprinted in the Banner 1960 and 1984 editions of *Diary and Life*, is a valuable addition to information on Bonar's life and character.

[12] *Diary*, p. 91 [p. 62].

[13] *Diary of Jessie Thain*, ed. Murdoch Campbell (Inverness: privately published, 1955), pp. 32-33, 54-55. It is stated, on the authority of Alexander Smellie, that M'Cheyne was engaged to Jessie Thain at the time of his death.

[14] Through his bachelor days at Collace his home was run by his sister Christian. When she died in 1862, he wrote: 'Christian was ten years with me at Collace, and I am certain she never once all that time spoke to me one unkind word or did one selfish act.' *Reminiscences*, p. 207.

[15] A recent writer represents Bonar's motives in going to Glasgow as the need 'to expand his circle of ecclesiastical influence' and to advance his prophetic beliefs. *Prisoners of Hope? Aspects of Evangelical Millennialism in Britain and Ireland, 1800-1880*, eds. Crawford Gribben and T. C. F. Stunt (Milton Keynes: Paternoster, 2004), p. 200. Bonar was premillennial in his prophetic beliefs (see his *Redemption Drawing Nigh*, 1847), in contrast with the prevailing postmillennialism of a majority of the Free Church of Scotland, but to say, as Gribben does, 'It was concern to maintain premillennial orthodoxy and biblical inerrancy that forced Andrew Bonar to abandon the Westminster Confession of Faith', is absurd. On the basis of a book, *The Development of the Antichrist* (1853), Gribben alleges Bonar engaged in 'a major revision of his earlier writings', evidently unaware that this work was not written by Andrew A. Bonar of Glasgow, but by Andrew Bonar Esq., a layman of Leamington.

[16] *Princes of the Church*, pp. 57-58. At the close of 1857, Marjory Bonar wrote, 'The roll of communicants was 136.' At that date numbers of churchgoers were not communicants; she speaks of the usual attendance as 'from 400 to 500'. Nicoll's figure may be more accurate; 'We remember him saying that for a year his average congregation did not amount to two hundred persons.' These were low numbers in that more churchgoing era.

17 Ferguson, *Life*, p. 242.

18 Something of what Bonar was as a pastor can be seen in his valuable little book, *The Visitor's Book of Texts; or, The Word Brought Nigh to the Sick and Sorrowful* (London: Nisbet, 7th ed., 1887; repr. Edinburgh: Banner of Truth Trust, 2010). This contains characteristic guidance such as the following: 'Persevere in declaring the good news of God's grace to the guilty. But we must never be formal in so doing. We must every time tell of what we have felt and have been using for ourselves.'

19 *Reminiscences*, p. 215 [p. 290].

20 Ferguson, *Life*, p. 215.

21 Ferguson, *Life*, p. 218.

22 C. H. Spurgeon, *Lectures to My Students,* (1875–94; repr. Edinburgh: Banner of Truth Trust, 2008), p. 45. Bonar added sermons and writings of M'Cheyne to the *Memoir* hence the original title, *Memoir and Remains of the Rev. Robert Murray M'Cheyne*. Gribben, in harmony with contemporary academic language, puts the book among 'popular pietistic textbooks', and sees its subject as 'a typical Romantic hero'. *Prisoners of Hope?* pp. 179, 191.

23 Contrary to plain evidence to the contrary, Gribben asserts of Bonar: 'His priorities made it already clear why he would be out of step with the celebration of the revival of 1859.' *Prisoners of Hope?* p. 200. Bonar's interests are portrayed by this author as so narrow that he feared lest revival could give support to postmillennial belief!

24 *Nettleton and His Labours: the Memoir of Dr Asahel Nettleton*, Bennet Tyler, remodelled in some parts by Andrew A. Bonar (1854; repr. Edinburgh: Banner of Truth Trust, 1974), pp. 449-50.

25 Andrew A. Bonar, *James Scott, A Labourer of God* (London: Morgan & Scott, n.d., c. 1885). Scott, a student for the ministry in the Free Church of Scotland, was enrolled by Moody to organize the Evangelistic Association which began in Glasgow at this time. He died at the age of 38.

26 This work consists of five letters by Bonar, 'slightly abridged', and only covering the weeks February 8 – March 13, 1874 (Randolph; New York, 1875).

27 Quoted by Marjory Bonar, *Reminiscences*, p. xiv.

[28] *James Scott*, pp. 111-12.

[29] *Ibid.*, p. 13. While Bonar was not critical of Moody's preaching there were areas where he had reservations. While Moody did not make a public response to the gospel a means of conversion (as happened in Arminian evangelism), his occasional practice of getting would-be converts to identify themselves at once publicly was a deviation without precedent in Scotland. Marjory Bonar wrote: 'Dr Bonar did not always approve of all the methods employed by those who were sent to carry on the work, but that did not hinder him from identifying himself with any such movement. He believed that God could work even where there might be much imperfection, and he and his people were never left unrefreshed when heavenly showers were falling', *Reminiscences*, p. 45 [p. 327].

[30] *Diary*, p. 353 [p. 255].

[31] *Reminiscences*, p. 152 [p.405].

[32] *Memoir and Remains*, p. 282. 'God will put all natural and literary qualifications in the dust, if there is not the simple exhibition of Christ' (p. 281). Bonar's *Diary*, p. 90, notes how he and M'Cheyne spoke together of how 'God works most by holy instruments.'

[33] Ferguson, *Life*, pp. 193, 182, 150, 218.

[34] *Ibid.*, p. 231.

[35] *Reminiscences*, p. 78 [p. 348].

[36] 'Election seems to me a most blessed truth this day, for therein I discover how I may cast off every lurking idea of my unfitness standing in the way of infinite fullness being mine. The poorer the materials, just the more thereby will he display his "wisdom" in forming out of me a wonderful vessel of glory!' *Diary*, p. 363 [p. 263].

[37] *Reminiscences*, p. 307.

[38] *Diary*, p. 147 [p. 104]. And see his address on 'The Pins of the Tabernacle', *Reminiscences*, pp. 286-8. 'This teaches us to be content with our lot.—The sons of Merari might say, "Why do our brethren the Kohathites carry the Ark?" Because God said it; that is all. He that serves most is the greatest in the kingdom. He who carries the pins may get the greatest reward.'

[39] *Diary*, p. 182 [p. 131].

[40] *Diary*, p. 291 [p. 210].

[41] *Reminiscences*, p. 39 [p. 322]. 'Is not this a lamentable state of things that there should be so much to get and so few to ask!' (p. 55 [p. 334]).

[42] *Princes of the Church*, p. 59.

[43] *Diary*, p. 279 [p. 202].

[44] *Ibid.*, p. 353 [p. 256].

[45] *Ibid.*, p. 138 [p. 97].

[46] *Ibid.*, p. 394 [p. 286].

[47] It is significant that Spurgeon takes up the subject of unction under the heading of 'Private Prayer': 'We not only ought to pray more, but we must. The fact is, the secret of all ministerial success lies in prevalence at the mercy seat. One bright benison which private prayer brings down upon the ministry is an indescribable and inimitable something, better understood than named; it is a dew from the Lord, a divine presence which you will recognize at once when I say it is "an unction from the holy One".' *Lectures to My Students*, p. 51.

[48] *Memoir and Remains*, p. 407.

[49] *Diary*, pp. 130, 132, 218 [pp. 91, 93, 156].

[50] Charles Bridges, *The Christian Ministry* (London: Seeley, 1830), pp. 379-80. Why these words were dropped in later editions of this classic I do not know. The book remains a classic.

[51] *Diary*, p. 344 [p. 248].

[52] *Reminiscences*, p. 36 [p. 320].

[53] *Memoir and Remains*, p. 324.

[54] *Reminiscences*, p. 51 [p. 330].

[55] *Ibid.*, p. 236.

[56] Daniel Lamont, *The Anchorage of Life* (London: Inter-Varsity Fellowship, 1946), pp. 209-10.

[57] *Diary*, p. 319 [p. 230]. I have written on 'The Tragedy of the Free Church of Scotland' in *A Scottish Christian Heritage*.

CHAPTER 3

[1] *Sword and the Trowel*, Issue 340.

[2] *An All-round Ministry*, p. 360.

[3] The source for this, and other unreferenced quotations below, will be found in my biography, *Archibald G. Brown, Spurgeon's Successor* (Edinburgh: Banner of Truth Trust, 2011).

[4] A later sermon from the same text will be found in *The Face of Jesus Christ* (Edinburgh: Banner of Truth Trust, 2012).

[5] *The Face of Jesus Christ*, p. 203.

[6] It was preached on September 24, 1876, and will be found in *Metropolitan Tabernacle Pulpit*, vol. 22, number 1,316. The first sentence reads, 'Our curiosity enquires into the condition of those who have newly entered heaven. Like fresh stars they have lit up the celestial firmament with an added splendour.'

[7] A notable earlier worker was the Congregational minister, Andrew Reed (1787–1862), whose life is told by Ian J. Shaw in *The Greatest Is Charity* (Darlington: Evangelical Press, 2005).

[8] On Spurgeon's death, newspapers had expected Brown to succeed him in 1892, but, apart from other considerations, the serious illness of Brown's third wife would have made that impossible. Brown was 'Spurgeon's Successor' in the sense that he continued to uphold all that Spurgeon held dear, and this was more significant than the three fruitful years which he spent at the Metropolitan Tabernacle.

[9] 'Let him speak of love, that is taken with love, that is captivated with love, that is carried away with love. If this man speaks of it, his speaking signifies something.' John Bunyan.

[10] The words are Spurgeon's. Brown said: 'A man may be sound as Calvin, and as eloquent as a Whitefield, and yet lack the one thing that proves him to be a child of God. "He that loveth not, knoweth not God."'

[11] Sermon on Proverbs 11:30.

[12] August 17, 1873.

[13] *Glory of the Ministry* (Revell: New York, 1911), p. 150.

[14] 'I am afraid lest some of you should be drifting into this heighty-flighty balloonism that is getting so wonderfully popular at the present day—the frothy spiritual life that has not any deep sense of personal sin about it. If you know yourself you will not know how to speak in sufficiently uncomplimentary terms about yourself' ('My Sins', sermon on Psa. 51:9).

[15] Ignorant of how truth leads to life, one newspaper praised Brown and condemned his message in these words: 'Apart from his noble social work, he is the East-end apostle of the most dismal gospel. The old Calvinism still masters his mind. That he should set up Distress Funds, Orphanages, Convalescent Homes, etc., is the beautiful contradiction in a good life to a sour creed.'

[16] *Face of Jesus Christ*, pp. 151-52. On prayer meetings Brown was known to say, 'Let everything else go rather than the meetings for pleading with God.' Both Brown and Spurgeon were disturbed at the way musical instruments were beginning to play such a part in evangelical worship and their thinking on the subject will be found in an appendix to my book, *Archibald G. Brown, Spurgeon's Successor* (Edinburgh: Banner of Truth Trust, 2011), pp. 375-91.

Chapter 4

[1] Iain H. Murray, *Diary of Kenneth A. MacRae* (Edinburgh: Banner of Truth Trust, 1980). Referred to in this chapter as *Diary*.

[2] Dr Lloyd-Jones shared a similar view of MacRae and of the *Diary*. It was only after MacRae's death that he preached in the Stornoway pulpit, at which time he told the people, 'My background is the same as yours. I feel as a man returned to his family, I also bemoan the fact that my first visit is taking place after the departure of Mr MacRae.'

[3] I found one copy in the library of John MacArthur's father in California.

[4] I quote here, and repeatedly in this chapter, from the *Diary*.

[5] *Dabney on Preaching* (repr. Edinburgh: Banner of Truth, 1979), p. 116.

[6] Alexandrina MacRae died in 1921, his father in 1929. He had been, Kenneth noted, 'a backslider', but in his long illness of later years 'his whole nature seemed to be changed in wonderful way. He never spoke of getting better and never complained.'

[7] *Diary*, p. 25.

[8] Personal letter from Spurgeon to Mrs Kennedy, published as an appendix to Alexander Auld, *Life of John Kennedy* (London: Nelson, 1887).

[9] MacRae's reading was similarly wide. His favourite book on preaching was that of the Methodist, Daniel P. Kidder, *A Treatise on Homiletics, Designed to Illustrate the True Theory and Practice of Preaching the Gospel* (New York, rev. ed. 1892). In his early ministry he devoured such titles as Spurgeon's *An All-round Ministry*, and Richard Baxter's *Reformed Pastor* (1656, repr. Edinburgh: Banner of Truth Trust, 1974, abridged ed.).

[10] Preface to a first Gaelic edition of Owen's title (Edinburgh, 1876). 'This book', wrote Kennedy, 'is the product of a past age. No living theologian could write it.'

[11] *'Apostle of the North': Life and Labours of the Rev. Dr John Mac-Donald* (London: Nelson, 1866). Reviewed in *Sword and the Trowel*, 1866, pp, 149-56.

[12] *Sword and the Trowel*, 1892, p. 7. This was the year of Spurgeon's death and the review was written 'in Menton, when laying back on a couch through weakness'. Some of the titles mentioned above have been reprinted. A favourite of MacRae's which has not, is William Findlater, *Memoir of the Rev. Robert Findlater* (Glasgow: Collins, 1840).

[13] Allan M. Blanch, *From Strength to Strength, A Life of Marcus Loane* (North Melbourne: Australian Scholarly, 2015), p. 36. For Loane on preaching, see Donald Howard, ed., *Preach or Perish: Reaching the hearts and minds of the world today*, (2008; PO Box 1149, Camden, 2570, Australia).

[14] Spurgeon writes in *Cheque Book of the Bank of Faith* (Sept. 11): 'Praise intoxicates if it be not preceded by abuse. Men who rise to eminence without a struggle usually fall into dishonour. The yoke of affliction, disappointment, and excessive labour is by no means to be

sought for, but when the Lord lays it on us in our youth it frequently develops a character which glorifies God and blesses the church.'

[15] Catherine MacRae was to write after her husband's death, 'Almost 48 years of happy wedded life is now ended. But nothing shall separate us from the love of God in Christ Jesus. He was a gentle, tender, and loving companion, husband and father.' Their only child, Mary, was born in 1921.

[16] In 1955 he spoke of eleven weekly prayer meetings in the congregation, the main one supported by 200 to 250. 'At the Saturday evening prayer meeting of the communion one could, and can, always look for an attendance of 800-1,000.' *The Resurgence of Arminianism* (privately published by MacRae), pp. 26-27.

[17] He is referring here to hanging on to Scripture, not to maintaining all traditions. It was his belief that 'the refusal of the church to adapt itself to the changed conditions in which it may find itself, has done infinite harm in the Highlands. It seems to think it is better to die in a rut than to try to get out of it.'

[18] In 1923, when financial support was difficult in Skye, some of his young people had to go to Glasgow to find work, they sent him a gift 'more precious than any other gift I ever received'. It was £7, prized by him 'more than if it were ten times its value'.

[19] John Kennedy, *The Days of the Fathers in Ross-shire* (repr., Inverness, 1927), p, 190.

[20] *Ibid.*, pp. 23-24.

[21] Nor did he confine his visiting to the households of his own congregation. He also visited the Stornoway 'poor house' for the mentally infirm, and the Sanatorium for those suffering from tuberculosis.

[22] One remedy is to keep a notebook always at hand to record texts which arrest in the course of general reading.

[23] Among exceptions were series on Colossians, and on 1 Peter chapter 1.

[24] W. G. Blackie, *For the Work of the Ministry* (London: Nisbet, 1885), p. 100.

[25] His own failure in this respect he would note at times in his diary, as after a sermon on Romans 9:25, 'I am afraid my discourse

lacked logical connection and point, that, in fact, it wandered unduly from the text.'

[26] The sermon notes show how methodical MacRae was. This sermon was numbered 2,092, and followed his usual practice by noting where he had preached it: '1. Stornoway, to congregation of 700 with liberty. 2. Govan, 11 Nov. 1962, 420 with liberty. 3. Bragar, 16 Nov. 1962, 70 with good measure of liberty.'

[27] James M. Garretson, *Thoughts on Preaching and Pastoral Ministry: Lessons from the Life and Writings of James W. Alexander* (Grand Rapids: RHB, 2015), p. 141.

[28] An invitation to meet A. W. Pink (then living in Stornoway) did not qualify and, as Pink had a similar guard on his afternoon hours, the two men never met! After Pink's death it is said that 'the Rev. K. A. MacRae was one of the closest friends' of his widow. Iain H. Murray, *Life of A. W. Pink* (Edinburgh: Banner of Truth Trust, 2004), pp. 248-49, 283.

[29] Probably a reference to 'The Use of Fear in Religion' in W. G. T. Shedd, *Sermons to the Natural Man* (1876; repr. Edinburgh: Banner of Truth Trust, 1977). Shedd's book on *Homiletics and Pastoral Theology* (New York: Charles Scribner's Sons, 1891) MacRae also valued.

[30] MacRae knew the difficulties. In a diary note of August 3, 1922, he wrote: 'Only an exceptional memory combined with great diligence of preparation can make preaching without notes uniformly successful.'

[31] *Works of Jonathan Edwards* (1834; repr. Edinburgh: Banner of Truth Trust, 1974), vol. 2, pp. 35-36.

[32] George Smeaton, *The Doctrine of the Holy Spirit* (repr. Edinburgh: Banner of Truth Trust, 1974), p. 52; of which book MacRae noted: 'As one reads this one can only say, there were giants in those days ... rightly regarded as the standard work on this doctrine.' This book was been reprinted in a new retypeset edition by the Trust in 2016, along with two other titles by fellow Scots authors: James Buchanan, *The Doctrine of Justification*; and Thomas J. Crawford, *The Mysteries of Christianity: Revealed Truths Expounded and Defended*.

[33] Referring to contemporary conditions, he reflected, 'We have preachers but men of prayer are pitifully few.'

[34] *Preaching & Preachers*, p. 319.

[35] One series of addresses on Revival in Scotland ran to 17 in number. Regrettably they have only survived in his outline of notes.

[36] See a reference to this on Dec. 30, 1933, *Diary*, p. 267.

[37] He feared a tendency in the denomination to substitute interest in mission work abroad to facing the situation at home. 'Our leaders are dreaming fantastic dreams of Foreign Mission expansion while the Highlands are slipping from their grasp.'

[38] *Diary*, p. 197.

[39] *Ibid.*, p. 283.

[40] *Ibid.*, p. 292. It might be wondered, given MacRae's location in the Western Isles, how he could generalise about the wider state of his denomination. But he was often on the mainland as, for instance, in 1936, when the General Assembly asked him to visit needy congregations for three months. With his characteristic diligence he preached in 38 churches.

Chapter 5

[1] *Preaching & Preachers*, 40th anniversary edition (Grand Rapids: Zondervan, 2011), p. 110.

[2] *Engaging with Martyn Lloyd-Jones*, eds. Andrew Atherstone and David C. Jones (Nottingham: IVP, 2001), p. 305. It is worthy of note that Lloyd-Jones said he had first learned of God's sovereignty in revival from John Wesley's *Journals*.

[3] *Studies in the Sermon on the Mount*, vol. 2 (London: IVF, 1960), p. 161.

[4] *Knowing the Times, Addresses Delivered on Various Occasions, 1942-1977* (Edinburgh: Banner of Truth Trust, 1989), pp. 35-36.

[5] Iain H. Murray, *D. Martyn Lloyd-Jones: The Fight of Faith, 1939–1981* (Edinburgh: Banner of Truth Trust, 1990), p. 742.

[6] *Exposition of Romans 7:1-8:4* (Edinburgh: Banner of Truth Trust, 1973), p. 114.

[7] *Fight of Faith*, pp. 739-40.

[8] *Ibid.*, p. 64. Elsewhere he said: 'Whatever authority I may have as a preacher is not the result of any decision on my part. It was God's hand that laid hold of me and drew me out.'

[9] Iain H. Murray, *D. Martyn Lloyd-Jones: The First Forty Years, 1899–1939* (Edinburgh: Banner of Truth Trust, 1982), p. 286.

[10] See below, p. 137.

[11] *Why Does God Allow War?* (London: Hodder & Stoughton, 1939), p. 92.

[12] 'Evangelism: A Very Modern Problem', in *Setting Our Affections upon Glory* (Wheaton, IL: Crossway, 2013), p. 116.

[13] For the same reason it was now urged that old-fashioned terms, such as justification and sanctification, should be avoided. To which Lloyd-Jones replied, 'When did people understand them? When did the unbeliever understand this language? The answer is, Never! These terms are peculiar and special to the gospel.' *Preaching & Preachers*, p. 142.

[14] *Exposition of Romans 5* (London: Banner of Truth Trust, 1971), pp. 113-14.

[15] In John 3:12, Jesus teaches that 'earthly things', i.e., man's fallen nature which necessitates a new birth, is to come before 'heavenly things'. The latter cannot be understood except in that order. Hence John 16:8, and, at length, Romans 1:16-3:19.

[16] *Old Testament Evangelistic Sermons* (Edinburgh: Banner of Truth Trust, 1996), p. xxiv. The preacher was not disheartened when he heard the complaint, 'This man preaches to us as if we were sinners.'

[17] John Piper, for instance, writing of the 'shock' received from Lloyd-Jones's sermons, says: 'I recall distinctly hearing George Verwer say at Urbana '67 that Lloyd-Jones's two volumes on the *Sermon on the Mount* were the greatest thing he had ever read. I bought the books and read them. The impact was unforgettable.' *Preaching & Preachers*, p. 154.

[18] He identified hyper-Calvinism with the belief that 'the gospel is only to be offered to those who are chosen and elect' (*Exposition of*

Romans 8:17-39, p. 188). He adds, 'Many in their ignorance regard that as Calvinism. But it is hyper-Calvinism.' God's sovereignty secures the salvation of the elect, but it does not cause the condemnation of others. Lloyd-Jones's understanding was the same as Spurgeon's on which I have written in *Spurgeon v. Hyper-Calvinism* (Edinburgh: Banner of Truth Trust, 1995).

[19] John Murray, *Redemption—Accomplished and Applied* (Edinburgh: Banner of Truth Trust, 2016 ed.), pp. 110, 111.

[20] Owen, *Works*, vol. 2. p. 150. John Calvin, *Tracts and Letters*, vol. 3 (Edinburgh: Banner of Truth Trust, 2009), pp. 260-61.

[21] *Living Waters, Studies in John 4* (Wheaton, IL: Crossway, 2009), p. 70.

[22] Calvin, *Tracts and Letters*, vol. 3, p. 260-61.

[23] D. Martyn Lloyd-Jones, *The All-Sufficient God: Sermons on Isaiah 40* (Edinburgh: Banner of Truth Trust, 2005), p. 85.

[24] D. Martyn Lloyd-Jones, *The Puritans: Their Origins and Successors* (Edinburgh: Banner of Truth, 1987), pp. 210-12.

[25] D. Martyn Lloyd-Jones, *Exposition of Romans 1* (Edinburgh: Banner of Truth Trust, 1985), p. 330.

[26] *Fight of Faith*, p. 737.

[27] *Evangelical Quarterly*, 1991, p. 71.

[28] Quoted in J. Graham Miller, *An A–Z of Christian Truth and Experience* (Edinburgh: Banner of Truth Trust, 2003), p. 82.

[29] D. Martyn Lloyd-Jones, *Exposition of Romans 8:5-17*, p. 168. Elsewhere he called pride 'the greatest of all temptations that assail a preacher', and warned, 'Many a preacher has been ruined by his congregation. Their praise, their encouragement of him as a man, has almost ruined him as a messenger from God.'

[30] *Preaching & Preachers* (London: Hodder & Stoughton, 1972; reprinted, with additional material, Grand Rapids: Zondervan, ed. Kevin DeYoung, 2011).

[31] D. Martyn Lloyd-Jones, *Knowing the Times* (Edinburgh: Banner of Truth Trust, 2008).

[32] Iain H. Murray, *Lloyd-Jones: Messenger of Grace* (Edinburgh: Banner of Truth, 2008), p. 101.

[33] *Ibid.*, p. 105.

[34] *Ibid.*, p. 103.

[35] On this point, as on a number of others, Dr Lloyd-Jones was of one mind with Archibald Alexander, who emphasized that man, created in the image of God, needs to have his mind addressed 'through carefully prepared, well organized, and clearly presented sermons'. James M. Garretson, *Princeton and Preaching: Archibald Alexander and the Christian Ministry* (Edinburgh: Banner of Truth Trust, 2005), p. 97.

[36] 'There should always be one evangelistic sermon in connection with each church once a week.' *Preaching & Preachers*, p. 163.

[37] This proportion of his ministry is not reflected in his published sermons. In part because it was thought that it would be Christians who would buy his sermons.

[38] *First Forty Years*, p. 304. The texts were, John 6:66-68, 'Will ye also go away?' and Matt. 7:13-14, 'Enter ye in at the strait gate.' The sermons included such questions as, 'Are you ready for the judgment? Have you a personal conviction of sin, and a personal knowledge of God?'

[39] *Fight of Faith*, pp. 335-36.

[40] *Preachers & Preaching*, p. 170.

[41] Lloyd-Jones believed that this high view of preaching gives a true preacher a very low view of his own efforts. He endorsed the words of J. H. Thornwell, 'Depend upon it that there is but little preaching in the world. My own performances in this way fill me with disgust.'

[42] *Ibid.*, pp. 340-41.

[43] In this case, as in others, it is unfortunate that schools of thought come to be identified with one man's name. Considerable variations are to be found under the classification of 'Amyraldian'. The best succinct survey known to the present writer is that by Roger Nicole in *The Encyclopedia of Christianity*, eds. Edwin Palmer and John Murray (Wilmington: Foundation for Christian Education, 1964), vol. 1, pp. 184-93. It was a loss to the church that this ambitious Encyclopedia did not proceed further than vol. 2 and the letters, Bi-Chuza.

[44] The latest example of this early belief known to us is in a sermon preached in 1935, when, speaking on the cross, he said, 'It is there the whole of humanity is focused. He is the representative of the whole of mankind, he died for all.' *Evangelistic Sermons* (Edinburgh: Banner of Truth Trust, 1983), p. 278. Printed posthumously unedited.

[45] Amyraldians commonly hold that Scripture is using anthropomorphic language when it speaks of a series of events in salvation, one subsequent to another, and therefore we should not speak of an order of divine decrees. Although election is to be considered as after redemption, the decree is one in God. We are not to think in terms of time. But that is precisely what Scripture would have us think, that there is a plan of salvation and an order in the plan of salvation: 'redemption through his blood' is in sequence to 'chosen in him' (Eph. 1:4-7), and 'justified' follows 'predestinate and called' (Rom. 8:29). Election is the cause of faith (Acts 13:48). Yet that this characterization of God necessarily makes him the author of sin is firmly denied.

[46] *God the Father, God the Son: Great Doctrines of the Bible*, vol. 1 (Wheaton: Crossway, 1996), p. 96.

[47] *Saved in Eternity: Studies in John 17:1-5* (Wheaton: Crossway, 1988), pp. 61-62.

[48] *Safe in the World: Studies in John 17:6-19* (Wheaton: Crossway, 1988), p. 41.

[49] *Romans: Exposition of Chapter 5* (London: Banner of Truth Trust, 1971), p. 224.

[50] *Ibid.*, p. 243.

[51] *Life in the Spirit in Marriage, Home and Work: Exposition of Ephesians 5:18-6:9* (Edinburgh: Banner of Truth Trust, 1973), pp. 145-46. This is not to deny that there are 'certain common, general benefits' deriving from the work of Christ, 'differentiated from special grace, which is the grace of redemption'. *God the Father*, pp. 362-63.

[52] The best explanation Lynch can give (p. 166) is that of Richard Baxter on which Dr Packer comments, 'Where orthodox Calvinism taught that Christ satisfies the law in the sinner's place, Baxter

held that Christ satisfied the Lawgiver and so procured a change in the law' (p. 262). 'Baxter here aligned himself with the Arminians and Socinians, denying that God in all circumstances required exact penal equivalent for each particular sin ... On this foundation the other Arminian bricks in his dogmatic structure were laid. He denied that Christ's death was a case of penal substitution, affirming that its whole effect was to procure a new law of grace for the world, and he insisted that faith is imputed for what under the new law it is—"evangelical righteousness"—and so is the proper ground of justification.' *Redemption & Restoration of Man in the Thought of Richard Baxter*, pp. 262, 398. Packer rightly calls Baxter's presentation of the atonement 'bewildering'. 'It involved re-definition right and left: terms like law, works, merit, righteousness, justification, imputation, instrument, all meant something different in Baxter from what they meant in the rest of Protestant literature.' *Ibid.*, p. 261.

[53] B. B. Warfield, *The Plan of Salvation* (Grand Rapids: Eerdmans, 1955), p. 94. Those who think that Calvinism has to distort John 3:16 to fit 'their scheme' should read his sermon on the text, 'God's Immeasurable Love' in *The Saviour of the World* (Edinburgh: Banner of Truth Trust, 1991).

[54] *Encyclopedia of Christianity*, vol. 1, p. 191.

[55] Dr Packer is making the same point when he says: 'Whether we call ourselves Calvinists hardly matters; what matters is that we should understand the gospel biblically. But that, we think, does in fact mean understanding it as historic Calvinism does.' Introductory Essay, *Death of Death*, p. 13.

[56] *Romans; Exposition of Chapter 9* (Edinburgh: Banner of Truth Trust, 1991), p. 164.

[57] *Puritan Principles: 1951-54 Puritan Papers (Notes & Abstract)* (Stoke-on-Trent: Tentmaker Publications, n.d.), pp. 7-8.

[58] *Fight of Faith*, p. 231.

[59] In much fuller form, its content will be found in Murray, *Redemption—Accomplished and Applied*. Lynch feels himself free to describe Murray's opposition to universal redemption as 'bizarre', 'extremely weak', and 'cavalier' (*Lamb of God*, pp. 17, 155-57).

[60] Tape-recorded conversation with Iain H. Murray in late 1970s.

[61] This remains in print (Edinburgh: Banner of Truth Trust, 2013).

[62] *The Apostles' Doctrine of the Atonement* (Edinburgh: Banner of Truth Trust, 2013), pp. 540-43.

[63] *The Cure of Church Divisions* (1670), p. 216. For which reason, among others, Banner publishes only some of the 160 books Baxter wrote.

[64] *Redemption & Restoration*, p. 398.

[65] *Confession of Faith of the Calvinistic Methodists, or the Presbyterians of Wales*, 'Of Redemption', p. 75.

[66] *God the Father, Great Doctrines of the Bible vol. 1* (Wheaton: Crossway, 1996), p. 94.

[67] *Saved in Eternity*, p. 63.

CHAPTER 6

[1] Ian R. K. Paisley, *W. P. Nicholson, Tornado of the Pulpit* (Belfast: Martyrs Memorial Productions, 1982), p. 7.

[2] J. C. Ryle, *Knots Untied: Being Plain Statements on Disputed Points in Religion from the Standpoint of an Evangelical Churchman* (1874; repr. Edinburgh: Banner of Truth Trust, 2016).

[3] Ernest Brown, *'By Honour and Dishonour': The Story of the Evangelical Presbyterian Church* (Belfast: Evangelical Book Shop, 2016). I am so heavily indebted to Mr Brown in this chapter that I will simply give page references to his history in square brackets as above.

[4] Grier on 'Benjamin Breckinridge Warfield' in *Banner of Truth*, Feb. 1971, p. 9.

[5] James W. Alexander, *Life of Archibald Alexander* (New York: Scribner, 1854), p. 649.

[6] *Ibid.*, p. 606.

[7] W. J. Grier, 'The Reformed Faith', *Banner of Truth*, May 1973, p. 5. For C. W. Hodge's address on 'The Significance of the Reformed Theology Today', given in 1921, see *Princeton and the*

Work of the Christian Ministry, Addresses Selected by James M. Garretson (Edinburgh: Banner of Truth Trust, 2012) vol. 2, pp. 591-602.

[8] J. Gresham Machen, *God Transcendent* (Edinburgh: Banner of Truth Trust, 1982), p. 115.

[9] *Tornado of the Pulpit*, p. 98.

[10] W. J. Grier, *The Origin and Witness of the Irish Evangelical Church* (Belfast: Evangelical Book Shop, 1945), p. 33.

[11] *Origin and Witness*, p. 36. For full information see Ernest Brown, *'By Honour and Dishonour'*.

[12] *Origin and Witness*, p. 37.

[13] *Ibid.*, p. 48.

[14] *Ibid.*, p. 58.

[15] *Ibid.*, p. 51.

[16] *Faith in an Unchanging Vesture: An Exposure of Modernistic Principles based on 'The Changing Vesture of Faith'*, by Professor J. E. Davey. Grier, who had hopes that his friend might train for the ministry, called the book, 'tremendously thorough and devastating, written in a warm, evangelical tone'. *Origin and Witness*, p. 54.

[17] The controversy compelled Grier to look more closely at dispensationalism, then a comparatively new teaching. This led to his articles on the subject which were ultimately published in book form as *The Momentous Event* (Belfast: Evangelical Book Shop, 1945). By 2016 the book had sold 54,611 copies, plus editions in German, Portuguese, French, Italian, and Japanese.

[18] *Origin and Witness*, p. 55.

[19] 'A Tribute to Rev. James Hunter', *Irish Evangelical*, May 1958. For the first fourteen years of the magazine Hunter usually wrote the leader.

[20] It remained the home of Dr John R. Gillespie who died in 1960 aged 88. No one served the church more faithfully and generously.

[21] Such was Macleod's esteem for Grier that when, on one occasion, he heard that Grier was staying in a hotel in Edinburgh, he went at once and insisted the visitor must stay with them. Macleod's *Scottish Theology in relation to Church History* (repr. Edinburgh: Banner of Truth Trust, 2015) remains a first-class guide for students.

²² *Irish Evangelical*, May 1958.

²³ It is recommended by D. Martyn Lloyd-Jones in *The Church and the Last Things* (Wheaton, IL: Crossway, 1998), p. 88, the third volume in the series *Great Doctrines of the Bible*.

²⁴ In 1944 the Irish Evangelical Church had added the *Westminster Confession of Faith* to its doctrinal standards (with some revision of chapters 23-25); in 1964, 'to identify much more specifically than the title Irish Evangelical Church could do', the denomination's name became, Evangelical Presbyterian Church [288] and the next year the magazine became the *Evangelical Presbyterian*.

²⁵ I have reflected on a distinction between 'Christian Unity and Church Unity' in *The Old Evangelicalism* (Edinburgh: Banner of Truth, 2005), chapter 7. I had met Professor Murray when he delivered the Campbell Morgan Bible Lecture on 'The Heavenly Priestly Activity of Christ' on June 18, 1958. Of this lecture, which was published for the day of its delivery, I sent a copy to Grier, and in his reply to me, he teasingly added after words of commendation on Murray's style, 'There are some sentences in this Lecture that one had to read over a few times to get the full significance. Perhaps it is because this is Monday morning!'

²⁶ See *Fight of Faith*, p. 500. There was no doctrinal difference between the three men. As David Ceri Jones has written of the 1950s, 'During these years he [ML-J] ensured, almost single-handedly, that much of Welsh Evangelicalism would be both theologically literate and guided in a thoroughly Calvinistic direction.' *Engaging with Martyn Lloyd-Jones,* p. 75. But England in the 1960s was not Wales in the 1950s.

²⁷ The address was printed in *Banner of Truth*, issue 128. The present writer will not forget having to go to my friend's room before the start of one Leicester Conference. When I entered, after knocking, it was to find him rising from his knees with his face glowing.

²⁸ Article by Grier in the *Presbyterian Journal* (Weaverville, NC), September 24, 1969. The editor reported that the author asked it to be published anonymously, 'It being almost dangerous to take a pen in hand in this matter.' The current Wikipedia articles on the 'Troubles in Ulster' is correct in saying: 'The conflict was primarily

political, but it also had an ethnic or sectarian dimension, although it was not a religious conflict.' This was not the picture which the IRA circulated in the American media.

[29] I would exempt Puritan authors of the seventeenth century from this statement, although he admired and recommended their teaching.

[30] He wrote 23 articles on the life of Calvin in the *Irish Evangelical*, 1954–56, and it was his unfulfilled hope to develop and revise these as a book. Edited by the Rev. Jonathan Watson, they were, however, published posthumously as *The Life of John Calvin* (Edinburgh: Banner of Truth Trust, 2012).

[31] The Banner of Truth Trust published Runia's *Reformation Today* in 1968.

[32] 'Impetration', a technical word used in seventeenth-century controversy. See John Owen, *Death of Death*, Book 2, chapters iv and v. Some wanted to speak of 'impetration' in terms of Christ procuring the benefit of redemption for *all* while its application was only for *some*. Reformed theology, generally, allowed no such distinction between impetration and application.

[33] There was a difference in Lloyd-Jones's later teaching when he said of the Jews, 'that in a national sense they are going to be converted'. *Exposition of Romans Chapter 11* (Edinburgh: Banner of Truth, 1998), p. 109.

[34] Another example against being more dogmatic than Scripture warrants was his non-acceptance of the view that psalms alone should be sung in public worship. This did not hinder his friendship with ministers who upheld that practice.

[35] Barclay told his readers of how wrong it was to look upon Jesus as 'the rescuer from the wrath of God'.

[36] A. A. Hodge, *Evangelical Theology* (Edinburgh: Banner of Truth, 1976), p. 402

[37] As reported in Wikipedia, around 3,600 were killed between 1969 and 1998. The latter year saw 'The Good Friday Agreement', which introduced 'power sharing' between Unionists and Republicans.

[38] His body was buried in the family grave at Dundonald. Catherine Grier died in 1991. Her home had been, in Bunyan's words,

'A Palace Beautiful, built by the Lord of the Hill for the relief and security of pilgrims.'

[39] The quotation is that of Dr Hyndman, a Belfast minister, after hearing the answer given in Fisher's *Catechism* to the Question, 'What are you by nature?' 'I am an enemy of God, a child of Satan and an heir of hell.' Grier, 'The Wrath of God', *Banner of Truth*, April 1971, p. 1.

[40] I am dependent here on Spurgeon's reading for May 11 in his *Cheque Book of the Bank of Faith* (a book long promoted by the Evangelical Book Shop and today published by Christian Focus). Ernest Brown tells us that Grier could tell the story of *Pilgrim's Progress* from memory.

[41] Grier, 'The Reformed Faith', *Banner of Truth*, May 1973, p. 3.

CHAPTER 7

[1] I have sought to give a biographical account in *John MacArthur: Servant of the Word and Flock* (Edinburgh: Banner of Truth Trust, 2011).

[2] John Watson, *The Cure of Souls, Yale Lectures on Practical Theology* (London: Hodder & Stoughton, 1896), pp. 235-36.

[3] John MacArthur, *Twelve Extraordinary Women* (Nashville; Nelson, 2005), p. 5.

[4] *John MacArthur: Servant of the Word and Flock*, p. 54.

[5] *Truth Endures, Landmark Sermons by John MacArthur, 1969–2009* (Panorama City, CA: Grace to You, 2009), p.104.

[6] MacArthur, *Ashamed of the Gospel* (Wheaton, IL: Crossway, 1993), p. 174.

[7] MacArthur, *Gospel According to Jesus* (Grand Rapids: Zondervan, 1988), pp. 84-85.

[8] MacArthur, *Hard to Believe* (Nashville: Thomas Nelson, 2003), p. 68.

[9] MacArthur, *Gospel According to the Apostles* (Nashville: Word, 2000), p. 74. He goes on to quote the words of A. W. Tozer,

'The formula "Accept Christ" has become a panacea of universal application, and I believe it has been fatal to many.'

[10] *Gospel According to Jesus*, p. 73.

[11] 'Striking Similarities Between Two Extraordinary Expositors', *The Master's Seminary Journal*, Spring 2011, p. 59. This same issue contains a bibliography of Dr MacArthur's Writings, 1973–2011, prepared by Dennis M. Swanson.

[12] MacArthur, *The Vanishing Conscience* (Nashville: Nelson, 1995), p. 11.

[13] *Hard to Believe*, p. 20.

[14] MacArthur, *Reckless Faith: When the Church Loses its Will to Discern* (Wheaton, IL: Crossway, 1994), p. 51.

[15] MacArthur points out that the contemporary evangelical call for relevance had a forerunner: 'the aim of the early modernists was simply to make the church more "modern", more unified, more relevant, more acceptable to a sceptical modern age'. *Ashamed of the Gospel*, p. xvi.

[16] MacArthur, *The Master's Plan for the Church* (Chicago: Moody, 1991), p. 48. See also pp. 235-53.

[17] *MacArthur: Servant of the Word and Flock*, p. 66.

[18] *Ibid.*, p. 172.

[19] *Gospel According to the Apostles*, p. 22.

[20] MacArthur, *The Truth War, Fighting for Certainty in an Age of Deception* (Nashville: Nelson, 2007), p. xiv.

[21] *Ibid.*, p. 149. The analysis in these pages is very disturbing reading. 'For many years now, evangelical leaders have systematically embraced and fostered almost every worldly, shallow and frivolous idea that comes into the church.'

[22] *The Gospel According to the Apostles*, p. 13.

[23] *Gospel According to Jesus*, Anniversary Edition (Zondervan, 2008), p. 9. He notes, 'By the time we finished Matthew, our congregation's collective devotion to the authority and seriousness of God's word was almost palpable.'

[24] On the insufficiency of the Apostles' Creed, see 'What Are the Fundamentals of Christianity?' in *Truth Matters*. Human nature has

not changed since B. B. Warfield wrote of the impatience in his day 'to state with precision the doctrinal presuppositions and contents of Christianity. The basis of this impatience is often a mere latitudinarian indifferentism.' *The Right to Systematic Theology* (Edinburgh: T & T Clark, 1897), p. 16.

[25] Spurgeon, *All-round Ministry*, p. 360.

[26] 'What Are the Fundamentals of Christianity?' in *Truth Matters*.

[27] These titles currently remain in print from the Banner of Truth Trust. The other titles in his list were, *The Valley of Vision* (Arthur Bennnet), *Knowing God* (J. I. Packer), *Studies in the Sermon on the Mount* (Lloyd-Jones), *Spiritual Growth* (A. W. Pink), *The Preacher's Portrait* (J. R. W. Stott).

[28] This principle, as his colleague Irvin Busenitz has written, is 'woven into the fabric' of his ministry. *Master's Seminary Journal*, Spring 2011, p. 131.

[29] 'A Humble Brother Whom God Has Exalted', *Master's Seminary Journal*, Spring 2011, pp. 133-4.

[30] *Monthly Record of the Free Church of Scotland*, April 2012, pp. 19-20.

[31] Archibald Alexander, *Practical Sermons* (Philadelphia: Presbyterian Board of Publications, 1850), p. 6.

[32] Richard Mayhew, *The Death of Death in the Death of Christ* (1679, repr., London: Ward, n.d.), p. 66. On the same page Mayhew says, 'The combination of sinners have not so much prejudiced the power of godliness as the contention of saints.'

General Index

Aaron, John, xiii, 28, 37
Alexander, Archibald, 178, 233, 258
— J. A. (son), 178, 204
Alliance News, 188
Allis, O. T. (Prof.), 176, 177
America, 35, 147
Amyraldianism, 154-68
Anglesey, 5, 8-12, 19, 24, 25
Arminian/ism, 27, 30, 138-9, 155, 248, 260
Arnold, Matthew, 136
Atonement, extent of, 27-34, 36-38, 154-68, 204
Auburn Affirmation, 176, 179
Australia, 88, 107-8
Australian Baptist, 88

Bala, 5-6, 11, 14, 15, 17, 29
Ball, Ella, 197
Bangor, N. Ireland, 172
Banner of Truth, 101, 164, 206
Banner of Truth Trust, 164-6, 198-99 (begun), 203, 205
Barclay, W., 205, 264
Bavinck, H., 204
Baxter, Richard, 155, 163-64, 166, 242, 259-60, 261
— Baxterian, 29, 243
Belfast, 171-3, 175, 180-81, 190-91, 195 (bombed), 207 (bombed again)
— Assembly's College 171, 175, 180, 184

— Knockdene Park South, 191, 193, 195
— Queen's University, 171, 173-5, 196
— Ravenhill Presbyterian Church, 173, 175, 181, 188
— Richview Presbyterian Church, 185-86
— Ulster Hall, 187-88
— YMCA Hall, 184
Bernal, J. D., 149
Bibles,
— Welsh and New Testaments, 17
— Gaelic, 106
Bigg, Annie (see Mrs A. G. Brown), 76, 78
Blackwood, S. Arthur (Sir), 76-77
Bob Jones University, SC, 216
Bonar, Andrew, 43-72
— Isabella (wife), 60
— Isabella (daughter), 60
— Marjory (daughter), 60, 64, 246, 248
— James (son), 60
— Mary Elizabeth (daughter), 60
Bonar, Horatius, 46, 49, 59, 69
Bridges, Charles, 69
British and Foreign Bible Society, 17
British Evangelical Council (BEC) 200, 206
British Medical Association, 153

General Index

MacKay, George, 107-8
Macleay, Kenneth, 102
Macleod, John (Principal), 196, 262
MacRae, Kenneth, 99-130, 252, 253, 254, 255
— Murdo (father), 104
— Catherine (wife), 101, 108, 125
Machen, J. Gresham, 177, 179-80, 185-87, 190, 194
Marchioness of Anglesey, 12
Manchuria, 181, 191
Matthews, W. R. (Dean), 149
Mentone, France, 95
Milford, Donegal, 172, 174
Mission of Inquiry, 48, 54-5 (book)
Methodists,
— Calvinistic, 4-5, 7, 9, 14, 18, 20-3, 27-9, 32-3, 37, 41, 103, 168, 238
— Wesleyan, 4, 27
Modernist, controversy, 176-7, 179, 187-88
Moody, D. L., 57-60, 248
Moody Monthly, 233
Moody-Stuart, Alexander, 59
Morgan, Edward, xi, 3, 8, 13, 21, 36
Moore, T. V., 199
Moule, H. C. G., 63, 107
Murray, John (Prof.), 149, 164, 177, 198, 200-1, 205 (and Israel), 206, 263
Music and worship, 74, 93-4, 144, 223, 228

New Zealand, 87
Nicole, Roger, 159, 167
Nicholson, W. P., 172-3, 175, 180-81, 185, 188, 194
Nicoll, W. Robertson (Sir) 45, 52, 54, 66
Newton, John, 17
New York, 59, 176

Nonconformity, 21, 29, 36
North Star, 130

Oxford, 18, 164
Owen, John, 33, 107, 144, 164, 165, 241, 243
Owen, W. T. 29, 37-8

Packer, J. I. 163-65, 167, 199, 259-60
Palestine, 48, 191
Patton, Francis L. (Prof.), 176
Perth, Scotland, 47-8, 54
Peru, 197
Philippines, 227
Pink, A. W., 204, 254
Piper, John, 256,
Poole-Connor, E. J., 200
Pratt, Josiah, 18
Prayer,
— Family, 23, 50
— Private, 23, 48, 53, 62, 66, 71, 114, 249, 255
Preachers,
— and university degrees, 20-21
— and Christ, 66-67, 93, 102-3, 115
— and Scripture, 71-2, 110-11, 220-22
— and love, 16, 46, 63, 64, 67, 88, 117
— and the Holy Spirit, 126-28, 153-4
— and prayer, 66 (see Prayer, Private)
— only instruments, 25-6
— and universal invitation to Christ, 30, 36, 143
— and humility, 64, 91-2,
— and unction, 17, 66, 67, 94, 104, 249
— texts or serial exposition, 67-9, 119, 151-2
Presbyterian Church in the USA, 172, 177

Index of Authors and Works Cited

ABOUT THE PUBLISHER

THE Banner of Truth Trust originated in 1957 in London. The founders believed that much of the best literature of historic Christianity had been allowed to fall into oblivion and that, under God, its recovery could well lead not only to a strengthening of the church, but to true revival.

Inter-denominational in vision, this publishing work is now international, and our lists include a number of contemporary authors along with classics from the past. The translation of these books into many languages is encouraged.

A monthly magazine, *The Banner of Truth,* is also published. More information about this and all our publications can be found on our website or supplied by either of the offices below.

THE BANNER OF TRUTH TRUST

3 Murrayfield Road   PO Box 621, Carlisle,
Edinburgh, EH12 6EL   Pennsylvania 17013
UK   USA

www.banneroftruth.org